Voce del Popolo:
Mussolini as Revealed in His Political Speeches
(November 1914–August 1923)

VOCE DEL POPOLO

Mussolini as Revealed in His Political Speeches

(NOVEMBER 1914–AUGUST 1923)

ANTELOPE HILL PUBLISHING

Antelope Hill first edition, first printing 2023.

Originally published as:
*Mussolini: As Revealed in His Political Speeches
(November 1914–August 1923)*
London and Toronto, J. M. Dent & Sons LTD
and New York, E. P. Dutton & Co., 1923.
Originally selected, translated, and edited by
Baron Bernardo Quaranta di San Severino.

Editing, with footnotes, and layout by Margaret Bauer.
Cover art by Swifty.

Antelope Hill Publishing | antelopehillpublishing.com

Paperback ISBN-13: 978-1-956887-99-0
EPUB ISBN-13: 979-8-89252-000-3

Dedicated to

The President of the Italian Senate, Tommaso Tittoni

By the Translator, Barone Bernardo Quaranta Di San Severino

Benito Mussolini pictured in the 1920s

Contents

Letter From Tommaso Tittoni

Rome
April 24th, 1923

My Dear Baron,

I gladly accept the dedication of your English edition of the speeches of Benito Mussolini.

I have always held in great esteem the sobriety of the world that does not sound alone, but, by creating, strikes home and leaves a deep mark in the mind of the listener. And such are the clear, incisive, impetuous words—disdainful of any showy rhetoric—of Benito Mussolini, the man in whom are united faith, energy and willpower, the qualities necessary to begin and carry out the reconstruction of Italy by restoring the public finance and the authority and prestige of the State. When listening to the words of Benito Mussolini, that which Dante says of the stream of Purgatorio is recalled to mind: "Tutte l'acque che son di qua più monde / parrieno avere in sé mistura alcuna / verso di quella, che nulla nasconde."[1]

With all good wishes for the success of your work, I remain—

Yours Sincerely,
Tommaso Tittoni

---

[1] "All of the purest waters here on earth, / when matched against that stream, would seem to be / touched by impurity; it hides no thing." Dante Alighieri, *Purgatorio*, trans. Mandelbaum, Canto XXVIII, 28–30.

Introduction: A Note on Italian Fascism

In an interesting article published last year in our press, Ettore Ciccotti shows that Italian Fascism does not represent an absolutely new political event, but is part of the general historic development of nations. In the first years of its appearance, it was compared to the *krypteia* of Sparta, to the *eterie* of Athens, and to similar phenomena, which are repeated as a manifestation of self-defense of strong and active groups or classes, uniting and forming centers of resistance; exercising thus, by their extended action, general functions of State in a period in which its protection is weak or inefficient, and shows signs of disintegration or degeneration. Other examples of this phenomenon can be found in the history of the Church and in the Italian Communes, in England, Germany, in the Clubs of the French Revolution, and in the rest of Europe. When in a nation that shows such signs that this form of vitality does not exist, we witness the general collapse of that nation, as in Russia at this moment, where only the radical uprooting of Bolshevism might lead to the general resurrection of the country.

The after-war period in Italy, as elsewhere, had caused complete apathy, slackness and disorder in Parliamentary State functions, characterized by many elaborate programs, but few facts. The Italian working classes, moreover, had been hypnotized by the nefarious gospel of Lenin, which had powerfully contributed to bring about the grave state of affairs in Italy in 1920, when the Communist peril had reached its acute stage. The continued strikes in all industries had caused prices to rise at a tremendous pace; the production of commodities had been reduced to a minimum; the enormous deficit in the railway and postal departments, the debt, and the general budget of the State were alarming, while foreign exchanges had reached fantastic figures. The arrogance of the Communist elements had become unbearable, and officers at times were obliged to dress in plain clothes in order not to be attacked by Bolshevists, while soldiers, Carabineers, and Guardie Regie were frequently insulted and in some instances even killed by Communists.

But the gallant fighters of the Trentino, of the Carso, and of the Grappa, the volunteers who had saved Italy and arrested the advance of the enemy on the Piave could not reconcile themselves to this state of affairs,[2] to the idea of watching with folded arms the complete loss of the fruits of victory for which half a million men had left their lives on the battlefields. These brave youths, with an indomitable courage, ready to face all, full of the purest ideals and passionate love for our country, representing a new force and a new Italy, had already in April 1919 grouped themselves together in a *fascio* (bundle), as the Fascio Nazionale dei Combattenti (National Fasces of Combatants), under the leadership of Benito Mussolini, who was the inspirer and organizer of the movement and had himself been their comrade at the front.

They became stronger every day and dealt the initial blow to Communism in 1921, when the first encounter took place between Fascists and Communists at Bologna, which marks the waning of Bolshevism and the rise of Fascism.

But it was not an easy matter for the new movement to make its way, as in its laborious progress it met with endless difficulties, and above all had to fight the apathy of the people and the general skepticism regarding it. Fascism had to deal with peculiar mentalities, to fight various organizations, including the State, which felt itself being undermined by this new political group, while its chief enemy, the Bolshevist faction, had made endless victims among its rank and file during the past.

It was not possible, however, for the Fascists to deal with the Communists otherwise than by using violence, as normal means would have been entirely inadequate against the seditious elements (made all the more arrogant by the manifest impotence of the State and the *laissez faire* attitude of public opinion), in view of the daily increasing number of crimes committed against property and peaceful individuals.

---

[2] Referring to the Second Battle of the Piave River (or Battle of the Solstice), June 15th–23rd, 1918, was a decisive victory for the Italian Army against the Austro-Hungarian Empire during the First World War.

Fascists, moreover, started a strong movement against the composition of the Chamber, maintaining that it no longer represented the nation, that it had grown prematurely old and must, therefore, be quickly dissolved and a new appeal to the electors be made as soon as possible. They had been deeply concerned, on the other hand, with the Italian economic crisis, which, according to Edmondo Rossoni, the able organizer and Secretary-General of the Syndicalist Corporations, could not be overcome without an increase in the production of commodities to be obtained by a more rigorous discipline in the labor question; thus, an economic victory followed the victory on the battlefields. The masses of the working classes, many of them previously Socialists and Communists, enrolled themselves among the Fascist syndicates scattered all over Italy and were able to settle various important disputes.

The alleged dissension between Fascism and the Italian Monarchy had always been a favorite weapon in the hands of the anti-Fascist elements. The Hon. Mussolini, in his speech at the great Fascist Mass Meeting at Naples on October 24th of last year (1922), clearly manifested his party feeling in the matter, as can be gathered by his own words uttered there.[3] The attitude of Fascism toward Monarchy clearly defined by its leader was very opportune, and contributed to the greater popularity of the movement throughout the country, where this institution rests on a solid base, represents Italian unity, and is today associated with its illustrious representative, King Victor Emmanuel III, an example of domestic virtue in private life, one of the most cultured men of our times, beloved by all classes, who at the front proved himself the first soldier among soldiers and gained the popularity of the whole nation.

The Army was secretly or openly greatly in favor of Fascism, the successful efforts of which to save the country from the Social-Communist factions it could not forget. The soldiers could, therefore, never have marched against the Fascists—who represented Italian patriotism. The very generals of the regular Army, such as Generals Fara, Ceccherini, Graziani, de Bono, and other Blackshirts, themselves directed the famous March to Rome.

With reference to religion, Mussolini's Government promised to

---

[3] See page 150.

respect all creeds, especially Catholicism. At Ouchy he said to the Press, "My spirit is deeply religious. Religion is a formidable force that must be respected and defended. I am, therefore, against anti-clerical and atheistic democracy, which represents an old and useless toy. I maintain that Catholicism is a great spiritual power, and I trust that the relations between Church and State will henceforward be more friendly." And while the Minister for Public Instruction, Senator Gentile, has introduced compulsory religious instruction in the elementary public schools, the Under-Secretary of the same Ministry, Hon. Dario Lupi, one of Mussolini's closest friends, issued, as one of his first acts, a timely and peremptory order to the school authorities requesting the immediate replacement of the crucifix and the picture of the king.

Fascism, which during the last months of 1922 had seen its membership increasing by leaps and bounds, finally won with a note of fanaticism the very heart of the country from the Alps to the southern shores of Sicily. Latterly it had exercised the functions of State almost undisturbed, and did not spare either institutions or individuals in the pursuit of its end. It had demanded and successfully obtained the dismissal of the pan-Germanist Mayor of Bolzano, Herr Perathoner; it had occupied the Giunta Provinciale of Trento, causing the removal of the Italian governor, maintaining that he had been too weak in his attitude toward arrogant pan-Germanists in that region; and had acted successfully as arbitrator in the labor dispute between Cantiere Orlando of Leghorn and the Government itself. It was no wonder, then, if after the big October meeting of last year at Naples and the March to Rome with the famous Quadrumvirate formed by General Cesare de Bono, Hon. Cesare Maria de Vecchi, Italo Balbo, and Michele Bianchi, then Secretary-General of the Party, Mussolini, the creator of this mighty movement, was summoned by the king to form the new Fascist Cabinet.

It might be a cause of surprise to the superficial observer, this sudden ascent to power of a party that, a few days before it took the Government into its hands, had been threatened with martial law, an order that the king wisely refused to sign, thus avoiding civil war. But whoever has followed the development and progress of Fascism during the last four years, considers its great strength and power in the country, its formidable membership (now over a million strong) compared with that of any other party (the Socialists are reduced to seventy thousand), and takes into account the high and patriotic principles on which this movement is founded will not wonder that the party got to power through an extra-parliamentary crisis. We cannot and must not forget that these Blackshirts—as the Fascists are called—have really saved Italy from Bolshevism, which was sucking her very life-blood, and that they are thereby entitled to the gratitude of our country and of the world at large. As Lord Rothermere writes:

> The Moscow conspirators, whose object was the overthrow of Western civilization, swept with a wide net. They made great headway in Germany, especially in Berlin; they seized Budapest under the direction of a convicted thief, but it was upon Italy they counted most, and when Mussolini struck against them in Italy, he was fighting a battle for all Europe.[4]

I do not think—and the Hon. Mussolini agreed with me in one of the conversations I had with him—that people abroad, especially in England and the United States, know much about Fascism. It had been diagnosed as a sporadic revolutionary movement, which sooner or later would be put down by drastic measures. Not many have realized that in this after-war period there is no more important historical phenomenon than Fascism, which, as our Prime Minister said, "is at the same time political, military, religious, economic and syndicalist, and represents all the hopes, the aspirations and requirements of the people." The popular air "Giovinezza" (Youth), the official song of the Fascists, with its thrilling notes, which magnetized the heart of the people; the characteristic Blackshirts with the shield of the *fascio* on their breasts; the *gagliardetti* (Fascist standards)—all these have largely contributed toward rousing a delirium of enthusiasm among the masses for the great cause.

But three other important elements account for the success of the National Fascist Party (as it is now officially constituted, with its Grand Council of Fascism), namely its military organization, its powerful press, and, above all, the personality of Mussolini himself, *Il*

---

[4] Harold Harmsworth, the first Lord Rothermere, "What Europe Owes Mussolini," *The Daily Mail*, May 1923.

Duce, as he is called. The military organization is entirely on Roman lines, with Roman names of legion, consul, cohort, senior, centurion, decurion, triari, etc. The symbol of Fascism is the same as that of the lictors of Imperial Rome—a bundle of rods with an axe in the center—and the Fascist salute is that of the ancient Romans—by outstretched arm. The coins being struck bear on one side the king's head and on the other the Roman *fascio*; in the same way special gold coins of one hundred lire will be issued shortly, to celebrate the first anniversary of the March to Rome. There is the most rigorous discipline, and the motto "No discussion, only obedience" has proved of immense value in all the sudden mobilizations and demobilizations carried out, often at a few hours' notice, which could give points to the best organized army in the world. On the occasion of the mass meeting preceding the March to Rome, which was attended by over half a million men, in less than twenty-four hours forty thousand left the town in perfect order and without the slightest hitch.

Fascism possesses a large press, which comprises five dailies, a large number of weekly, fortnightly, and monthly publications, a publishing house in Milan.

But the decisive factor in the great victory of Fascism is due to the personality of the great leader of this army of Italy's salvation, the very soul of this mighty movement.

Few public men of our time have had a more rapid, brilliant, and interesting career than Benito Mussolini, the son of a blacksmith. He is the youngest of his predecessors in this office, as he was born only forty years ago at Predappio, in the province of Forli, where the villagers still call him simply Our Benit. He was deeply attached to his mother, Rosa Maltoni, and her death caused him intense sorrow. He has one sister, Edvige, and a younger brother, Arnaldo, who, since the elder one has become Prime Minister, has taken his place as editor of *Il Popolo d'Italia*. Mussolini first worked in his father's forge and then, having occupied for a time the position of village schoolmaster, immigrated to Switzerland, from which country he was, however, expelled on account of articles he had written advocating the Marxist doctrines. Returning once more to Italy, he became an active member of the Socialist Party and finally editor of its organ, the *Avanti!*. Upon the outbreak of war in 1914, with his keen political insight, Mussolini saw the necessity of Italian intervention and in consequence was forced to leave the official Socialist Party, giving up all the positions he held in it. He founded his *Popolo d'Italia* and began fiercely to sound the trumpets of war, inciting his country to abandon her neutral attitude and to throw in her lot with the Allies. He gained his end, and in 1915 he went to the front as a simple soldier in the 11th Bersagliere Regiment. In 1917, as the result of the bursting of a shell, he received thirty-eight simultaneous wounds; he was obliged to go to the hospital, promoted on the field, and invalided out of the Army. He then returned to Milan, and having resumed the editorship of his paper, *Il Popolo d'Italia*, began his political battles and continued to fight through its columns, spurring his countrymen on to final victory.

With no exaggeration it can be stated that since the advent to power of Mussolini every day has seen a steady advance in the direction of the rebuilding of the country within and a notable enhancement of our prestige abroad. His strenuous everyday work is inspired by an indomitable determination to make Italy worthy of the glories of Vittorio Veneto, strengthened and disciplined, and he will spare neither himself nor those around him in his attempt to bring about its realization.

He wishes to secure Italy's rightful position in the world. Mussolini's foreign policy of dignity, honesty, and justice has already been outlined in his opening speech before the Chamber, and can be summarized thus: "No imperialism, no aggressions, but an attitude that shall do away with the policy of humility that has made Italy more like the Cinderella and humble servant of other nations. Respect for international treaties no matter what cost. Fidelity and friendship toward the nations that give Italy serious proofs of reciprocating it. Maintenance of Eastern equilibrium, on which depends the tranquility of the Balkan States and, therefore, European and world peace."

It is enough to cast an eye on the numerous legislative and administrative work accomplished by Mussolini's Government in these first eleven months to convince oneself that he is in deep earnest as to the vast program of reconstruction he means to carry through. With reference to domestic matters, the Fascist Government has passed a great number of bills and projects of laws concerning the Electoral Reform Bill approved by the Chamber last July: radical reform of the entire school system; institution of the National Militia; abolition of the Guardie Regie (which was a poor substitute for the Carabineers);

industrialization of public services (posts, telegraphs, railways); abolition of death taxes between near relations; enactment of Decree on the Eight-Hour Work Bill; reformation of the Civil Law Codes; reduction of Ministerial departments, now only nine, which formerly were sixteen; formation of the recent Ministry of National Economy, under which are grouped various others, Industry, Agriculture, Labor, etc.; and reduction of the national debt by over a billion, a comforting contribution toward the balance of the Budget, as is gathered by the speech delivered in June, at Milan, by the Minister of Finance, Hon. De Stefani.

Mussolini has established a real discipline (there are no more strikes since the Fascist Government is in power), fully restored the authority of the State, and has shown himself to be the most practical anti-waste advocate the world has yet known. As to foreign policy, he has adhered to the Washington Disarmament Conference, signed conventions relative to the laying of cables for a direct telegraphic communication with North, Central, and South America, negotiated important commercial treaties with Canada, Russia, Spain, Lithuania, Poland, Siam, Finland, Estonia, etc., and exercised beneficial influence in the Ruhr conflict and in the Lausanne Conference, being an element of equilibrium for the new afterwar international policy in the world.

The selection of his speeches contained in this volume is not a mere translation, since, in fact, the exact equivalent of this book as it has been arranged, classified, and edited is not to be found in any other language. These speeches, with the addition of the valuable prefatory notes, almost all of which have been supplied to me by one who has been closely associated with Mussolini during the whole of his political career, serve, in my opinion, as could no biography, to reveal the mind, character, and personality of Mussolini himself. Delivered at intervals throughout the various stages of his career, from Socialist to Fascist Prime Minister, they enable the reader to follow intimately the events that led up to the Fascist Revolution and its leader's attainment of his present strong position. The forcible and sober style of his character, shorn of every unnecessary word, betrays the dynamic force and intense earnestness of this man, who has been compared to Cromwell for his drastic and dictatorial methods in the Chamber and to Napoleon for his eagle-like perception, for his decisiveness, and his marvelous power of leadership.

Mussolini is a volcanic genius, a bewitcher of crowds. He seems a regular warrior, with an indomitable daring, great physical and moral courage, and he has seen death near him without wavering. He is the real type of Roman emperor, with a severe bronzed face, but which hides a kind and generous heart. He is what people call a real self-made man and is a great lover of the violin and of all kinds of sport: fencing, cycling, flying, riding, and motoring. Mussolini gets all he wants and quickly, and, as all his party do, knows exactly what he *does* want.

Apart from all that has been said, the present collection of speeches, besides showing Mussolini's strong hand in the difficult art of statesmanship, displays clearly in almost every page (and so, possibly, the book may also appeal to others than politicians) additional important elements that are not usually found in a volume of political speeches, namely a richness of sympathy for mankind, a blunt straightforwardness, a gentleness of soul together with exceptional moral strength, and pure idealism, which lift him not only above party politics, but also high above the average of mankind.

Such is the builder of New Italy, and the enthusiasm and deep confidence that Mussolini has inspired in our country, and the unanimous approval his work has prompted abroad, are a good omen for Italy's future fortunes and for the welfare of the world at large.

Bernardo Quaranta di San Severino

Siena, Via S. Quirico, N.1.
October 1923

Manifesto Issued by Mussolini After He and His Party Succeeded to the Government

National Fascist Party

Fascists of all Italy!

Our movement has been crowned with success. The leader of our Party now holds the political power of the State for Italy and abroad. While this New Government represents our triumph, it celebrates, at the same time, our victory in the name of those who by land and by sea promoted it; and it accepts also, for the purpose of pacification, men from other parties, provided they are true to the cause of the Nation. The Italian Fascists are too intelligent to wish to abuse their victory.

Fascists!

The supreme Quadrumvirate, which has resigned its powers in favor of the Party, thanks you for the magnificent proof of courage and of discipline you have given, and salutes you. You have proved yourselves worthy of the fortunes and of the future of your Fatherland.

Demobilize in the same perfectly orderly manner in which you assembled for this great achievement, destined—as we firmly believe—to open a new era in the history of Italy. Return now to your usual occupations, as, in order to arrive at the summit of her fortunes, Italy needs to work. May nothing disturb the glory of these days through which we have just passed—days of superb passion and of Roman greatness.

Long live Italy!

Long live Fascism!

The Quadrumvirate
Italo Balbo, Michele Bianchi, Emilio De Bono,
and Cesare Maria De Vecchi

PART I

MUSSOLINI THE SOCIALIST

Do Not Think That by Taking Away My Membership Card You Will Take Away My Faith in the Cause

November 25th, 1914, Milan
Before the meeting of the Milanese Socialist Section, which had
decreed Mussolini's expulsion from the official Socialist Party

In the fearless militarism of the dramatic speech with which this volume begins, the Socialistic activity of Benito Mussolini ends—of Benito Mussolini, who from the autumn of 1914 could have been considered the recognized and acclaimed leader of the Italian Socialist Party. He had attained with giant strides the highest rank in the Party's hierarchy, namely the editorship of the *Avanti!*, the chief organ of the political and syndicalist movement. He had been a clever and aggressive writer in a weekly provincial paper of Forli, called *La lotta di classe* (Class struggle), and an ardent Sunday orator for the ville of Romagna. He had revealed himself a comrade of tremendous power at the Congress of Reggio Emilia, held in the summer of 1912, where he delivered a memorable speech bitterly criticizing the flaccid mentality of Reformism then dominating the Party.

It was within two months of his success at Reggio Emilia that the revolutionary leaders, feeling the need of strong men, entrusted to Benito Mussolini the editorship of the *Avanti!*, which was the most powerful weapon of the Party.

The following speech was delivered before a furious crowd of not less than three thousand holders of membership cards, who hastened from other centers adjacent to Milan, amid a diabolical tumult in an atmosphere of organized hostility, which was the more violent by contrast with the fanatical devotion Benito Mussolini had evoked during the two years in which he had been the undisputed mouthpiece of the Party.

This atmosphere of intolerance and hatred had been fostered by the neutralist adversaries who had succeeded to the management of the *Avanti!* after the present head of the Italian Government had left the Party.

As is known, the excited meeting held in the spacious hall of the Casa del Popolo closed with a resolution for the expulsion of the new heretic, which

3

was passed, except by a negligible minority of about fifty supporters, who afterwards stood by Mussolini in the victorious campaign for intervention.

◆ ◆ ◆

My fate is decided, and it seems as if the sentence were to be executed with a certain solemnity. (Voices: "Louder! Louder!")

You are severer than ordinary judges who allow the fullest and most exhaustive defense even after the sentence, since they give ten days for the production of the motives of appeal. If, then, it is decided, and you still think that I am unworthy of fighting any longer for your cause—("Yes! yes!" is shouted by some of the most excited among the audience)—then expel me. But I have a right to exact a legal act of accusation, and in this meeting the public prosecutor has not yet intervened with regard either to the political or to the moral issues. I shall, therefore, be condemned by an "order of the day," which means nothing. In a case like this, I ought to have been told that I was unworthy to belong any longer to the party for definite reasons, in which case I should have accepted my fate. This, however, has not been said, and a great many of you—if not all—will leave this room with an uneasy conscience. (Deafening voices: "No! no!")

With reference to the moral question, I repeat once more that I am ready to submit my case to any Committee that cares to make investigations and to issue a report.

As regards the question of discipline, I should say that this has not been examined, because there are just and fitting precedents for my changed attitude, and if I do not quote them it is because I feel myself to be secure and have an easy conscience.

You think you are signing my death warrant, but you are mistaken. Today you hate me, because in your heart of hearts you still love me, because. . . . (Applause and hisses interrupt the speaker.)

But you have not seen the last of me! Twelve years of my party life are, or ought to be, a sufficient guarantee of my faith in Socialism. Socialism is something that takes root in the heart. What divides me from you now is not a small dispute, but a great question over which the whole of Socialism is divided. Amilcare Cipriani can no longer be your candidate because he declared, both by word of mouth and in writing, that if his seventy-five years allowed him, he would be in the trenches fighting the European military reaction that was stifling revolution.

Time will prove who is right and who is wrong in the formidable question that now confronts Socialism, which it has never had to face before in the history of humanity, since never before has there been such a conflagration as exists today, in which millions of the proletariat are pitted one against the other. This war, which has much in common with those of the Napoleonic period, is not an everyday event. Waterloo was fought in 1814; perhaps 1914 will see some other principles fall to the ground, will see the salvation of liberty, and the beginning of a new era in the world's history—(loud applause greets this fitting historical comparison)—and especially in the history of the proletariat, which at all critical moments has found me here with you in this same spot, just as it found me in the street.

But I tell you that from now onwards I shall never forgive nor have pity on anyone who in this momentous hour does not speak his mind for fear of being hissed at or shouted down. (This cutting allusion to the many prominent absentees is understood and warmly applauded by the meeting.)

I shall neither forgive nor have pity on those who are purposely reticent, those who show themselves hypocrites and cowards. And you will find me still on your side. You must not think that the middle classes are enthusiastic about our intervention. They snarl and accuse us of temerity, and fear that the proletariat, once armed with bayonets, will use them for their own ends. (Mingled applause, and cries of "No! no!")

Do not think that in taking away my membership card you will be taking away my faith in the cause, or that you will prevent me from still working for Socialism and revolution. (Hearty applause follows these last words of Mussolini, uttered with great energy and profound conviction. He descends from the platform and makes his way down the great hall.)

PART II

MUSSOLINI THE MAN OF THE WAR

For the Liberty of Humanity and the Future of Italy

December 13th, 1914, Scuole Mazza, Parma

This speech was delivered under the stress of great excitement. The most ardent supporters of active neutrality were assembled at Parma, a citadel of revolutionary syndicalism, which opposed Party Socialism, and the majority of whose members, after the outbreak of the European War, sided against the Central Empires and in defense of intervention. Among these we remember Giacinto Menotti Serrati, then editor-in-chief of the *Avanti!*, and Fulvio Zocchi, a ridiculous and malignant demagogue, now removed from political life.

But, notwithstanding this pressure from outside, the people of Parma, mindful of their Garibaldian and anti-Austrian traditions, sided enthusiastically with Mussolini and Alceste De Ambris, the leader of syndicalism and member of Parliament for the city, who had been the first to support the section of the extremists.

◆ ◆ ◆

Citizens, it is in your interest to listen to me quietly and with tolerance. I shall be brief, precise, and sincere to the point of rudeness.

The last great continental war was from 1870 to 1871. Prussia, guided by Bismarck and Moltke, defeated France and robbed her of two flourishing and populous provinces. The Treaty of Frankfurt marked the triumph of Bismarck's policy, which aimed at the incontestable hegemony of Prussia in Central Europe and the gradual Slavization of the Balkan zones of Austria-Hungary. One recalls these features of Bismarck's policy in trying to understand the different international crises that took place in Europe from 1870 up to the bewildering and extremely painful situation of today. From 1870 onwards there were only remoter wars among the peoples of Eastern Europe,

9

such as those between Russia and Turkey, Serbia and Bulgaria, Greece and Turkey, or wars in the colonies. There was, in consequence, a widespread conviction that a European or world war was no longer possible. The most diverse reasons were put forward to maintain this argument.

Illusions and Sophisms. It was suggested, for example, that perfecting the instruments of war would destroy its possibility. Ridiculous! War has always been deadly. The perfecting of arms is relative to the progress—technical, mechanical, and military—of the human race. In this respect the warlike machines of the ancient Romans are the equivalent of 420 mm caliber mortars. They are made with the object of killing, and they do kill. The perfecting of instruments of war is no hindrance to warlike instincts. It might have the opposite effect.

Reliance was also placed on "human kindness" and other sentiments of humanity, of brotherhood and love, which ought, it was maintained, to bind all the different branches of the species "man" together regardless of barriers of land or sea. Another illusion! It is very true that these feelings of sympathy and brotherliness exist; our century has, in truth, seen the rapid multiplication of philanthropic works for the alleviation of the hardships both of men and of animals, but along with these impulses exist others, profounder, higher, and more vital. We should not explain the universal phenomenon of war by attributing it to the caprices of monarchs, race-hatred, or economic rivalry; we must take into account other feelings, which each one of us carries in his heart, and which made Proudhon exclaim, with that perennial truth that hides beneath the mask of paradox, that war was of "divine origin."

It was also maintained that the encouragement of closer international relations—economic, artistic, intellectual, political, and sporting—by causing the peoples to become better acquainted, would have prevented the outbreak of war among civilized nations. Norman Angell had founded his book upon the impossibility of war, proving that all the nations involved—victors and vanquished alike—would have their economic life completely convulsed and ruined in consequence. Another illusion laid bare! Lack of observation. The purely economic man does not exist. The story of the world is not merely a page of book-keeping, and material interests—luckily—are not the only mainspring of human actions. It is true that international relations have multiplied, that there is, or was, freer interchange—political and economic—between peoples of different countries than there was a century ago. But parallel with this phenomenon is another, which is that the people, with the diffusion of culture and the formation of an economic system of a national type, tend to isolate themselves psychologically and morally.

Internationalism. Side by side with the peaceful, middle-class movement, which is not worth examination, flourished another of an international character, that of the working classes. At the outbreak of war this class, too, gave evidence of its inefficiency. The Germans, who ought to have set the example, flocked as a man to the Kaiser's banner. The treachery of the Germans forced the Socialists of the other countries to fall back upon the basis of nationality and the necessity of national defense. The German unity automatically determined the unity of the other countries. It is said, and justly, that international relations are like love; it takes two to carry them on. Internationalism is ended; that which existed yesterday is dead, and it is impossible to foresee what form it will take tomorrow. Reality cannot be done away with and cannot be ignored, and the reality is that millions and millions of men, for the most part of the working classes, are standing opposite one another today on the blood-drenched battlefields of Europe. The neutrals, who shout themselves hoarse crying "Down with war!" do not realize the grotesque cowardice contained in that cry today. It is irony of the most atrocious kind to shout "Down with war!" while men are fighting and dying in the trenches.

The Real Situation. Between the two groups, the Triple Entente and the Austro-German Alliance, Italy has remained neutral. In the Triple Entente there is heroic Serbia, who has broken loose from the Austrian yoke; there is martyred Belgium, who refused to sell herself; there is republican France who has been attacked; there is democratic England; there is autocratic Russia, though her foundations are undermined by revolution. On the other side there is Austria, clerical and feudal, and Germany, militarist and aggressive. At the outbreak of war Italy proclaimed herself neutral. Was the "exception" contemplated in the treaties? It seems as if it were so, especially in view of the recent revelations made by Giolitti. If the neutrality of the Government meant indifference, the neutrality of the Socialists and the economic organizations had an entirely different character and significance. The Socialist neutrality intended a general strike in the case of alliance with Austria, no practical opposition in the case of a war against her. A distinction was made, therefore, between one war and another. Further, the classes were allowed to be called up.

If the Government had mobilized, all the Socialists would have found it a natural and logical proceeding. They admitted, therefore, that a nation has the right and duty to defend itself by recourse to arms, in case of attack from outside. Neutrality understood in this way had necessarily to lead—with the progress of events, especially in Belgium—to the idea of intervention.

The Bourgeoisie is Neutral. It is controversial whether Italy has a bourgeoisie in the generally accepted sense of the word. Rather than the bourgeoisie and lower classes, there are rich and poor. In any case, it is untrue that the Italian middle classes are, at the moment, jingoist; on the contrary, they are neutral and desperately pacifist. The banking world is neutral, the industrial classes have reorganized their business, and the agrarian population, small and great, are pacifists by tradition and temperament; the political and academic middle classes are neutral. Look at the Senate! There are perhaps exceptions, young men who do not wish to stagnate in the dead pool of neutrality, but the middle classes, taken as a whole, are hostile to war and are neutral. As a conclusive proof, compare the tone of the middle-class papers today with that shown at the time of the Libyan campaign and note the difference. The trumpet-call which then sounded for war is muffled now. The language of the middle-class press is uncertain, wavering, and mysterious, neutral in word but, in effect, in favor of the Allies. Where are the trumpets that summoned us in September 1911? The secret is out, and ought to make the Socialists, who are not stupid, stop and think. On the one side are all the conservative and stagnant elements, and on the other the revolutionary and the living forces of the country. It is necessary to choose.

We Want the War! But *we* want the war and we want it *at once*. It is not true that military preparation is lacking. What does this waiting for the spring to come mean?

Socialism ought not, and cannot, be against all wars because in that case it would have to deny fifty years of history. Do you want to judge and condemn in the same breath the war in Tripoli and the result of the French Revolution of 1793? And Garibaldi? Is he, too, a jingoist? You must distinguish between one war and another, as between one crime and another, one case of bloodshed and another. Bovio said, "All the water in the sea would not suffice to remove the stain from the hands of Lady Macbeth, but a basinful would wash the blood from the hands of Garibaldi."

Guesde, in a congress of French Socialists held a few weeks before the outbreak of war, declared that, in case of a conflagration, the nation that was most Socialist would be the victim of the nation that was least. To prove this, notice the behavior of the Italian Socialists. Look at them in Parliament. Treves lost time by quibbling. At one moment he exclaimed, "We shall not deny the country." In fact the country cannot be denied. One does not deny one's mother, even if she does not offer one all her gifts, even if she does force one to earn one's living in the alluring streets of the world. (Great applause.)

Treves said more: "We shall not oppose a war of defense." If this is admitted, the necessity of arming ourselves is admitted. You will not open the gates of Italy yet to the Austrian army, because they will come to pillage the houses and violate the women! I know it well. There are base wretches who blame Belgium for defending herself. She might have pocketed the money of the Germans, they say, and allowed them a free passage, while resistance meant laying herself open to the scientific and systematic destruction of her towns. But Belgium lives, and will live, because she refused to sell herself ignobly. If she had done so, she would be dead for all time. (Great applause, and cries of "Long live Belgium!" The cheering lasts for some minutes.)

The War of Defense. When do you want to begin to defend yourselves? When the enemy's knee is on your chest? Wouldn't it be better to begin a little earlier? Wouldn't it be better to begin today when it would not cost so much, rather than wait until tomorrow when it might be disastrous? Do you wish to maintain a splendid isolation? But in that case we must arm, arm and create a colossal militarism.

The Socialists, and I am still one, although an exasperated one, never brought forward the question of irredentism, but left it to the Republicans. We are in favor of a national war. But there are also reasons, purely socialist in character, which spur us on toward intervention.

The Europe of Tomorrow. It is said that the Europe of tomorrow will not be any different from the Europe of yesterday. This is the most absurd and alarming hypothesis. If you accept it, there is some absolute meaning for your neutrality. It is not worthwhile sacrificing oneself in order to leave things as they were before. But both mind and heart refuse to believe that this spilling of blood over three continents will lead to nothing. Everything leads one to believe, on the contrary, that the Europe of tomorrow will be profoundly transformed. Greater liberty or greater reaction? More or less militarism? Which of the two groups of Powers, by their victory, would assure us of better conditions of liberty for the working classes? There is no doubt about the answer. And in what way do you wish to assist in the triumph of the Triple Entente? Perhaps with articles in the papers and "orders of the day" in committee? Are these sentimental manifestations enough to raise up Belgium again? To relieve France? This France which bled for Europe in the revolutions and wars from 1789 to 1871 and from 1871 to 1914? Do you then offer to the France of the "Rights of Man" nothing but words?

Against Apathy. Tell me—and this is the supreme reason for intervention—tell me, is it human, civilized, socialistic, to stop quietly at the window while blood is flowing in torrents, and to say, "I am not going to move, it does not matter to me a bit"? Can the formula of "sacred egoism" devised by the Hon. Salandra be accepted by the working classes? No! I do not think so. The law of solidarity does not stop at economic competition; it goes beyond. Yesterday it was both fine and necessary to contribute in aid of struggling companions; but today they ask you to shed your blood for them. They implore it. Intervention will shorten the period of terrible carnage. That will be to the advantage of all, even of the Germans, our enemies. Will you refuse this proof of solidarity? If you do, with what dignity will you, Italian proletarians, show yourselves abroad tomorrow? Do you not fear that your German comrades will reject you, because you betrayed the Triple Entente? Do you not fear that those in France and Belgium, showing you their land still scarred by graves and trenches, and pointing out with pride their ruined towns, will say to you: "Where were you, and what did you do, O Italian Proletarians, when we fought desperately against the Austro-German militarism to free Europe from the incubus of the hegemony of the Kaiser?" In that day you will not know how to answer; in that day you will be ashamed to be Italian, but it will be too late!

The People's War. Let us take up again the Italian traditions. The people who want the war want it without delay. In two months' time it might be an act of brigandage; today it is a war to be fought with courage and dignity.

War and Socialism are incompatible, understood in their universal sense, but every epoch and every people has had its wars. Life is relative; the absolute only exists in the cold and unfruitful abstract. Those who set too much store by their skins will not go into the trenches, and you will not find them even in the streets on the day of battle. He who refuses to fight today is an accomplice of the Kaiser and a prop of the tottering throne of Franz Joseph. Do you wish mechanical Germany, intoxicated by Bismarck, to be once more the free and unprejudiced Germany of the first half of last century? Do you wish for a German Republic extending from the Rhine to the Vistula? Does the idea of the Kaiser, a prisoner and banished to some remote island, make you laugh? Germany will only find her soul through defeat. With the defeat of Germany the new and brilliant spring will burst over Europe.

It is necessary to act, to move, to fight and, if necessary, to die. Neutrals have never dominated events. They have always gone under. It is blood that moves the wheels of history! (Frantic bursts of applause.)

Either War or the End of Italy's Name as a Great Power

January 25th, 1915, Milan

The progress of Milanese, which is to say of Italian interventionalism, thanks to the authority and the influence of the Lombard metropolis, the throbbing heart of the country, begins with the meeting held in the great hall of the Istituto Tecnico Carlo Cattaneo. At this meeting there were present forty-five "fasci" called Fasci d'Azione Rivoluzionaria,[5] formed almost entirely in the principal regional and provincial centers. Among the most notable supporters were a group of soldiers of the 61st and 62nd Infantry, the poet Ceccardo Roccatagliata Ceccardi, and the old Garibaldian patriot Ergisto Bezzi, called the "Ferruccio" of the Trentino.

◆　◆　◆

I thank you for your greeting and am happy and proud to be present at this meeting, which represents, perhaps, in these six months of a neutrality of commercialism and smuggling, branded with Socialism, a new fact of the utmost importance and significance.

While listening to the reports made here, my mind carried me back to the congresses of the First International, when the representatives of the various sections of the different countries prepared written reports that gave full details as to the situations of their respective peoples. This was a splendid means of coming to a closer understanding. I pass now to speak of the international state of affairs.

---

[5] Literally "Fasces of Revolutionary Action" or figuratively "League of Revolutionary Action." Founded on December 11th, 1914, they held their first meeting here in Milan on January 25th, 1915. At this time the members are referred to as "fasci," not "fascisti" (fascists) until late April.

The diplomatic and political situation cannot be spoken of without the military. The military situation is stationary, although, today, it is clearly in favor of the Germans, who occupy the whole of Belgium, with the exception of 880 square kilometers, who hold ten rich and populous departments of France, and a great part of Russian Poland. Besides, the recent attack upon Dunkirk and the activity of the submarines and dirigibles show that the Germans are still full of fight and wish to carry the war on literally to the utmost limits of their powers of attack and defense. Thus the intervention of Italy is not late. I think the right moment has come now, when the military situation hangs in the balance. There is neither advance nor retreat on either side, for which reason it would be a good thing to decide the game by the introduction of a new factor, the intervention of Italy and Romania.

The principal international events of this week have been the Berchtold resignations, the consideration of intervention by Romania, and the treaty of the Triple Entente for the regulation of Russia's financial difficulties.

Russia. It really seems to me that there was a moment of slackness in the pursuit of the war on the part of Austria and Russia. It is enough to call to mind a short paragraph in an official Russian paper, the *Russkoe Slovo*, in order to realize that there was a time when Russia wavered.

"It is true," says the paper, "that on September 4th, Russia, France, England, Belgium, and Serbia undertook not to make peace individually; but this pledge brings with it the necessity of supporting the expenses of war in common, especially now that Turkey has come to the help of the Central Powers. Our treasury is empty. Where can we obtain that money which is more important than men? If England refuses, we shall be obliged to end the war in any way convenient to Russia." Really threatening words these, of which England, however, understood the meaning and immediately took steps to prevent their realization by launching the loan of 15 billion in favor of Russia to be subscribed to in the capitals of the Triple Entente. And, in fact, immediately after the announcement of the loan, the tone of the official papers changed, and there was no more talk of making a separate peace.

Austria. There were other symptoms of restlessness in Austria. Clearly, up to the present, Austria has been sacrificed the most. She has lost Galicia and been defeated by the Russians and Serbs.

It may be then that the resignation of Berchtold is an indication that Austrian politics are taking a new direction. In what sense? I do not think in the pacifist sense. Austria is tied to Germany, and Germany leans upon Austria and Hungary. Burian's journey to the German General Staff was made, I think, with the object of obtaining military aid for Hungary. Austria and Hungary are preparing themselves against Romania, because this nation will probably intervene before Italy.

Romania. Romania has 4 million men concentrated in Transylvania under the rule of Austria-Hungary; she is a young nation with a perfect army of 500,000 men, and she will be obliged to end her hesitation, probably owing to the fact that the Russians are at her frontier. Nothing would embarrass the Romanians as much as this, since they remember that in 1878 the Russians occupied Bessarabia. When the Russians, therefore, are in Transylvania, the intervention of Romania will be decided at once.

Vlorë. One fact that has a certain importance where Italy is concerned is the occupation of Vlorë, which has come about in curious circumstances with the occupation of Sazan and the landing of the marines before the Bersaglieri.[6] I do not think that there are really rebels in Albania; and I think that Italy will stop at Vlorë. I do not think either that Vlorë will run any serious risk, because the Albanians have rifles but no artillery. Albania does not exist in the true sense of the word, as the Albanians are divided both by race and tribe, and I do not think that an organized movement is to be feared.

Switzerland. One point that we must take into consideration is the position of Switzerland—a point, to my mind, rather obscure. It is true that we can feel, to a certain extent, reassured by the fact that the president of Switzerland at the moment is an Italian.[7] But without a doubt a restless state of mind prevails among the German element there. The voice of race calls louder than the voice of political union: the German Swiss lay down laws; they circulate pamphlets that say "Let us remain Swiss"; they go in search of the Swiss spirit, but I think

---

[6] The Italian variations of Valona and Saseno were used in the original publication. For clarity in English, these have been changed to Vlorë and Sazan, the Albanian names by which they are internationally known.

[7] Giuseppe Motta, president for the calendar year of 1915.

that it would be difficult to find it. In any case, it is certain that they make acid comments on the articles in *Popolo d'Italia!* Taken as a whole it can be said that a Pan-German movement has developed in German Switzerland, which manifests open sympathy toward the Central Powers.

Zahn, a Swiss writer, in this way published an ode and sent money to the German Red Cross. A political personality of Basel sent information about the troops and the Swiss defense to the *Frankfurter Zeitung*. The novelist Schapfer, of Basel, went to Berlin to extol Germany and to sing "Deutschland Über Alles" at a public meeting. The journalist Schappner advocated in the *Neues Deutschland* that Switzerland should abandon her neutral position in order to help Germany and have as compensation Upper Savoy, the Gex region, and a part of Franche-Comté so that she might form an advanced post of Germany toward the south, declaring at the same time an alliance with Austria-Hungary, which would enable Switzerland to extend her boundaries also toward Italy.

The *Neue Zürcher Nachrichten* has even gone to the extent of taunting Belgium with her unhappy fate, saying that the neutrality of Belgium would have been violated by her own Government, calling her the betrayer of Germany, and saying that Germany had every right to punish her.

These are all documents that are worthwhile knowing about, because they denote a state of mind that might have a surprise in store for us. Switzerland is made up of twenty-four cantons, in one of which the Italian language is spoken, but I don't think that much reliance can be placed on that fact. For the rest, I know that the General Staff preoccupies itself a good deal with the possibility that, either through love or fear, Switzerland will allow the Kaiser's troops to pass through Swiss territory, in which case they would then find themselves at once in Lombardy.

The Dilemma of Italy. This meeting, therefore, asks for the repudiation of the Treaty of the Triple Alliance as the first step to mobilization and war. Otherwise, if the treaty is still in force, you can see how it can be interpreted in any sense. At first it bound us to intervene on the side of Austria and Germany, and we were taxed with being traitors when we declared ourselves neutral. Today it proves that it is our duty to remain neutral. Treaties then are interpreted according to the letter, according to the spirit, and according to the convenience of those who have to interpret them! Necessity demands, therefore, the explicit repudiation of the Treaty of the Triple Alliance. Perhaps this can be made the *casus belli*. We are not diplomats, but it is certain that if Italy repudiates the Treaty of the Triple Alliance, Germany will ask for explanations, and if, at the same time, there was mobilization against Austria and Germany, we should be able to reach the stage in which a solution by arms would be forced upon us. For us the *casus belli* was magnificent and solemn; it was that created by the violation of the neutrality of Belgium. Italy ought to intervene in the name of *jus gentium*, in the name of her own national security. She has not been able to do so then, but now we must decide. "Either war or the end of our name as a great power." Let us build gambling-houses and hotels and grow fat. A people can have this ideal also, which is shared by the lower zoological species!

In reality the German working classes have embraced the cause of Prussian militarism, and so, my friends, the chief reason for remaining neutral falls to the ground. You Italian Socialists are preparing to commit the same crime of which you accuse the German Socialists. We, in the meantime, question the right of the German Socialists to call themselves Socialists anymore. The International compact is only of value when it is signed and respected by all the contracting parties. Since the Germans are the first to have broken it, the Italians are no longer under obligation to hold by a contract that might mean their ruin.

It is a fact, however, that Italy is "still bound to the Triple Alliance." This Government of ours is pusillanimous, because the repudiation of the Triple Alliance does not mean a declaration of war or even mobilization. But, meanwhile, this would prove that the Italian people vindicate their right to independence of action in this period of history.

The Revolutionary War. To say that we are causing a revolution in order to obtain war, is to say something that we cannot maintain. We have not the strength. We find ourselves face to face with formidable coalitions, but the fasces of action have this object, to create that state of mind that will impose war upon the country.

Tomorrow, if Italy does not make war, a revolutionary position will be inevitably decided and discontent will spring up everywhere. Those same men who today are in favor of neutrality, when they feel themselves humiliated as men and Italians, will ask the responsible powers to account for it, and then will be our chance. Then we shall have our war. Then we shall say to the dominant classes, "You have not proved yourselves capable of fulfilling your task; you have deceived us and destroyed our aspirations. Your first care should have been the completion of the unity of the country, and you have ignored it. You have been warned about it by democracy in general and by the Republican Party particularly." This will be a case which will surely end in condemnation, in condemnation that cannot be other than capital. And then perhaps we shall issue from this harassing period of history. Every day we feel that there is something in Italy that does not work, that there is a cog missing in the gear, or a wheel that does not go round. The country is young, but its institutions are old, and when— if I may be allowed to quote once more from Karl Marx, the old Pan-Germanist—a conflict between new forces and old institutions begins to shape itself, which means that the new wine cannot any longer be kept in the old skins, or the inevitable will occur. The old forces of the political and social life of Italy will fall into fragments. (Loud applause.)

To the Complete Vanquishing of the Huns

December 1st, 1917, Sesto San Giovanni

After the Caporetto disaster,[8] the patriotic organizations of Milan had consolidated their union, previously undermined by the opponents of war, who, thanks to the leniency of the Government, had been able to work in the interest of the enemy. They developed the existing sphere of propaganda, advocating resistance within the country. One of the centers most infected by neutralist opposition was undoubtedly Sesto San Giovanni, a large borough of the working classes at the gates of Milan, completely controlled by Social-Communist administration.

Mussolini, having just left the military hospital, where he had been lying ill as a result of the many wounds he received as a Bersagliere of the 11th Regiment, spoke in this hostile citadel as only he could speak; and it is certainly beyond question that his frank and incisive eloquence was mainly instrumental in dispersing the bitter anti-war feelings fomented by stubborn and impudent Socialist neutralism.

◆   ◆   ◆

Workmen and citizens! The other evening, after three years' silence, I spoke to the audience of La Scala,[9] an imposing audience and a large hall, but I prefer this friendly gathering of workmen and soldiers, because, in spite of everything, I am, and shall always remain, one with the masses who produce and work, and the implacable adversary of every parasite.

---

[8] The Italians lost the Battle of Caporetto (also called the Twelfth Battle of the Isonzo, the Battle of Kobarid or the Battle of Karfreit) fought on their front against the Central Powers. The battle took place from October 24th to November 19th, 1917.
[9] The Teatro alla Scala opera house in Milan.

The International Illusion. I am here to talk to you of the war, and to remind you of an article, which some of you will still remember, in which, in a certain degree, I foresaw this truce. "A truce of arms" I called it then, and I repeat these words today. When one speaks of war, one must do so with a clear conscience and without all those useless ornaments of speech typical of an old, artificial style of literature. We must remember that while we stand together here to think of them, the best among our men, our brothers, your sons, and your husbands are consuming themselves, suffering and perhaps dying for us, for our country and for our civilization! We wished for the war, it is true, but because the arrogance of other men imposed it upon us. We had entertained the illusion that it was possible to realize the international dream among the peoples, but, while we were sincerely putting our faith in this beautiful chimera, the German "Internationals," with Bebel at their head, were declaring themselves to be first Germans, and afterwards Socialists! And in the International Congresses the Germans always systematically refused to bind themselves to decisive action with the Socialists of other countries, under the specious pretext that the retrograde constitution of their country did not allow them, without jeopardizing their organization, to conclude international agreements. They held too much by their organizations, by their 101 deputies and by the fat and swollen purse of marks, which is the only thing which has been saved from German Socialism. (Loud applause.)

While Germany was preparing for war by organizing formidable means of dominion and massacre, nobody in England, France, Italy, or Russia dreamed of the imminence of the terrible scourge.

The True Germany. We had a very wrong idea of Germany. We only knew the Germany of the flaxen-haired Gretchens and of home-sick novels, and not that of von Bernhardi, Harden, and the Hohenzollerns.[10]

It was Germany who wanted the war. Harden said so in an ill-considered outburst of sincerity. The Socialists, who claimed more land for the expansion of the German people, wanted it; spectacled professors incapable of synthesis, but terrible in analysis, prepared it; the military caste imposed it. The pretext for the unchaining of these

---

[10] Friedrich von Bernhardi, Maximilian Harden, and the House of Hohenzollern.

forces was soon found. Two revolver shots in 1914, some bombs thrown, two imperial corpses hurried away in a court coach were the pretext. The war, for which the Central Powers were prepared, blazed up on all sides.

The Socialist Intervention. We Socialists who were in favor of intervention advocated war, because we divined that it contained within it the seeds of revolution. It is not the first instance of revolutionary war. There were the Napoleonic Wars, the War of 1870, the enterprises of Garibaldi, in which, had we lived in those days, we should have joined in the same spirit and the same faith.

Karl Marx, too, was a jingoist. In 1855 he wrote that Germany would have been obliged to declare war against Russia; and in 1870 he said of the French, "They must be defeated! They will never be sufficiently beaten." And when in 1871 the Socialists of France, with Latin ingenuousness, after declaring the Republic, sent a passionate appeal to the Germans for peace, Karl Marx said, "These imbeciles of Frenchmen claim that for their rag of a republic we should renounce all the advantages of this war."

One Does Not Deny One's Country. It is possible to remain a Socialist and be in favor of certain wars. When the country is in danger, it is not possible to remain pacifist. A man cannot ignore his country any more than a tree can ignore the earth which provides it with sustenance. (Applause.) Our people have understood it, and you, who carry in your veins some drops of the warrior-blood of those men of Legnano who drove away Barbarossa, of the people of the Cinque Giornate,[11] join with me today in inciting our soldiers to free our land from the shame of servitude. (Applause.) To deny one's country, especially in a critical hour of her existence, is to deny one's mother!

It was thought that the soldiers' strike would bring peace. But, when our soldiers found that the enemy, instead of throwing down their rifles, mounted cannons and field-guns, instead of fraternizing, massacred old men, women, and children, and far from returning to their own country, advanced into ours, they only waited until a large enough river divided them from the adversary to place before them once again the impassable barrier of the Italian forces. (Loud applause.)

---

[11] The Five Days of Milan insurrection in 1848.

Our setback is not due to fear of the Germans. The victors of eleven battles, the soldiers of the Carso, Bainsizza, Monte Santo, Cucco, and of Sabotino do not fear spiked helmets. The armies of all the combatant countries have had moments of bewilderment, but not one recovered itself as quickly as we have. After only one week of retreat, our troops faced the enemy again and forced them back.

A Resolute Resistance. We have skirted the abyss; we might have been lost, but we have saved ourselves. While the Germans were hoping for still further revolution, the soldiers reestablished the force of resistance that had been weakened, and now at the front the only fraternity is that of rifle shots. (Applause.)

When the storm is passed we shall be proud of having done our duty. Wilson, convinced pacifist, was drawn into the war by an elevated humanitarian motive, which made him feel that to prolong the war was an act of intolerable complicity with the Germans, and he gives us an example.

The war will end with our victory, but in order to win, you, workmen, must produce more. We must have guns, shells, rifles, and bombs in great quantities. Arms and munitions, at this moment, represent our salvation. Tomorrow, when our factories again produce ploughs and spades and instruments for agriculture, we shall have the joy of a duty done. Today, and until the barbarians are defeated forever, instruments of war must increase in number under the impulse of your decisive will to win. (Loud applause and demonstration of affection and sympathy.)

No Turning Back!

February 24th, 1918, Augusteo, Rome[12]

The speech delivered at the Augusteo in Rome may be included among those made by the most fervent patriots to rouse the country to a resolute effort after the Caporetto disaster. It was a summons to resistance, and a strong indictment against the heads of the Government in Italy, which was responsible for the moral collapse that took place in the Army, due to the evil influences of blackmail and neutralist Parliamentarism at work in the country. The salient feature of this meeting was the leaving of the hall by the generals representing the Corpo d'Armata (Army Corps) and the Ministry of War. But it was entirely owing to this meeting of exasperated patriots that the general policy of the then Prime Minister ceased to be lenient to the enemy's sympathizers and that active resistance paved the way to the victory of the country in arms.

◆   ◆   ◆

I wonder if there is anyone among you who remembers a meeting in favor of intervention in the war, which we held three years ago in one of the squares in Rome? We were dispersed by the police, but we were in the right. We moved on, and history moved on with us.

Three cities created history. But it does not matter. It is always the cities that create history; the villages are content to endure it. We, after three years of war, notwithstanding Caporetto, solemnly and truly reaffirm all that was deep, pure, and immortal in those days in May.

---

[12] The inner portion of the Mausoleum of Augustus, which was converted into a concert hall in 1907 and restored as an archeological site in 1936.

Remember! It was just in May 1915 that Italy was not afraid of knowing how to live, because she was not afraid of knowing how to die!

The Mistake of May. But we made a great mistake then, which we have since paid for bitterly. We, who wished for the war, ought to have taken command of the situation. (Loud applause.) The Italian people—which is not the plebeian crowd that gets drunk in taverns, for twenty centuries of history have not civilized us for nothing—the Italian people had, even then, a vague apprehension of the dangers that threatened its mission.

In May 1915 the nation as a whole presented a marvelous concentration of human force. We men of '84, when we forded the Upper Isonzo, thought that it was never again to be crossed by the Germans. When we gained the other side, with one accord we shouted: "Long live Italy!" (Loud applause from the whole assembly, who echo the cry.) It was fine human material, which we handed over to those men who carried on war as if it were a tiresome task more tedious than the rest. We gave it over—for a war which, after twenty centuries of history, was the first war of the Italian people—to men who did not understand it, to men who represented the past, to bureaucrats who have spilled exceedingly too much ink over the trials and sufferings of the people.

But we are here to say to you: Gentlemen! the Germans are on the Piave, the Germans have broken down one gate of the Veneto and are in the process of breaking down the other. The moment has come to see if our hearts are made of steel. (Enthusiastic applause.)

I know these soldiers, because, as a simple soldier myself, I have lived among them, leading the life of a simple soldier. I have seen them under all the different aspects of military life. I have seen them in the barracks, in the hard, bare military transports while going to the front, in the trenches, in the dugouts under ceaseless bombardment when the shells rained down death; I have seen them when every heart has stopped beating, awaiting the command of the officer, "Over the top"; I know them, these sons of Italy, and I tell you, they have not been merely soldiers, they have been saints and martyrs! (Loud burst of applause.)

The Causes of Caporetto. How then did Caporetto happen? Let us search our consciences courageously as a great people.

Ah! yes! At first, it may have had a military reason, not later. Later we were face to face with a gigantic hallucination. (Applause.) Great words were flashed across the horizon. The formula of "salvation" had come from Russia, and from Rome came a fierce outcry against the war, saying that it was "a useless massacre." You cannot conceive the profound disturbance this outcry caused in the minds of the multitude. And, as if that were not enough, without anyone having the courage to take summary proceedings against the authors, another sacrilegious message came from Parliament: "No more trenches next winter." And, it is true, we are not any longer in the trenches beyond the Isonzo; we are on this side of the Piave.

Justice for All. All this was the result of a falsehood that lay at the bottom of our national life. The words "political liberty" had been said. Ah! liberty to betray, to murder the country, to pour out more blood, as said the man in France.[13] (General applause. Cries of "Long live Clemenceau!") This political liberty is a paradox. It is criminal to think that men are requisitioned, dressed, armed, and sent to be killed while every liberty of speech and power of protest is denied them, that they are terribly punished for the slightest act or word not in keeping with given orders, while at the same time, behind, in the secret meeting-places, in the club-houses of brutalized drunkards, plans are allowed to be matured and words to be spoken that are death to the war. (Loud general applause.)

But did you not feel, after October 24th,[14] that there was a great change in us, both collectively and individually? Did you not feel that the vultures had torn away the flesh and fixed their claws in the open wounds? Did you not understand that we were going back to '66? Did you not take into account the danger that the military system of '66 would be accompanied by the same diplomatic maneuvering that we have not yet expiated? One does not deny one's country, one conquers it! (Warm applause.)

The Example of Russia. Take a lesson from what has happened in Russia. The Latin sages used to say that Nature does not work by sudden leaps. I think, on the contrary, that she does sometimes. But in Russia they wanted to make things move too fast. They got rid of

---

[13] Georges Clemenceau.
[14] 1917, the beginning of the Battle of Caporetto.

Tsarism in order to form the democratic republic of Rodzianko and Milyukov. That was in itself a big step, and I pass over the intermediate action of the Grand Duke Michael. But, not satisfied with this republic, they wished to become more Socialist and called for Kerensky. Kerensky went, because he was a mere figurehead—(Laughter)—and now there are other people who still want to make things move too fast. But now the Germans, under the pretense of a future pseudo-democracy, have unmasked their brutal and barbarous annexationist projects. At Petrograd, it is said, all citizens must dig trenches, and those falling under suspicion of vagabondage or espionage will be shot immediately.

An Iron Policy. But meanwhile the Germans advance, and I think they are impelled by three motives: military, political, and dynastic. I think that the Hohenzollerns propose to put the Romanovs back on the throne. Well! I don't care if they do! As the Russian people have proved that they don't know how to live under a regime of liberty, let them live in slavery. But, in the meantime, the defection of the Russians increases our task.

It is not the moment to bewail idly or to follow a weak policy. I seek ferocious men! I want the fierce man who possesses energy—the energy to smash, the inexorable determination to punish and to strike without hesitation, and the higher the position of the culprit the better. (Loud applause from the assembly, which understands the allusion.)

You send the simple soldier, burdened with a family, full of cares, and whom you have never taught anything about the country, to court-martial because he has disobeyed some order. If you put this soldier with his back against the wall, I approve of what you do, because I am a believer in rigid discipline. But you must not have two kinds of law. If there is a general who infringes the Sacchi decree, strike him too. If there is a deputy who, after the experience of Caporetto, says again that war is a "useless massacre," I tell you that he, too, ought to be arrested and punished! (Ovation.)

Whoever has been to the front and lived in the trenches knows what an effect the reading of certain speeches and Parliamentary reports had upon the minds of the soldiers. The poor man in the trenches asked himself, "Why must I suffer and die, if they are still discussing at Rome whether there ought to be war, if those who are at the head of affairs there do not know whether or not it is a good thing to be fighting?" That is deplorable and criminal talk, gentlemen! And now, even after Caporetto, after defeat, irresponsible people are allowed to make public anti-war demonstrations. (Loud applause.)

Ghosts! After Caporetto men showed themselves again whom we thought to have swept away forever. But we have driven them back into their holes, because we are still on our legs.

Yes! Many of our comrades have not come back from the Carso and from among the Alps. But we carry their sacred memory in our hearts. I think of the indescribable torture of mind of those men of the Third Armata, when they had to abandon the Carso. I think they must have cried out, "For what reason, as the result of what unexpected catastrophe, are we forced to abandon these rocks?" Because in the end one loves the tracks, the stones, the trenches, and the dugouts among which men have lived and suffered. We love the Carso, this heap of stones dotted with little crosses, which mark the graves of those fallen in the cause of the liberty of our country. (Applause.) We love the Carso, from which we can view the coveted coastline, the riviera of our Trieste. We still carry, alive and splendid, the torch of the dead, the torch of those who fell in the face of the enemy. And we are not moved by motives of gain. We want clear and explicit recognition of the fact that we have done our duty. And we find ourselves still in the breach, that we may tell this people, in case they have forgotten, that there is no turning back. There is no possibility of choosing. Worry your brains as you will, there is nothing else to be done, nothing else can be thought of!

Until Victory. The game is such that we must go on, because there is no other solution than this: victory or defeat! And it is the life or death of the nation that is at stake. Also those who assumed power with different ideas, with the intention of mending the situation, have had to change their minds. There is no turning back; we must win!

The warning has come from Russia. The Russian rulers tried to turn back and make peace. They have talked for days, weeks, and months without coming to any conclusions, because if Maximalism had sent lawyers more or less smart, Prussia had sent armed generals who from time to time tapped the pavement with their swords so that German rights might be the better understood. Then they accepted peace. But Prussia, thirsty for land, the Prussia of the Hohenzollerns, insatiable and implacable, marches into Russia and occupies territory.

If there is anybody today who does not wish for peace, who prevents talk of peace, who wants to continue the war, you must not seek him among the people, but at Berlin in the company of Hindenburg and Ludendorff. These are the enemies of mankind and to these one does not kneel. No! The Latin race holds itself upright! (Ovation.)

We who desired the war and make it our boast that we did so, we who do not go humbly soliciting electoral divisions, we shall not follow the cowardly demagogic example of those who wish to ingratiate themselves with the people. Democracy does not signify descent. It means ascent. It means raising up those who are down. And so for all the sacred and youthful blood that has been shed, which we have not forgotten, and for the sake of all that is still to be shed, let us renew the solemn pact of our faith in the certainty of victory.

No! Italy will not die, because Italy is immortal! (Frantic applause.)

The Fatal Victory

May 24th, 1918, Teatro Comunale, Bologna

On this occasion the principal speaker was the editor of *Il Popolo d'Italia*, who had recovered his physical efficiency after severe wounds received on the Carso, and had a real influence in securing victory because of the encouragement he gave to the spirit of resistance within the country.

Bologna was then a stronghold of the opponents of war, on account of the net of political and syndicalist organization stretching throughout the province, and of Socialist supremacy in the communes and dependent administrations. It is, unfortunately, well known that the State had by then ceased exercising any authority other than merely formal in this province.

A mark of Socialist power, which proves also the profound anti-national feeling of the defeated politicians who today stammer so many lying excuses, is offered by the absolute prohibition of manifestations calculated to glorify the Italian Army.

Mussolini's speech at the Comunale temporarily reunited the sane sections of Bologna to the rest of Italy, then in great anxiety for her fate and future.

◆ ◆ ◆

Combatants and Citizens! Will you allow me to pass over without unnecessary delay the polemics which preceded my coming to this city? If, as says our great poet Carducci, "one does not seek for butterflies beneath the arch of Titus," one does not seek for them either beneath the arches of this, our ancient and magnificent town of Bologna, especially as one would probably not find butterflies at all, but bats dazed and frightened by this glorious May sunshine.

The form of my speech will not surprise you. In those days, three years ago, all the Italy that was conscious of life and possessed of will-power, the only Italy which has a right to transform her chaotic succession of events into history, burned with an intense ardor—our ardor. I have noticed now for some time that there are opportunists who are trying to open a door for eventual responsibilities and who are carefully and laboriously cataloguing the reasons why Italy could not remain neutral.

Destiny and Will. Very well! I admit that there has been fatality, I admit this compulsion, which was the result of a number of causes which it is useless to dwell upon, but I add that at a certain moment we imprinted the mark of our will upon this concatenation of events, and today, after three years, we are not penitent of what we have done. We leave this weak, spiritual attitude to those who seek applause, seats in Parliament, and personal satisfaction; those who thoroughly despise, as I do, all parliamenteering and demagogism, are far away from all this.

What Machiavelli says in Chapter VI of *The Prince*, about those who, by their own inherent qualities, attained the position of princes, Moses, Cyrus, Romulus, and Theseus, can be applied not only to the individual, but also to the nation. So says the Florentine Secretary:

> And in examining their actions and lives one cannot see that they owed anything to fortune beyond opportunity, which brought them the material to mold into the form which seemed best to them. Without that opportunity their powers of mind would have been extinguished, and without those powers the opportunity would have come in vain.[15]

As to the Italian people in that glorious May, it can be said that without the opportunity of the war the virtue of our people would have been lost; but without this virtue the opportunity of the war would have come in vain.

I have found an echo of the thought of Machiavelli in the book of Maeterlinck, the great Belgian poet, the poet who, perhaps, more than any of his contemporaries, has given expression to the most delicate and complex movements of the human soul. Maeterlinck in his book *Wisdom and Destiny* admits the existence of a mechanical,

---

[15] Niccolò Machiavelli, *The Prince*, trans. W. K. Marriott (New York: E. P. Dutton & Co., 1908), Ch. 6, para. 3, pg. 46-7.

external fate, but says that a human being can react against it:

> The event in itself is pure water that flows from the pitcher of fate, and seldom has it either savor or perfume or color. But even as the soul may be wherein it seeks shelter, so will the event become joyous or sad, become tender or hateful, become deadly or quick with life. To those round about us there happen incessant and countless adventures, whereof every one, it would seem, contains a germ of heroism; but the adventure passes away, and heroic deed is there none. But when Jesus Christ met the Samaritan, met a few children, an adulterous woman, then did humanity rise three times in succession to the level of God.[16]

The war has been as a jet of pure water for our nation. It has been deadly for Spain, for instance, but life-giving to us. We desired it. We chose. Before making our choice we argued and struggled, and the struggle sometimes assumed the aspect of violence; but we won, and now we are proud of those days, and are glad to think that the memory of the crowds who filled the streets and squares of our cities disturbs those who were defeated and those who even today, by the most insidious means, try to extinguish the sacred flame and the faith of our people. They accepted this war as one accepts a heavy burden, and their leader, followed by the curses of the people, withdrew, like an old feudal lord, to his remote native country, and we can only wish that he will always remain there.

Enough of Old Age! But, as I am never tired of repeating, we young men made one fatal mistake then, which we have paid for bitterly; we entrusted this ardent youth of ours to the most grievous old age. When I say old age, I do not establish merely a chronological fact. I think some people are born old, that there are those at twenty who are in a mental and physical decline, whereas some men—the marvelous Tiger of France,[17] for instance—at seventy have all the vibration and fire of virile youth. I speak of the old men who are old men, who are behind the times, who are encumbrances. They neither understood nor realized the fundamental truths underlying the war.

Besides the people, the meaning of this war in its historical aspect and development has been perceived by two classes of men: the poets

---

[16] Maurice Maeterlinck, *Wisdom and Destiny*, trans. Alred Sutro (New York: Dodd, Mead and Company, 1918), § 8, pg. 28–9.

[17] Georges Clemenceau.

and the industrial world. By the poets, because with their extreme sensitiveness they grasp truths that remain half veiled to the ordinary person; and by the industrial world, because it understands that this war is a war of machines. Between the two let us also put the journalists, who have enough of the poet in them not to belong to the industrial world, and are enough of the industrial world not to be poets. And the journalists have often forestalled the Government. I speak of the great journalists who keep their ears open, on the alert to catch vibrations from the outside world. The journalist has sometimes foreseen what those responsible, alas! have recognized too late.

Quality versus Quantity. This war has so far been one of quantity. Now, it is realized that the masses do not beat the masses, an army does not vanquish an army, quantity does not overcome quantity. The problem must be faced from another point of view—that of quality. This war, which began by being tremendously democratic, is now tending to become aristocratic. Soldiers are becoming warriors. A selection is being made from the armed mass. The struggle, now carried on almost exclusively in the air, has lost the characteristics it had in 1914.

The first novelist who foresaw the problems of the war of quality was H. G. Wells. Read his book *War and the Future: Italy, France and Britain at War*.[18] It is in this book that he advised the exploitation of the "quality" of the Latin and Anglo-Saxon races. Because, whereas the Germans only work in close formation, only give good results through the automatism of the masses, the Latin feels the joy of personal audacity, the fascination of risk, and has the taste for adventure, which, says Wells, is limited in Germany to the descendants of the feudal nobility, while with us it is to be found also among the people.

Another truth which those responsible realized late was that, in order to win the armies, the people must be won, that is to say, that the armies must be taken in the rear. This would be difficult where Germany was concerned, as she is ethnically, politically, and morally compact. But we are face to face with an enemy against whom we could have acted in this way from the very start. We ought to have penetrated the mosaic of the Austrian State.

---

[18] The Italian edition has a different title: *La guerra su tre fronti* (The War on Three Fronts).

A Great People. Among the peoples who cannot be taken in the rear by surprise, is ours. My praise is sincere. The people in the trenches are great, and those who have not fought are great. For deficiency you must look among those old men of whom I spoke just now.

I have lived among our brave soldiers in the trenches and listened to them talking in their little groups. I have seen them during their bad times and in epic moments of enthusiasm. And when, after that sad October 24th, there was a certain distrust of them, I would not allow it, because it seemed to me impossible that the soldiers, who had won battles in circumstances more difficult than those prevailing in any other theater of war, had become all at once weak cowards, who fled at the mere crackling of a machine gun. And it was not so, because if it had been, no river would have stopped the invading forces, and if we stopped them on the Piave, it means we could have resisted also on the Isonzo. (Applause.)

I was reading in the train last night a book of poems written in the trenches by a Captain Arturo Arpigati. The literature of the war is the only readable literature, but it must have been written by men who have really been at the front. In this verse I recognized my one-time fellow soldiers, the humble and great soldiers of our war. Here it is:

Col vecchio suo magico sguardo	As of old, by her magic glance,
il Dovere, nume d'acciaio	Duty, of the steel hand,
gli inconsci anche soggioga.	Enchains even the ignorant.
benché ne balbettino il nome,	While they stammer her name,
ecco, essi, la madre difendono	Lo! they defend their mother,
ed è la madre di tutti;	Who is the mother of all.
e sono essi la Guerra,	And they are the war,
e sono essi la Fronte,	And they are the battle front,
sono essi la Vittoria;	And they are the victory.
dai loro elmetti ferrei	From their steel helmets,
spicca il volo la gloria:	Glory is reflected:
essi martiri e santi,	They are the martyrs and saints,
sono l'eroica Patria, essi. I Fanti!	They are the heroic Homeland. The Infantrymen!

But the highest praise of the people in arms is contained in the thousand bulletins of the Supreme Command. The unarmed also deserve praise, both those in cities—inevitably nervous and restless by reason of the association of thousands of human beings and the contact of thousands of temperaments—and those in the country. From the Po Valley to the Tavoliere delle Puglie (Table of the Apulias), from the vine-clad hills of Montferrat to the plains of the Conca d'Oro, the houses of the peasants stand empty, and with the houses the stables. The women have seen the father and the son depart together, the thoughtful territorial of over forty and the adventurous youth. It is useless to expect from the humble people of the proletariat a highly developed sense of nationality. It cannot possess what we have never done anything to cultivate. From the people who have exchanged the spade for the gun we simply ask for obedience, and the Italian people, the people of the country and of the factories, obey. A sad episode, some signs of restlessness are not enough to spoil this picture. It had been said that we should not hold out six months, that at the announcement of the names of the dead the families would rebel, that the sight of the maimed at the street corners would rouse the people to action. Three years have now passed—three long years. The mothers of the fallen take a sacred pride in their grief. The maimed do not ask to be called "glorious," and refuse to be pitied. Food is scarce, but the people still resist. The troop trains go to the front adorned with flowers as in May 1915. The dignity and peace in the towns and in the country is simply marvelous! The national crisis, which lasted from August to October 1917, and which is summed up in the two names of Turin and Caporetto, has been in a certain sense salutary. It was the repercussion of the great crisis that hurled Russia into the abyss.

The Russian Tragedy. Was there any definite motive in the Leninist policy that led Russia to make the "painful, forced, and shameful Peace of Brest"? Yes! there was. The Maximalists really believe in the possibility of revolution by "contagion." They hoped to infect the Germans with the Maximalist bacillus. They did not succeed; Germany is refractory. The very "minoritaries" are far from proclaiming themselves Bolshevists. And more, these "minoritaries," who ought to represent the fermenting yeast, are continually losing ground. In three elections there have been three overwhelming defeats. The "majoritaries" triumph. They are the same now as in August 1914, accomplices of Pan-Germanism. They want to win. After Brest-Litovsk the Socialists lay low; after the Treaty of Bucharest they kept silence.[19]

We have seen what have been the results in Russia of the Leninist gospel; we have seen how the German Socialists, who accepted "neither annexations nor indemnities and the right of the people to decide their own fate," have interpreted this doctrine. The Germans took possession of 540,000 square kilometers of territory in Russia with a population of 55 million; then they went on to Romania and plundered her. If the Treaty of Brest-Litovsk was shameful for Russia, the Treaty of Bucharest was not. The Romanians were taken in the rear and could not resist.

In the meantime, Georgy Chicherin, the Commissioner for Foreign Affairs, used the radio. A cynic might remark that if the Roman Republic had a Cicero in a critical hour of her history, Russia has a Chicherin, whom, contrary to the former, nobody takes seriously, because it is impossible to take seriously those who do not know how to take up arms in the defense of their own rights.

The Russian experiment has helped us enormously, both from the socialist and the political points of view. It has opened many eyes which had persistently remained closed. It must be realized that if Germany wins, complete and certain ruin awaits us. Germany has not changed her fundamental instincts. They are the same as those that Tacitus describes to perfection in his *Germania* in these words: "The Germans do not live in villages, but in separate houses, set wide apart the better to protect them against fire. To shield themselves from the cold, they live in underground dwellings covered with manure or clothe themselves in the skins of small animals, of which they have a great number. Strong in war, but persistent drunkards and gamblers, armed with spears and well supplied with horses, they prefer to gain wealth, when it suits them, by violence rather than by the working of their lands."[20]

In his *Agricola* this Roman writer notes a contrast between the Germans and the Britons nineteen centuries ago which is still the same today, that is, that while the Britons fight for the defense of their country and their homes, the Germans fight for avarice and lust.

---

[19] The Treaty of Brest-Litovsk, by which Russia withdrew from the First World War, was signed on May 3rd, 1918. Likewise, Romania withdrew with the Treaty of Bucharest, signed on May 7th, 1918, both mere weeks before this speech.

[20] Paraphrased and condensed from various sections of *Germania*.

These same tribes, driven once to Legnano, have resumed their march beyond the Rhine and are preparing once more to take up the offensive against us. But the "lust" of which Kuhlmann speaks will not carry the Germans beyond the Piave.

We Are on Our Feet. According to German calculations, the Italian nation, as the result of Caporetto, ought to fall into a state of chaos. Instead, it is on its feet. What vicissitudes may not this last phase of the war bring with it? Will Germany, who has not been able to beat us by ourselves, beat the formidable combination of nations who face her?

We are one with France, whose soldiers have performed wonders of heroism. And this France, which we knew so little, because we had looked for her only in the cabarets of Montmartre, not frequented by Frenchmen at all but by adventurers from all over the world, has written for us the most splendid pages of heroic deeds. She has known how to rid herself of insidious dangers, to give the death-blow to the plotters of treachery, both great and small, and to make the rifles of the executionary squadrons crackle, a sound which, to one who loves his country, is sweeter than the harmonies of a great opera. Also we, in Italy, must act inexorably where traitors are concerned, if we are to defend our soldiers from attack from behind. Where the existence of the nation and of millions of men is involved, there cannot and must not be a moment's hesitation about sacrificing the lives of one, ten, or a hundred men.

We are one with England, who repeats the words of Nelson, "England expects that every man will do his duty."[21]

And we are one with the United States. This is internationalism, the real, true, and lasting internationalism, even if it has not got the formulas, dogmas, and chrism of Socialism made official. It is in the trenches, where soldiers of different nationalities have crossed six thousand leagues of ocean to come and die in Europe.

You must allow me to be optimistic about the outcome of the war. We shall win because the United States cannot lose, England cannot lose, France cannot lose. The United States has a population of 110 million; one single levy can produce a million recruits. America, like

---

[21] Vice-Admiral of the Royal Navy Horatio Nelson, 1st Viscount Nelson at the commencement of the Battle of Trafalgar on October 21st, 1805.

England, knows that the wealth of society is at stake.

As long as we are in this company there is no danger of a ruinous peace. Not to arrive at the goal of peace means to be crushed; but when we arrive there, we, too, can look the enemy in the face and say that we, too, small, despised people, army of mandolinists, have held out to the end, wept, suffered, but resisted, and have thus the right to a just and lasting peace!

Convalescence. I am an optimist and see the Italy of tomorrow through rose-colored glasses. Enough of the Italy of the hotel keeper, goal of the idle with their odious Baedekers in their hands;[22] enough of dusting old plaster work; we are and we wish to be a nation of producers.

We are a people who will expand without aiming at conquest. We shall gain the world's respect by means of our industries and our work. It will be the august name of Rome that will still guide our forces in the Adriatic, the Gulf of the Mediterranean, and in the Mediterranean, which forms the communication between three continents.

Those who have been wounded know what convalescence means. There comes a day when the surgeon no longer takes his ruthless but life-giving knife from the tray, no longer tortures the suffering flesh. The danger of infection is over, and you feel yourself reborn. A second youth begins. Things, men, the voice of a woman, the caress of a child, the flowering of a tree—everything gives you the ineffable sensation of a return. New blood surges through your veins and fills you with a feverish desire to work.

The Italian people too will have its convalescence, and it will be a competition for reconstruction after destruction. The flag of the disabled is a symbol of a change in their moral and spiritual life. Just think that certain rascals thought to take advantage of them for their infamous speculations. But the disabled answered, "We will not lend ourselves to this shameful game; we do not intend to accept from your charity and sympathy help that would humiliate us." And they do not curse their fate, they do not complain, even if they are without an arm or a leg; even those who have lost the divine light of their eyes hold their peace. In vain the enemy hoped to profit by the state of mind of these people. They reply to this by saying that all they had they gave

---

[22] Baedeker referring to the Baedeker travel guides.

for their country, and today they do not wish to be a burden upon her, and so they work and train themselves and give further proof of their devotion to the sacred cause.

The Returning Battalions. I no longer see relegated to some far future time the day upon which the banners of the disabled will precede the torn and glorious standards of the regiments. And around the standards will be collected the veterans and the people. And there will be the shadow of our dead, from those who fell on the Alps to those who were buried beyond the Isonzo, from those who stormed Gorizia to those who were mowed down between Hermada and the mysterious Timavo, or upon the banks of the Piave. All this sacred phalanx we sum up in three names: Cesare Battisti, who wished deliberately to face martyrdom, and who was never so noble as when he offered his neck to the Hapsburg executioner; Giacomo Venezian, who left the austere halls of your Athenæum in order to go and meet his death upon the road to Trieste; and Filippo Corridoni, born of the people, a fighter for the people, and who died for the people on the first rocky ridges of the Carso.

The returning battalions will move with the slow and measured tread of those who have lived and suffered much and who have seen innumerable others suffer and die. They will say, we shall say:

"Here upon the track that leads back to the harvest field, here in the factory that now forges the instruments of peace, here in the tumultuous city and the silent country, now that the duty was done and the goal reached, let us set up the symbol of our new right. Away with shadows! We, the survivors, we, the returned, vindicate our right to govern Italy, not to her destruction and decay, but in order to lead her ever higher, ever on, to make her, in thought and deed, worthy to take her place among the great nations that will build up the civilization of the world of tomorrow."

In Honor of the American People

April 8th, 1918, Milan, on the occasion of the popular demonstrations

The exaggerated welcome lavished upon President Wilson during his visit to Italy is well known,[23] and of all cities Milan accorded him the most generous hospitality. Benito Mussolini, who on that occasion was specially entrusted with the task of addressing the President of the United States on behalf of the Lombard Association of Journalists, had prepared the mind of the Milanese eight months before, by a speech delivered in Piazza Cordusio, extolling the generous and brotherly effort of the great and vigorous American people.

◆   ◆   ◆

Citizens! Time does not allow long speeches. I do not speak of time by the clock, but of historical time, which for some few weeks has quickened its beat. Today throughout Italy demonstrations are taking place worthy of this unique moment in the history of humanity. (Applause.)

The people of Bergamo go to Pontida to renew the vows made by the League of the Lombard Communes seven centuries ago, when they took the field against Barbarossa; at Rome an imposing demonstration is in progress beneath the shadow of the imperial walls of the Coliseum; while here the people of Milan, by their numbers and enthusiasm, express the keen sympathy they feel for the noble American Democracy. It was a year ago today that America, having loyally waited for the Germans to come to their senses, unsheathed her sword and joined the battle. (Applause.)

Six thousand leagues of ocean have not prevented the United

---

[23] January 1st–6th, 1919 in Rome, Genoa, Milan, and Turin.

States from fulfilling her definite duty. The importance of her intervention does not consist only in the fact that America gives us, and will give us, men, ammunition, and provisions. There is something deeper in the intimate reassurance given us as men and civilized people, as America would never have embraced our cause if she had not been firmly convinced of the right and justice of it. (Applause.)

Citizens! It is for us a source of pride and satisfaction to be associated with twenty-three other nations in this war against Prussian militarism. But it must also be a satisfaction for the United States to fight side by side with a great and powerful England who does not tremble before the varying chances of war, beside a France who is almost sublime in her heroism—(Applause)—and beside the new Italy, who has now definitely taken her place in the world struggle. (Applause.)

As Italy discovered America, so America and the rest of the New World must discover Italy, not only in the great towns, pulsating with life and humming with industry, but also in the country, where the humble laborers wait with quiet resignation for the dawn of a victorious and just peace to appear on the horizon.

There cannot be anybody now, even the most ignorant, who can sincerely believe that Germany did not want the war, and that Germany does not wish to continue the war in order that she may turn the world into a lot of horrible Prussian barracks. (Applause and cries of "Death to Germany!")

This is our conviction, and also the conviction of the Americans, a great people numbering more than 100 million, who have a vast wealth at their command and who have already submitted themselves to the magnificent discipline of war.

An old story comes into my mind. When Christopher Columbus turned the prows of his three poor little ships toward unknown lands and far-off shores, there were those who called him mad and moonstruck, and certainly sometimes during those three months of wandering a sense of despair invaded the hearts of those men lost in the midst of the unknown ocean. But one morning the crew up aloft saw something new upon the horizon. It was a dark, vague line. They shouted "Land! Land!" and three months of misery were forgotten in one delirious moment.

The day will come when from our blood-stained trenches will arise another such cry, the cry of "Victory! Victory!" And there will be the right and just peace for all the nations!

Citizens! On behalf of the Committee of the Wounded and Disabled Soldiers, I thank you for your solemn demonstration and I ask you to join with me in giving three cheers for America and for Italy. (Warm applause and cheers.)

The League of Nations

October 20th, 1918, Milan

Immediately after the end of the war, a group of journalists and politicians, belonging for the most part to the Republican and Radical democracy, took the initiative in a movement supporting the future work of the League of Nations. Later, however, this initiative had to be abandoned by those who were loyal to victory, because it seemed clear to them that the pseudo-idealism of the Allies would prejudice the legitimate interests of the Italian nation. The following speech, however, shows clearly the generosity of Italian ex-soldiers disappointed by the realism of other countries' national aspirations.

❖　◆　❖

The Executive Committee of the Wounded and Disabled Soldiers has asked me to speak on the order of the day expressing support of the idea of the League of Nations, which, already preconceived in Italy, is now so nobly advocated by President Wilson, and which proclaims the determination of the Italian people to cooperate effectively in bringing about its realization. I shall do so shortly, as the question is not new, but is already understood throughout the country.

The disabled soldiers have taken the initiative, and it is significant, as only those who have suffered most from the war have the right to say what the peace ought to be, not those who have willfully opposed it and would have led us to defeat or—not wishing that the people should suffer defeat—to continuous war.

This is the hour particularly suited to the discussion of these problems. Already a League of Nations seems to be in the process of realization; in the trenches the different peoples are mixed up and are associating with each other. The humblest peasant, dreaming of return to his native village after the hard experiences of the trenches, has widened his spiritual horizon and, for a time, breathes a world atmosphere.

In the other nations, the question has already come under discussion in the papers, the universities, and the Parliaments. It could be said that Italy was behindhand, but we might reply that in a certain sense we have forestalled the others. There have been epochs in our history when Italian thought has been almost too universal, but I think perhaps at those times the universality of our literature, our philosophy, our art, of our spirit, in fact, was our highest and noblest title to greatness.

But, without returning to the Middle Ages, two men of the nineteenth century, Cattaneo and Mazzini, prove that Italian thought led, and that the other nations followed the furrow we were the first to plough.

This war may be divided into two periods: the first, from the outbreak of hostilities to the American intervention; the second, from the American intervention up to today. In the first, the war has a national and territorial character. The names of Metz, Trento, Fiume, and Zara occur frequently, and can be said to sum up our aims. The territorial questions come first. The systemized jurisdiction of the world is not yet spoken of; the war is worldwide in its direct and indirect repercussion in as far as England has already made use of her colonies, since Australians and Indians came to fight in Europe, but it is not yet worldwide in its extension and aims. The second period began with the April of '17. Already, in the first period, English politicians had begun to disregard the territorial problems, but this process was shaped, hurried on, and definitely settled by the intervention of America. But in my modest opinion, the national and territorial questions must not be underrated too much; that would be to play into the hands of the anti-war agitators and the Germans. These are questions of justice. It is a good thing to remember that Wilson, in all his messages, though he certainly made a transposition of values, never failed to establish that vindication of national rights, without which the settlement of Europe and the world of tomorrow in general could have no definite meaning.

When we speak of a League of Nations we must take into account certain dispositions. Cesare Lombroso used to divide men into two categories: the misoneists and the philoneists: the misoneists, who accept the revealed truths, lean upon them, and sleep upon them; and the philoneists, who are restless, impatient spirits and as necessary to the world as the wheels and shafts to a cart. For the first the so-called kingdom of the impossible has always extensive boundaries, but the war has enormously reduced that kingdom. That which yesterday was a misty, fantastic utopia, today has become reality and fact.

Our enemies talk too much about the League of Nations. There are furious "Wilsonites" of the latest kind in Austria and in Germany. Now I must say that seeing this kind of people bleating like lambs makes a certain impression on me. (The simile is that of a Republican German paper printed at Berne.) They are the same who burned the cities of Belgium, who sank ships without leaving a trace, or gave orders to that effect; they are the same who carried off men and women in their retreat. They shout "League of Nations," but we cannot be mixed up with them. There is evidently an underlying motive. But they will be unmasked by the victorious armies of the Entente.

Some people say, "Would not this League of Nations be a substitute for victory?" No! on the other hand, it presupposes victory. Wilson has talked of absolute victory.

It is said, in a Socialist review, that a League of Nations is impossible if the Allies gain a military victory, because the desire for revenge would lurk in the depths of the German mind. Now there are three hypotheses as regards the way in which the conflict may end. The first is the victory of the enemy, and this has already fallen through. If this had come about, there would not have been a League of Nations, but a master at Berlin and slaves in the rest of Europe, which would then have become a German colony. The second is a war that ends in neither victory nor defeat, and this is the most repugnant and inhuman of all, as it would leave all the problems unsolved, and give a peace that was only a truce. The third is the solution that is now shaping itself gloriously upon the horizon: our victory. There is no danger of the spirit of revenge being fostered by the Germans tomorrow, because we allies in war would remain allies in peace. Germany will find herself face to face with the same coalition that defeated her, and will have to resign herself to the *fait accompli*. The League of Nations will be formed without Germany, against Germany, or with Germany when she has expiated her crime by being defeated.

Some people say, "Does it not seem very dangerous to go back to universality, after the experiences of the past?" Ernest Renan must have been up against this problem when he wrote:

> The nation which works out social and religious problems in its own bosom is almost always weak politically. Every country which dreams of a kingdom of God, which lives for general ideas, which pursues a work of universal interest, sacrifices through the same its individual destiny, enfeebles and destroys its rôle as a terrestrial country.[24] It was thus with Judea, Greece and Italy. It will, perhaps, be thus with France.[25]

Renan was a great man, but his prophecy has not been fulfilled. France during the nineteenth century entertained universal ideas, but with the outbreak of war she recovered her national spirit. Internationalism may be dangerous when a single nation advocates it, but today all the nations of the world are seeking each other, in order to lay the foundations of a lasting and pacific means of coexistence. Besides this, the racial, historical, and moral sense of every nation has been developed by the war. It is not a paradox but a reality that the war, while it has made us find ourselves and exalted the national spirit, has, at the same time, carried us beyond those boundaries which we have defended and conquered.

There is no danger of the leveling of the national spirit as the result of contact with other nations. Solid foundations are needed for national unity, and for this reason the condition of the working classes must be raised. No nation can become greater in which there are enormous masses condemned to the conditions of life of prehistoric humanity.

Another paradox of this war is that the nations fighting against the Germans have not yet formed a peace alliance. The peace manifesto to the peoples of the world ought to have come from Versailles. This could help, among other things, to make the German crisis more acute. It has not been done yet. The people intuitively felt the necessity. Sometimes truths are arrived at more quickly by intuition than

---

[24] Ernest Renan, *English Conferences*, trans. Clara Erskine Clement (Boston: James R. Osgood and Company, 1880), Third Conference, 73–4.
[25] While quoted as one, this last sentence does not appear in the above source. Mussolini may be paraphrasing.

by reasoning, and the people felt that that was the path to follow. And we are upon that path today. Not long ago, Clemenceau said that the liberation of France must be the liberation of humanity.

It is true that to put the idea of the League of Nations into practice would present difficulties, especially at first. According to me, the problems that will have to be faced and solved are of a political, economic, military, and colonial order. In a month's time you will have reports upon these subjects, and I do not wish to tire you with hasty anticipations.

We have arrived at a decisive point in history. While we are gathered here, the battle is raging; there are millions and millions of men who are fighting their last fight. Let us swear that all this has not been in vain, but that these sacrifices must mark a new phase in the history of humanity. Let us say to ourselves that all that can be tried will be tried, in order to make the purple flower of liberty spring from the bloodshed in the cause of freedom, and that justice shall reign sovereign over all the peoples of the renewed world!

In Celebration of Victory

November 11th, 1918, Milan,
Before the Monument of the Cinque Giornate

Milan, notwithstanding its multi-colored local Socialism, had ever remained the burning heart of the country's resistance and spent herself lavishly for the war. After the memorable day of Vittorio Veneto she gave herself up to unrestrained manifestations of patriotic joy.[26]

Benito Mussolini—the ardent advocate of intervention in the harassing times gone by, the indomitable fighter in the Carso trenches, and the fervent advocate of resistance in the hour in which the enemy's friends were crying for "peace at any price"—Benito Mussolini may well be considered as one of the principal artificers of victory.

The people of Milan felt this in the triumphant rejoicings, and the editor of *Il Popolo d'Italia* was acclaimed by public gratitude for his part in the union of hearts.

◆ ◆ ◆

My brothers of the trenches, Citizens! I have never before felt my inefficiency as an orator as deeply as I do now in the face of the greatness of the events and your memorable and imposing manifestation. What can I say to you, when this manifestation is already more than a speech, a hymn—more than a hymn, an epos?

We have arrived at this day after many hardships. I see here, gathered round the monument of the Cinque Giornate, which is the altar of Milan, those who fought first and last, those of the trenches who

---

[26] The Battle of Vittorio Veneto (October 24th–November 4th, 1918) was a decisive Italian victory and the final offensive launched on the Italian front of the First Word War.

are the survivors of the sacrifice of devotion, who marked with their blood the destinies of the country, and the disabled who feel themselves no longer maimed since Italy has become great. I see beside them the refugees, who will soon return to their lands and deserted hearths. I remember what I said last year; we must love these brothers of ours, warm them by our firesides, and still more in our hearts. And I see the people of Milan joined together like all the Italian people in a superb act of love.

How many different events in the course of a year! Do you remember these days a year ago? Do you remember last year at La Scala when we swore that the Germans should not pass the Piave? And they did not pass, and the then line of resistance became afterwards the line of advance toward victory. Even in the darkest hours I did not despair, and paid homage to the fighters. We saw in those days the first poilus and tommies;[27] it was the Entente coming to cement the Alliance in our trenches. After a year of faith and sacrifice has come victory.

We think with gratitude of the fine leaders who led us on to victory, but also, still more, of the anonymous mass of soldiers, our marvelous people, who resisted the invasion on the Piave, and from the Piave sprang forward to rout the enemy.

Remember it here—here where we held the first meeting for war—here, with Filippo Corridoni. (The crowd give a prolonged ovation to the memory of Filippo Corridoni.) We wanted the war, because we were obliged to want it, because it was imposed by historical necessity. Today we have realized all our ideals; we have secured our national aims; the Italian flag today flies from the Brenner to Trieste and Fiume and Italian Zara. We did not know then that there were Italian infantry on the other side of the Adriatic. Now, in all the cities and villages on the eastern shore, the Italians have planted the flag of their country, because that shore, which is Italian, must remain Italian.

We have also accomplished the international aims of our war. When we said, four years ago, that the red flag must wave over the castle at Potsdam, the dream appeared madness. Today the Kaiser has fled, and with the passing of the Hohenzollerns passes militarism.

The most magnificent political panorama that history records

---

[27] French and English troops respectively.

unfolds itself before the eyes of the astonished world. Empires, kingdoms, and autocracies crumble like castles built with cards. Austria no longer exists; tomorrow there will no longer be Imperialist Germany. We, with the sacrifice of our blood, have given the German people liberty, while the German people have made a holocaust of their blood in order to deliver us over to the chain of imperialism and military slavery. Upon the ruins of the old world is outlined the dream of a League of Nations.

Victory must also see the realization of the aims of war within the country—that is to say, the redemption of labor. From now onwards the Italian people must be the arbiters of their destinies, and labor must be redeemed from speculation and misery.

Citizens! At Trento there is the statue of Dante with his hand outstretched toward the Alps. It seemed before that the reproach of the great poet: "Ahi serva Italia, di dolore ostello, / nave sanza nocchiere in gran tempesta,"[28] rang out admonishing the country. But Italy today is no longer a slave, she is the mistress of herself and her future. She is no longer a rudderless ship in a storm, because a glorious horizon has been opened up by her victory.

And the people are the rudder of this ship, which, between three seas and three continents, sails serenely and securely toward the port of supreme justice in the light of the redeemed humanity of tomorrow. (Prolonged applause.)

---

[28] "Ah, abject Italy, you inn of sorrows, / you ship without a helmsman in harsh seas." Dante Alighieri, *Purgatorio*, trans. Mandelbaum, Canto VI, 76–7.

PART III

Mussolini the Fascist Friend of the People

Workmen's Rights After the War

March 20th, 1919, before the workmen of Dalmine

The episode of Syndicalist strife, during which the present prime minister addressed a crowded meeting of ironworkers, is often recalled as a kind of reproach by Italian Socialists. They would like to attribute to Mussolini and to Fascist syndicalism the initial responsibility for that dark period in our national life, which had its dramatic expression in the occupation of the factories.

But the methods of protest adopted by the patriotic Italian workmen of Dalmine (Bergamo), although primitive on account of the moral immaturity and technical incapacity of the proletariat at that time, were provoked by the insolence of employers. For the rest, the protest was kept within the bounds of correct and calm expression.

A significant item in the story, which reveals the state of mind of the workers, is the following: tricolor flags, which were then frequently insulted by organizations of workmen under the thumb of the Socialist Party, flew from all chimney-tops during the occupation of Dalmine works, while in the workshops below the work itself throbbed cheerfully and briskly.

◆

I have often asked myself if, after the four years of terrible though victorious war in which our bodies and minds have been engaged, the masses of the people would return to move in the same old tracks as before, or whether they would have the courage to change their direction. Dalmine has answered. The order of the day voted by you on Monday is a document of enormous historical importance, which will and must give a general direction to the line taken by all Italian labor.

The intrinsic significance of your action is clearly set forth in the order of the day. You have acted on the grounds of class, but you have not forgotten the nation. You have spoken for the Italian people, and not only for those of your class of metal workers. In the immediate interests of your category you might have caused a strike in the old style, the negative and destructive style; but, thinking of the interests of the people, you have inaugurated the creative strike that does not interrupt production. You could not deny the nation after having fought for her, when half a million men have given their lives for her. The nation, for which this sacrifice has been made, cannot be denied, because she is a glorious and victorious reality. You are not the poor, the humiliated, the rejected, as the old rhetorical sayings of the Socialists would have you be; you are the producers, and it is in this capacity that you vindicate your right to treat the industrial owners as equals. You are teaching some of them, especially those who have ignored all that has occurred in the world in the last four years, that for the figure of the old industrial magnate, odious and grasping, must be substituted that of the industrial captain.

You have not been able to prove your capacity for creation, on account of shortness of time and of the conditions made for you by the industrial leaders; but you have proved your goodwill, and I tell you that you are on the right road, because you are freed from your protectors, and have chosen from among yourselves the men who are to direct you and represent you, and to them only you have entrusted the guardianship of your rights.

The future of the proletariat is a question of willpower and capacity, not of willpower only and not of capacity only, but of both together. You are free from the yoke of political intrigue. Your applause tells me that it is true. I am proud of having fought for intervention. If it were necessary, I would carve in capital letters upon my forehead, so that all cowards might see, that I was among those in the glorious May of '15 who demanded that the shame of the neutral Italy of those days should cease.

Now that the war is over, I, who have been in the trenches and witnessed daily for long months the revelation, in every sense, of the valor of the sons of Italy—I say, today, that it is necessary to go out and meet the returning workers and those, who were no shirkers, who labored in the factories with minds open to the necessities of the hour. And those who do not see this necessity, involved by the new order of things, or deny it, are either stupid or deluded.

I have never asked, and today less than ever, anything from you or anybody. And so I have no anxiety or misgivings as to the effect that my words will have upon you. I tell you that your action has been original, and is worthy, on account of the motives of sympathy that inspired it.

Another observation. Upon the flagstaff of your building you have run up your flag, which is the tricolor, and around it you have fought your battle. You have done well. The national flag is not merely a rag, even if it has been dragged in the mud by the bourgeoisie, or by their representatives; it still remains the symbol of the sacrifice of thousands and thousands of men. For its sake from 1821 to 1918 innumerable bands of men suffered privation, imprisonment, and the gallows. Around it during these years, while it was the rallying-point of the nation, was shed the blood of the flower of our youth, of our sons and brothers. It seems to me that I have said enough.

As regards your rights, which are just and sacred, I am with you. I have always distinguished the mass which works from the party which assumes the right, nobody knows why, of representing it. I have sympathy with all the working classes, not excluding the General Federation of Labor, though I feel myself more drawn toward the Italian Union of Workmen. But I say that I shall not cease fighting against the party that during the war was the instrument of the Kaiser. They wish at your expense to try their monkey-like experiments, which are only an imitation of Russia. But you will succeed, sooner or later, in exercising essential functions in modern society, though the political dabblers of the bourgeoisie and semi-bourgeoisie must not make stepping-stones of your aspirations so as to arrive at winning their little games.

They may have said what they liked to you about me; I do not mind. I am an individualist, who does not seek companions on his journey. I find them, but I do not seek them. While this despicable speculation of the jackals rages, you, obscure workers of Dalmine, have cleared the way. It is labor that speaks in you, and not an idiotic dogma or an intolerant creed. It is that labor that in the trenches established its right to be no longer considered as labor, necessarily accompanied by poverty and despair, because it must bring joy, pride in creation, and the conquest of free men in the great and free country of Italy within and without her boundaries. (Enthusiastic applause.)

Sacrifice, Work, and Production

February 5th, 1920, Milan, before the Fascio Milanese Combattimento

◆

If it were possible, before voting on the orders of the day, to put into practice the system of democracy, we ought to have summoned the Assembly. But when events follow one another with lightning speed, it is not possible to carry out this system of absolute Democracy.

We have, therefore, voted the orders of the day, and wait for you to ratify them. We have brought forward three, and done so from a point of view essentially Fascist. I dare to say that one is born a Fascist, and that it is difficult to become one. All the other parties and associations argue on a basis of dogmas and from the standpoint of definite preconceptions and infallible ideals. We, being an anti-party, have no preconceptions. We are not like the Socialists, who always think that the working masses are in the right, and we are not like the Conservatives, who think that they are always in the wrong. We have got above all this and have the privilege of moving on the ground of pure objectivity. Voting these "orders of the day," after a serious and elaborate discussion, we have kept before us three classes of facts or elements. First, we have kept in mind the general interests of the nation, particularly as regards the recent strikes. Secondly, we have considered the subject of production, because if we kill production, if today we render sterile the fount of economic activity, tomorrow there will be universal poverty. Thirdly, we have been guided, in voting these orders of the day, by our disinterested love for the working classes.

All Must Sacrifice Themselves. I agree with those who recommend the spirit of sacrifice also to the working classes; I agree, because we do not only say to the working men that they must wait, while still working, for better times to come in order to break the vicious circle in which they move; we also say that, generally speaking, capital must be controlled. In this connection I announce to you that in a short time a manifesto will be issued in which it will be once more asserted that, in order to solve the financial problem, it is necessary to resort to a threefold measure: first, the partial confiscation of all wealth over a certain amount; secondly, the heavy taxation of inheritance; and thirdly, the confiscation of super war profits.

No Pessimism. I am not a bit pessimistic about the future of the Italian nation. If I were, I should retire from public life. But as I am profoundly optimistic, I think that with the January strikes over we have passed the critical period of our social crisis.

You will tell me that February has not brought much light; we have the strike of fifty thousand textile workers belonging to the Popular Party, which shows that black Bolshevism has the same destructive and anti-social character as the other Bolshevism. But it seems to me that the social crisis is stabilizing itself while awaiting solution. If we can get over these next six or eight months without catastrophe, if we can increase our trade with the East, if the workmen can be made to understand that we cannot take our money there but must send our manufactured goods, and that only thus will the high rate of living be diminished, because only from the East come those raw materials of which we stand in need, it is certain that the workmen will repudiate the more destructive than constructive weapon of strikes and settle down to serious work.

Sure Repentance. Our position as regards the syndicalist movement is not reactionary, as has been said by some purposely malicious adversary. I wrote some very bitter articles during the strikes, but these articles, which were so incriminating, brought me approval that was very significant. If there is a man in the Italian Union of Workmen who has worked seriously, it is the republican Carlo Bazzi, who has recently founded the Syndicate of Cooperation, which is the necessary counterwork to the Socialist cooperative movement. Now Bazzi wrote my brother a letter which contained these words[29]: "I fully subscribe to Mussolini's article 'You are immortal, Cagoia.'" This is enough

---

[29] His brother being Arnaldo Mussolini, editor of Il Popolo d'Italia.

for me. But, at the same time, I do not require that everybody shall agree with me, and that there shall be no one who differs. I am always ready to persuade myself of my mistake when I am in the wrong. But I do not think that our work can be valued now. I think that within five- or six-months' time there will be quite a few Socialists who will recognize that I am the only Socialist that there has been in Italy for the last five years; and I am not being paradoxical, even if I add that the Socialist Party on the whole is detestable. I think, too, that a great many elements of the Center and followers of Filippo Turati are beginning to recognize it even now, and that in a short time the working classes will admit that the days of April 15th and July 20th–21st, with all our violent opposition, were providential and miraculous, because, having put the stake between the wheels of the runaway coach, we prevented that what has happened in Hungary should happen in Italy.

Production Necessary. Today it is said that poverty should not be socialized, but that is what we said two years ago, just as today it is said that there must be increased production, as we said two years ago. And when history comes to be written, as it will be shortly, then our work will be judged very differently from that of the Socialists and the responsible elements in the working classes.

The discussion of this evening, I think, might end with a declaration upon these four points:

1. The meeting ratifies the "orders of the day" voted by the Executive Committee and the Central Committee.

2. The meeting reaffirms its solidarity with the just demands of the postal telegraphists and the railway men and all the State employees (because I have never been tired of repeating that we are against the strike, but not against the demands of the staff).

3. The meeting votes a warning to the Government that the working of the State services must be made really efficient, whether it be by removing the bureaucratic management or by industrialization. (And I think that autonomous organizations can be formed of the postal, telephone, and railway services, in which the agents would have a large direct representation.)

4. Finally, the meeting votes its sympathy with all the working-class elements who are agitating against the Socialist Party and urges them to gather together in a compact body so that, though hitherto it has not been possible, from today onwards it may be possible, even

in Italy, to live and work and struggle without being slaves to the new tyrannies, without the necessity of being compelled to become a mere member in a flock of membership cardholders like a flock of sheep.

We Are Not Against Labor, But Against the Socialist Party, In as Far as It Remains Anti-Italian

May 24th, 1920, Milan, second National Fascist meeting

The following is not a conventional speech, but represents a sincere act of faith, made in the darkest hour through which Italy passed, the hour which followed upon the sweeping electoral and political triumphs of 1919, when communal and provincial administrations were divorced from the Liberal policies.

The subversive newspapers of the day regarded that second Fascist meeting as a useless attempt at galvanization, since the movement which was destined later to conquer the State seemed then merely to lead to a blind alley. Such is the futility of newspaper prophecies!

◆   ◆   ◆

Words, at certain times, can be facts. Let us act, then, in such a way that all the words we utter now may be potential facts today, and reality tomorrow.

Five years ago, at this time, popular enthusiasm burst forth in all the streets and squares of the towns of Italy. Looking back now and studying the documents of those times, I can state, with certainty and a clear conscience, that the cause of intervention was not taken up by the so-called middle classes, but by the best and healthiest part of the Italian people. And when I say the people, I mean also the proletariat, because nobody could imagine that the thousands and thousands of citizens who followed Corridoni were all from the middle class. I remember that one Agricultural Chamber of Labor, that of Parma, declared in favor of intervention on the part of Italy with a great

65

majority. And even admitting that the war was a mistake, which I do not admit, he who scorns the sacrifice which has been made is despicable.

If you want to go back and make a critical examination, I am ready to argue with anybody and to maintain: First, that the war was desired by the Central Powers, as has been confessed by the politicians of the German Republic and confirmed by the imperial archives. Secondly, that Italy could not have remained neutral, and thirdly, that if she had, she would find herself, today, in a worse condition than she actually does.

On the other hand, we who intervened must not be surprised if the sea is tempestuous. It would be absurd to expect that a nation that had just passed through so grave a crisis would recover itself in twenty-four hours. And when you think that after two years we have not yet got our peace, when you think of the weakness of those who govern us, you will realize that certain crises of doubt are inevitable. But the war gave that which we required of it—it gave us victory.

Let Us Idealize Labor. When, not long ago, you hissed the song of the sickle and the hammer, you certainly did not mean to disdain these two instruments of human labor. There is nothing more beautiful and noble than the sickle, which gives us our bread, and nothing finer than the hammer, which shapes metals. We must not despise manual work. We must understand that if it is overrated today, it is because mankind, as a whole, is suffering from a lack of material goods. It is natural, therefore, that those who produce these necessities are excessively overrated. We do not represent a reactionary element. We tell the masses not to go too far, and not to expect to transform society by means of something that they do not understand. If there is to be transformation, it must come when the historical and psychological elements of our civilization have been taken into account.

Let Us Unmask the Deceivers. We do not intend to oppose the movement of the working classes, only to unmask the work of mystification which is carried on by a horde of middle-class, lower-middle-class, and pseudo-middle-class men, who think that they have become the saviors of humanity by the mere fact of being possessed of a card of membership. "We are not against the proletariat, but against the Socialist Party in as far as it continues to be anti-Italian." The

Socialist Party continued, after the victory, to abuse the war, to fight against those who had been in favor of intervention, threatening reprisals and excommunication. Well, I, for my part, shall not give way. I laugh at excommunication, and as for reprisals, we shall answer with sacred reprisals. But we cannot go against the people, because the people made the war. We cannot look askance at the peasants, who today are agitating for the solution of the land question. They commit excesses, but I ask you to remember that the backbone of the infantry was the peasantry.

Repentance. We do not deceive ourselves by thinking that we shall succeed in sinking completely the now wrecked ship of Bolshevism. But I already note signs of repentance. I think that someday the working classes, tired of letting themselves be duped, will turn to us, recognizing that we have never flattered them, but have always told them the brutal truth, working really in their interests. If, today, Italy has not fallen into the Hungarian abyss, it is due to us, because we have saved them by active interposition and by our life.

We have then one clear duty, which is to understand the social phenomenon developing before our eyes, and to fight the deceivers of the people and maintain a sure and immovable faith in the future of the nation.

Toward Equilibrium. There has been a period of lassitude immediately following all great historical crises. But afterwards, little by little, the tired muscles recover. All that which before was neglected and despised becomes once more honored and admired. Today nobody wants to talk of war, and it is natural. But when a certain period of time has elapsed, things will change, and a large part of the Italian people will recognize the moral and material value of victory; they will honor those who fought and will rebel against those Governments which do not guarantee the future of the nation. All the people will honor the great Arditi.[30] It was the Arditi who went to the trenches singing, and if we returned from the Piave and the Isonzo, if we still hold Fiume, and are still in Dalmatia, it is due to them.

Three martyrs, among the thousands who were consecrated to the war, clearly defined what were to be the destinies of the nation.

---

[30] An elite special force used in the First World War. From *ardire*, "to dare," the name Arditi roughly translates to "The Daring Ones."

Battisti tells us that the boundary of Italy should be at the Brenner; Sauro that the Adriatic must be an Italian sea and commercially Italo-Slav; while Rismondo tells us that Dalmatia is Italian.[31] Very well! Let us swear upon the standard which bears the sign of death, of that death which gives life, and the life which does not fear death, to keep faith to the sacrifice of these martyrs! (Loud applause.)

---

[31] Cesare Battisti (February 4th, 1875–July 12th, 1916), Nazario Sauro (September 20th, 1880–August 10th, 1916), and Francesco Rismondo (April 15th, 1885–August 10th, 1915).

Fascism's Interests for the Working Classes

April 4th, 1921, Prato della Marfisia, Ferrara

The manifestations of enthusiasm culminating in the meeting at the Prato della Marfisia solemnly confirmed the triumphant development of Fascism at Ferrara, the red province *par excellence*. On that occasion some fifty thousand *contadini*,[32] who had come on foot from the remotest centers of the vast province, spent the day acclaiming the "leader of the Blackshirts" and the new faith in Italy. A noteworthy feature was that many red flags belonging to the disbanded and defeated Socialist leagues were deposited before Mussolini and thereupon trampled underfoot by the crowd.

❖　◆　❖

People of Ferrara! and I say *people* intentionally, because that which I see before me now is a marvelous gathering of the people, in both the Roman and Italian sense of the word. I see among you children who are upon the threshold of life, and not long ago I shook hands with an old Garibaldian, a survivor of that heroic Italy which was born at Nola in 1821, when two cavalry officers hoisted the flag of liberty against the Bourbons, and which triumphed at Vittorio Veneto with the great and magnificent victory of the Italian people. I see also among you factory hands and their brothers of the fields.

We, Fascists, have a great love for the working classes. But our love, in as far as it is pure, is seriously disinterested and intransigent. Our love does not consist in burning incense and creating new idols and new kings, but in telling upon every occasion and in every place the

---

[32] Contadini are Italian peasants, rustics, or farmers.

plain truth, and the more this truth is unpalatable the greater the need to speak it out.

We, Fascists, hitherto slandered and maligned, wished to continue the war in order to obtain freedom of movement in Italy, and although not giving way to a sense of weak demagogism, we are the first to recognize that the rights of the laboring classes are sacred, and even more so the rights of those who work the soil. And here I can give hearty praise to the Fascists of Ferrara, who have undertaken with facts, and not with the useless words of the politicians, that agrarian revolution which must gradually give the peasants the possession of the soil. I strongly encourage the Fascists of Ferrara to go on as they have begun, and to become the vanguard of the Fascist agrarian movement in all Italy.

How does it come about that we are said to be sold to the middle classes, capitalism, and the Government? But already our enemies dare no longer continue this accusation, so false and ridiculous is it. This impressive meeting would move a heart harder than mine, and shows me that you have done justice to those base calumnies put into circulation by people who believed in the eternity of their fortunes, while in reality they had barricaded themselves in a castle, which must fall with the first breath of a Fascist revolt. And this Fascist revolt—and we could also use the more sacred and serious word *revolution*—is inspired by indestructible and moral motives and has nothing to do with incentives of a material nature. We, Fascists, say that above all the competition and those differences that divide men—and which might almost be called natural and inevitable, since life would be extraordinarily dull if everybody thought in the same way—above all this there is a single reality, common in all, and it is the reality of the nation and of the country to which we are bound, as the tree is bound by its roots to the soil that nourishes it.

Thus, whether you like it or not, the country is an indestructible, eternal, and immortal unity, which, like all ideas, institutions, and sentiments in this world, may be eclipsed for a time, but which revives again in the depths of the soul, as the seed thrown in the soil bursts into flower with the coming of the warmth of spring. We have thus, by our furious blows, broken the unworthy crust beneath which lay imprisoned the soul of the proletariat. There were those among the proletariat who were ashamed to be Italian; there were those who, brutalized by propaganda, shouted "Welcome to the Germans!" and also "Long live Austria!" They were for the most part irresponsible but sometimes wicked! Well we, Fascists, want to bring into every city, into every part of the country, even the most remote, the pride and passion of belonging to the most noble Italian race, the race which has produced Dante, which has given Galileo, the greatest master-pieces of art, Verdi, Mazzini, Garibaldi, and d'Annunzio to the world, and which has produced the people who won Vittorio Veneto.

And not this only. We do not intend to push the working classes backwards. All that which they have won and which they will win is sacred. But they must acquire these conquests by material and moral improvement. We, Fascists, do not speak only of rights, we speak also of duty, as Mazzini would have wished. We have not only the verb "to take," we have also the verb "to give," because sometimes when our country calls, whether she be threatened by an internal or external enemy, we exact both from our adherents and from those who sym-pathize with us readiness even for the supreme sacrifice. And you, Fascists of Ferrara, have consecrated the Fascist ideals with martyr-dom.

If the idea of Fascism had not contained in itself great potentiality, nobility and beauty, do you think that it would have spread with this tremendous impetus? Do you think that seven lives would have been given for it, lives which point out to us the path of perseverance and victory? A short time ago I went to your cemetery. One by one we visited the graves and threw our flowers upon them. Those seconds of silence we passed there were pregnant with feeling. Each one of us felt that within those graves were the bodies of young men in the flower of their days, men who were certainly loved and who had be-fore them all the possibilities of life. They are dead; they have fallen. But we, in this great hour of your history, O people of Ferrara, will recall them one by one in the orders of the day; and since they are not dead, because their mortal clay is transformed in the infinite play of the possibilities of the universe, we ask of the pure, bright blood of the youth of Ferrara the inspiration to be true to our ideals, to be faithful to our nation. And so we are content that our flags, after hav-ing saluted the dead, smile on life, because the working people of Fer-rara, and of all Italy, have found the true path that had been forgotten, have cast off all those ignoble politicians who had filled their heads with lying fables.

We, O Italians of Ferrara, have no need to go beyond our boundaries, beyond the seas, in order to find the word of wisdom and of life. We do not need to go to Russia in order to see how a great people may be massacred. We do not need to turn the pages of the Muscovite gospels, gospels which the prophets themselves are reviling since, overwhelmed by the reality of life, they are denying them. We have no need to imitate others, because brilliant original minds are to be found in Italy in all branches of civilization and learning. And if there is to be Socialism, it cannot be the bestial, tyrannical Socialism of yesterday; it can only be the Socialism of Carlo Pisacane, of Giuseppe Ferrari and Giuseppe Mazzini.

Here, O people of Ferrara, is your history, your life, and your future. And we, who have undertaken this hard battle, which has cost us tens and hundreds of lives, we do not ask you for salaries, we do not ask you for votes. We only ask you for one thing: that you shall shout with us "Long live Italy!" (Loud applause.)

My Father Was a Blacksmith and I Have Worked with Him; He Bent Iron, But I Have the Harder Task of Bending Souls

December 6th, 1922, Milan, before the workmen of the iron foundries, in answer to Engineer Vanzetti, the manager

On the occasion of his first visit to Milan after assuming the Premiership of the Council, the city where he had lived and the center of his victorious political strife, Mussolini was urgently summoned to the works of the Lombard Iron Foundries (Acciaierie Lombarde), where he was welcomed with enthusiastic demonstrations of support and appreciation. During the stormy years of 1919–20 these very works were the scene of extraordinary events.

◆

I am particularly glad to have seen these works, already known to me by what has been accomplished in them in the last five strenuous years. I am not going to make a speech, but, as has always been—and always will be—my way, I shall tell you things clearly as they are, things that will interest you.

The Government over which I have the honor of presiding is not, cannot, and does not wish to be anti-proletariat. The workmen are a vital part of the nation; they are Italians and, like all Italians, when they work, when they produce, and when they live orderly lives, must be protected, respected, and defended. My Government is very strong and does not need to seek a great deal of outside support; it neither asks for it nor refuses it. If the workmen's organizations choose to give me support, I shall not reject it. But we shall have to come to a clear understanding and to make definite agreements in order to avoid dissension later.

I was deeply moved just now while I was visiting the factory, and seemed for an instant to be living again the bygone days of my youth. Because I do not come of an aristocratic and illustrious family. My ancestors were peasants who tilled the earth, and my father was a blacksmith who bent red-hot iron on the anvil. Sometimes, when I was a boy, I helped my father in his hard and humble work, and now I have the infinitely harder task of bending souls. At twenty I worked with my hands—I repeat, with my hands—first as a mason's lad and afterwards as a mason. And I do not tell you this in order to arouse your sympathy, but to show you how impossible it is for me to be against the working class. I am, however, the enemy of those who, in the name of false and ridiculous ideologies, try to dupe the workmen and drive them toward ruin.

You will have the opportunity of realizing that more valuable than my words will be the acts of my Government, which, in all that it does, will be inspired by and keep before it these three fundamental principles:

First: The Nation, which is an undeniable reality.

Secondly: The necessity of Production, because greater and better production is not only the interest of the capitalist but also of the workman, since the workman, together with the capitalist, loses his livelihood and falls into poverty if the productions of the nation do not find a market in the trade centers of the world.

Thirdly: The Protection of the Legitimate Rights of the Working Classes.

Keeping these three essential principles in sight, I intend to give peace to Italy and to make her more respected at home and abroad.

Nobody wants to go in search of adventures that will imperil the lives and wealth of the citizens, but, on the other hand, neither do we wish to follow a policy of renunciation nor allow Italy to be the last considered among the nations. In order that we may be listened to in international conferences—conferences that are of the greatest importance to you workmen—it is necessary that the most rigid discipline be maintained at home, as no one will listen to us if we have a disturbed and unsettled country behind us.

You, workmen, must not think that it is only the head of the Government who is speaking to you now, but a man who knows you well and who is known by you, a man who understands your value and what you can and what you cannot do. But, as the head of the Government, I tell you that this one over which I preside is serious, strong, and sure of itself, and no slow-moving bureaucracy; it is a Government that wishes to act in the interests of the working classes, interests that will always be recognized when they are just.

The workmen thought that they could, and ought to, disassociate themselves from the life of the nation, and this has been a great mistake. They ought, instead, to be a most intimate part of the nation, so that all our long and laborious toiling may not be miserably lost.

This is the message that comes from our dead, who, hovering above us, repeat this command.

The Italian people must somehow find that medium of harmony necessary for the reconstruction and development of civilization; and if there be rebellious and seditious minorities they must be inexorably stamped out.

Treasure up these words in your hearts and remember the motto of the Fascist Syndicates: *The country must not be denied but conquered.*

I raise my glass with you and drink to the future and the fortunes of Italian industry, that it may take a glorious place in the eyes of the whole world.

Labor to Take the First Place in New Italy

January 6th, 1923, Rome, before a representative
gathering of Fascist dock workers from Genoa,
who had presented him with an illuminated address

You must certainly be aware of the fact that I take a great interest in your city—an interest which dates from 1915 when Genoa, together with Milan and Rome, led the way to revolution; because the revolution that has brought the Fascists into power began in May 1915, was continued in October 1922, and goes on still, and will go on for some time. I am very pleased to accept your message, and I thank you with sincere cordiality.

◆　　◆　　◆

I must tell you that the Government over which I have the honor of presiding never has had, never can, and never will have the intention of following a so-called anti-labor policy. On the contrary, I want to praise the working classes, who do not put obstacles in the way of the Government, who work, and who have practically abolished strikes. They have redeemed themselves, because they no longer believe in the Asiatic Utopia that came from Russia; they believe in themselves, in their work; they believe in the possibility, which for me is a certainty, of a prosperous Italian nation.

You have been directly interested in this greatness of the nation, and you, who come from such a live center as Genoa, are the most suited to feel this ferment of new life, all this active preparation for a new destiny.

The Government, as you see, governs for all, over the heads of all, and, if necessary, against all. It governs for all, because it takes into account all general interests; it governs against all, when any group, whether of the middle class or of the proletariat, tries to put its interests before the general interests of the nation. I am sure that if the working classes—of which you are the aristocratic minority—continue to give this noble exhibition of tranquility and discipline, the nation, which was upon the verge of ruin, will recover itself completely.

I do not say things that have not been well considered and thought over, and, after two months of government, I tell you that if the Fascist revolution had been postponed for another few months or perhaps only another few weeks, the nation would have fallen into a state of chaos. All that we are performing now is really work in arrears; we are freeing the citizens from the weight of laws that were the result of a foolish demagogic policy; we are freeing the State from all those superstructures that were suffocating it, from all the economic functions that it was unfitted to perform; we are working to balance the budget, which means reestablishing the value of the lira, which means taking a position of dignity and influence in the international world.

The Italy we wish to make, which we are building up day by day, which we shall succeed in making, as it is our aim and our immovable determination to do, will be a magnificent creation of power and of wisdom. You can rest assured that in this Italy the workman—and all labor both of the brain and of the hands—will take, as is right, the first place.

PART IV

MUSSOLINI THE FASCIST

The Three Declarations at the First Fascist Meeting

March 23rd, 1919, Milan, first Fascist meeting

In the spring of 1919, the most critical period through which Italy has passed, the attempt initiated by Benito Mussolini to summon the men prepared to fight Bolshevism, that apparently triumphant beast, seemed absolute madness. A handful of bold spirits, for the most part ex-soldiers coming from the extreme interventionist sections, responded to the appeal. But the gravity of the moment and the danger of physical sacrifice to which they exposed themselves were not sufficient to lessen their ardor and determination for an immediate counter-offensive. This had its conclusive expression in the assault upon and the burning of the offices of the newspaper *Avanti!*, which took place on a day of general strike, when two hundred thousand workmen marched defiantly through the streets of Milan.

◆ ◆ ◆

First of all, a few words about the proceedings. Without too much formality or pedantry, I will read you three declarations that seem to me worthy of being discussed and voted upon. Then in the afternoon we will resume the discussion of the declaration of our program. I tell you at once that we cannot go into detail. Wishing to act, we must take salient facts as they exist.

The first declaration is as follows:

The Meeting of March 23rd first salutes with reverence and remembrance the sons of Italy who have fallen for the cause of the greatness of the country and the liberty of the world, the maimed and disabled, and all the fighters and ex-prisoners who fulfilled their duty, and declares itself ready to uphold strongly the vindication of rights, both material and moral, advocated by the Association of Fighters.

As we do not wish to form a party of ex-soldiers, because something in that line has already been done in various cities in Italy, we cannot say exactly what this program of vindications will be; those interested will do so. We declare simply that we will uphold them. We do not wish to classify the dead, to look into their pockets to find out to which party they belonged; we leave this sort of occupation to the official Socialists. We include in one single loving thought all the fallen, from the general to the humblest soldier, from the most intelligent to the most ignorant and uncultured. But you must allow me to remember with special, if not exclusive, affection our dead, those who were with us in the glorious May: the Corridoni, Reguzzoni, Vidali, Deffenu, and our Serrani—all that marvelous youth which went to fight and remained to die. Certainly when one speaks of the greatness of the country and the liberty of the world, there may be someone who will sneer and smile ironically, because it is the fashion now to run down the war, but war must be either wholly accepted or wholly rejected. If this line is to be taken up, it will be for us to do so and not the others. Besides, wishing to examine the situation in the light of facts, we say that the active and passive sides of so immense an undertaking cannot be established with cut-and-dried figures. One cannot put on one side the "quantum" of that which has been accomplished and that which has not; the "qualifying" element must be taken into account.

From this point of view we can, with complete certainty, maintain that the country is greater today, not only because it extends as far as the Brenner—reached by Ergisto Bezzi, to whom my thoughts turn—(Applause)—not only because it extends as far as Dalmatia; Italy is greater, even if small minds try their little experiments, because we feel ourselves greater inasmuch as we have the experience of the war, inasmuch as we willed it, it was not forced upon us, and we could have avoided it. The choosing of this path was a sign that there are elements of greatness in our history and our blood, because if it were not so, we, today, should be the least important people in the world. The war has given us that for which we asked. It has yielded its negative and positive advantages: negative, in as far as it has prevented the

Houses of Hapsburg and Hohenzollern from dominating the world—and this result, which all can see, is enough in itself to justify the war; and positive, because in no nation has reaction triumphed. Everything moves toward a stronger political and economic democracy. In spite of certain details that may injure the more or less intelligent elements, the war has given all that we asked.

And why do we speak of ex-prisoners also? It is a burning question. Evidently there were those who surrendered themselves, but those are called deserters. The large majority of the mass that fell prisoner did so after having fought and done their duty. If this were not so, we could begin to brand Cesare Battisti and many brave and brilliant officers and men who had the misfortune to fall into the hands of the enemy.

The National Vindications. Second declaration:

> The Meeting of March 23rd declares that it will oppose imperialism in other peoples that would be prejudicial to Italy, and any eventual imperialism in Italy that would be prejudicial to other nations, and accepts the fundamental principle of the League of Nations, which presupposes the geographical integrity of every nation. This, as far as Italy is concerned, must be realized on the Alps and the Adriatic with the annexation of Fiume and Dalmatia.

We have 40 million inhabitants and an area of 111,000 square miles, divided by the Apennines, which reduce still further the availability of the land capable of cultivation. In ten- or twenty-years' time we shall be 60 million, and we have just over half a million square miles of land in the way of colonies, which to a large extent is barren, and to which we certainly can never send the surplus of our people. But, if we look around, we see England, with 47 million inhabitants, and a colonial empire of 21 million square miles, and we see France, with a population of 38 million, and a colonial empire of just under 6 million square miles. And I could prove to you with figures that all the nations of the world, not excluding Portugal, Holland, and Belgium, have colonies they cling to, and are not in the least disposed to relinquish for all the ideologies that come from the other side of the ocean. Imperialism is at the base of the life of every people who desires economic and spiritual expansion. That which distinguishes the different kinds of imperialism is the method adopted in its pursuit. Now the method that we choose, and will choose, will never resemble the barbaric penetration of the Germans. And we say, either everybody idealist or nobody. One cannot understand how people who are well off can preach idealism to those who suffer, because that would be very easy. We want our place in the world because we have a right to it. I reaffirm the principle of the League of Nations, but we must beware lest this principle mean only protection of the material interests of wealthy nations.

In View of the Elections. Third declaration:

> The Meeting of March 23rd pledges the Fascists to prevent by every means in their power the candidature of neutralists of any party.

You see I pass from one subject to another, but there is logic in it, an underlying thread. I am not an enthusiast for ballot-paper battles, so much so that for some time I have abolished the chronicles of the Chamber, and nobody is sorry. My example, too, has caused other papers to do the same, within the limits of strict necessity. It is clear in any case that the elections will take place before the end of the year. The date and the system to be followed are not yet known, but this year these electoral campaigns and ballot-paper battles will take place.

Now, whether one likes it or not, the war having been of late the dominant event of our national life, it is clear that in these elections the subject of the war cannot be avoided. We shall accept the battle precisely on the topic war, because not only have we not repented of that which we have done, but we go further and say, with that courage which is the result of our individuality, that if the same condition of things which existed in 1915 were repeated in Italy, we should demand war again as in 1915.

Now it is very sad to think that there are those who formerly were in favor of intervention and who now have changed. Only a few have done so, and it has not always been for political reasons. Some have changed for those reasons, and this I do not wish to discuss, but there has also been defection due to physical fear. "In order to pacify these people let us cede Dalmatia, let us renounce something!" But their calculations have piteously failed. We shall not only refuse to take up this political line, but we shall not give way to that physical fear which is simply absurd. One life is of the same value as another, and one barricade is as good as another. If there is to be a fight, we shall engage also in that of the elections.

There have been neutralists also among the official Socialists and the Republicans. We shall go and examine the passports of all these people, both the ultra-neutralists and those who accepted the war as a painful burden; we shall go to their meetings, we shall present candidates and find every possible means of routing them. (Prolonged applause.)

Outline of the Aims and Program of Fascism

July 22nd, 1919, Liceo Beccaria, Milan

The evening before the general international strike of July 20th and 21st, 1919, called by the federal organizations as a reaction to the rash movement, the National Socialists, the Republicans, the Democrats, and the Fascists met in order to share the responsibilities for possible complications and to demonstrate the inconsistency of so-called revolutionary attitudes.

This manifestation, according to the intention of its organizers, had also the object of marking the beginning of a political concentration of the Left, composed of ex-interventionists. But the attempt afterwards failed, chiefly on account of want of understanding on the part of the Republican Party, and because of the development of the spiritual crisis within the mass of Italian Fascism.

◆　◆　◆

I think that it will depend upon the sincerity and loyalty with which we join in this meeting whether it will become a historical event, or a little fact of everyday life destined to pass without leaving any trace.

This being the case, it will not surprise you if I speak with a frankness almost brutal. I add at once that the friendly confusion of this moment of reunion after schisms and separations will not eliminate the necessity of settling certain personal and political questions; otherwise, this union, which we wish to be eminently fruitful, cannot be other than painfully sterile.

What are we looking for, we who are members of U.S.M., the Fascio of Fighters, the Association of Fighters, the Association of Arditi, the Union of Demobilized, the Association of Volunteers, the Association of Garibaldians, the Republican Party, the Italian Socialist Union, the

Corridoni Club, etc.—we who are together represented in the Committee of Intesa e Azione (Understanding and Action) which was formed at the time of the movement against the high cost of living? We are looking for the least common denominator for this understanding and action. Shall we find it? Yes! We come from different schools; we have different temperaments, and temperaments divide men more widely than ideas; we belong to an individualist people; but all this does not prevent something else bringing us together and binding us both in these present contingencies and in that which has to do with the action of tomorrow.

The Basis of Unity. There can be a thousand shades of ideas among us, but upon one important point we are all agreed, and that is in regarding the Socialist manifestation as a bluff, a comedy, a speculation and blackmail. Also we are all agreed in making a differentiation between the Socialist Party and the mass of the workmen. The Socialist Party has usurped up to yesterday the name of being a pure revolutionary organization, of being the protector and the exclusive, genuine representative of the working masses. This is all nonsense and must be cleared up. Referring to statistics, we find that out of 42 million Italians, hardly sixty thousand were enrolled in the Socialist Party in August 1919, and the dominating element is a group composed of lower-middle-class people in the most philistine sense of the word.

In the unlikely and absurd event of a triumph on the part of the Leninist revolutionaries, ten of these idiots would be, tomorrow, the ten Ministers of the Italian nation. The Socialist Party is one thing, and the organized mass of working men another, and the disorganized mass yet another and seven times larger than the rest put together.

We must not allow ourselves to approach the working classes in the sometimes unctuous, sometimes theatrical, manner of the demagogues. The masses must be educated and for this reason must have the straight truth. Many of the crowds the Socialists sway are not worthy of blandishments, because they consist of masses of brutes infected and barbarized by the Red gospel. Our working-class colleagues know all about it, because they have had to leave certain factories. We must not present ourselves to the masses as charlatans, promising Paradise within a short time, but as educators who do not seek either success, popularity, salaries, or votes.

Produce! Produce! Produce! The Admonition of Merrheim. The way in which the working masses should and must be spoken to has been shown us by Alphonse Merrheim, one of the thinking heads of French syndicalism. Last January he made a very important speech, and it would be a good thing to run over those parts of it which are now of most importance, especially those touching upon the relations between economics and politics and the necessity of production:

> The militant Socialists must tell the truth, and all the truth, to the masses, even if the truth brings hatred and slander. Now the truth is for all those who reflect, that the bad conditions of life, which are the trouble of the masses, are not going to be remedied by a solution based on an increase of wages, which is not only inoperative, but entirely in opposition to economic laws. The masses must be told that the regime of production and distribution of commodities must undergo a transformation, if efficacious and lasting remedies are to be found for existing bad conditions, and that this can be arrived at by means of the force of organization. . . .
>
> It is pleasant to provoke loud applause by telling the audience at meetings that we are overstocked with commodities, and that they can consume without limit and enjoy comfort by imposing wages proportionate to their desires without increasing production.
>
> Courage lies in repeating to the masses that each man is at the same time a producer and consumer, and that the continued increase of production is necessary and indispensable.
>
> Courage lies in saying that it is not only impossible to satisfy those normal needs, natural to everyone, without normal production, but that it is absolutely impossible to obtain general comfort for everyone if at the same time individual production in the general interest is not increased.
>
> Courage lies in proclaiming that the purely political revolution, which inflames the people's minds, would not solve the social problem, the solution of which has been precipitated and rendered essential by the war.
>
> Courage lies in repeating untiringly to the masses that the revolution which must be brought about must be economic, and that it is not to be brought about in the streets by a delirious crowd destroying for the sake of destruction.
>
> Courage lies in saying that an economic revolution draws its substance from labor, and that it is strengthened, advanced, and carried out by the intensification of production whether in the fields or in the

factories, and by a further utilization of scientific processes and methods of production.

The Italian Situation. We agree upon a third point, in connection with existing circumstances, that is in maintaining that our national situation is critical, though far from being desperate. Briefly, it is this. From July 1st we have been defaulting debtors of England. Since July 31st other financial agreements with the United States must be faced. To save the situation, a loan of 1 billion dollars (7 to 8 billion lire) must be arranged. The railways have a coal supply for only fifteen more days. There are enough provisions for another twenty days, that is to say until the end of the month. Two million tons of food must be imported to save us from immediate hunger. But these financial and economic agreements depend upon the political ones at Paris.

The possibility, almost a certainty, has presented itself to us of obtaining large concessions in Asia Minor, with the coal mines of Heraclea. Clemenceau has made difficulties about it, but Lansing told him that he could not see any obstacle, given that Italy approved of the exploitation of the Saar mines on the part of France. We may also obtain oil wells in Armenia.

But these acquisitions in the East are in their turn subordinate to the Adriatic agreements. The solution of the problem of Fiume is already compromised by the work of the preceding Delegation, which had already accepted the principle of a Free State. But the project of Tardieu presented future dangers as far as the safeguarding of the Italian character of Fiume is concerned, because the Italian majority in the city would be overwhelmed by the mass of Slavs in the country. It is a question, then, of reducing these dangers to the smallest possible limits by the introduction of another plan, which would substitute for the idea of a Free State that of a Free City with limited boundaries.

In Dalmatia it is only possible for us to save the centers that have an Italian majority, with guarantees for the safeguarding of those Italian minorities scattered in the other centers. The eventual loss of Sebenico,[33] which had strategic and not national value, would be compensated for by some other strategic point to be given to Italy.

---

[33] Also called Šibenik, a city in Dalmatia, now in Croatia.

Lansing said that this would be eventually sought for in the Mediterranean.

Given this situation, it is no exaggeration to say that the general Socialist strike is a real attempted crime against the nation. And note: I could understand a strike that had as its object the setting up of the Soviet in Italy, but I do not understand or admit this one, which is without aim, object, or justification. It must and will fail, because the leaders themselves are in the *cul de sac* of this dilemma: either tragedy, because the State at this moment has its repressive machinery in full working order; or comedy, in the event of a revolt on the part of the workmen already outlined, and due to their being tired of serving a Socialist Party mostly composed of middle-class elements.

Perhaps it is worthwhile in passing to confute the objection in the *Stampa* of Portogruaro, which would like to deny our right of rising up against the strike on the ground that we were in favor of war. "What," it says, "is the damage done in two days of strike compared with that done in four years of war?" We crush these gentlemen with the reply that four years of neutrality would have damaged us more, besides having been to our lasting and ineffaceable moral shame.

Reactionaries and vice versa. For me revolution is not an attack of St. Vitus' dance or an unexpected fit of epilepsy. It must have force, aims, and above all, method. In 1913, when the Socialist Party was already rotten, it was I who put into circulation the words that made the pulses of the big men of Italian Socialism beat: "This proletariat is in need of a bath of blood," I said. It has had it, and it lasted for three years. "This proletariat is in need of a day of history." And it has had a thousand.

It was necessary then to shake up the masses, because they had fallen into a state of weakness and insensibility. Today this situation exists no longer. Today the only way not to live in fear of a revolution is to think that we are now in the full swing of one, that it began in August 1914 and that it is still going on. It is not a question, as some think, of entering into a revolution as one passes from a state of tranquility to a state of action. The task of really free spirits is different. If this great and immense process of changing the world stagnates or becomes confused, we can hasten it on; but if it is already progressing at a frantic rate, then our task is to apply the brakes and slow it down, in order to avoid disintegration and ruin. To be revolutionaries, in certain circumstances, time and place, can be the pride of a lifetime, but when those who speak of revolution are a lot of parasites, then one must not be afraid, in opposing them, to pass as a reactionary. One is always a reactionary and revolutionary for somebody. Fritz Adler, revolutionary in the time of Sturck, is a reactionary today compared with the Communists. I am not afraid of the word. I am a revolutionary and a reactionary. Really, life is always like this. I am afraid of the revolution that destroys and does not create. I fear going to extremes, the policy of madness, at the bottom of which may lie the destruction of this our fragile mechanical civilization, robbed of its solid moral basis, and the coming of a terrible race of dominators who would reintroduce discipline into the world and reestablish the necessary hierarchies with the cracking of whips and machine guns.

The Compass. At the same time, as regards reaction and revolution, I have a compass in my pocket that guides me. All that which tends toward making the Italian people great finds me favorable, and—*vice versa*—all that which tends toward lowering, brutalizing, and impoverishing them finds me opposed.

Now Socialism comes into the second category. I find it odd that my friend Carli, the founder of the National Association of Fighters and a valiant soldier, puts the Socialists among the advanced parties, storming them with a succession of "whys," as he did in the last number of the *Roma Futurista*.

I deny the title of vanguard to Socialism. I deny the use and timeliness of any cooperation with this party. I maintain that a reactionary party in 1914, '15, '16, '17, and '18 cannot become revolutionary in '19. I maintain that this serenading of the Socialists is useless, and this making of advances not clean. One day, in the culminating moment of the history of humanity, they embraced the cause of reaction represented by the Germany of the Hohenzollerns and Sudekum. Besides, it is idiotic and dangerous to lavish blandishments upon the official Socialists; we cannot reconcile ourselves with these people. There have been those who have attached themselves to the movement of today, but the Socialists have disdained that help, because they are megalomaniacs and nourish, among other things, the fatuous vanity of splendid isolation.

The Revision of the Treaty of Versailles. The Peace of Versailles is not a sufficient motive for the courted collaboration. Things must be made clear. The Socialists talk of annulling the peace; we wish simply to revise it. We do not condemn wholesale a peace which a German, and not one of the most insignificant, Edward Bernstein, has called nine parts just. The revision of the peace must not mean condemnation of the war. The Florentine Republican Union has published a manifesto that defines the limits of protest against the Treaty of Versailles:

> We do not wish to conceal that, although requiring radical amendments, the Treaty is, after all, the consecration of the fall of four Imperial autocracies, the fall of numerous dynasties, the creation of as many republics, the reestablishment of Poland, the reconquest of Alsace and Lorraine, and of Trento and Trieste by Italy, and of Jerusalem by civilized Europe. All this would suffice, as long as emendations were made, to bear witness to the supreme sanctity of the Italian intervention in the atrocious war let loose by the brutal German Hohenzollerns and Hapsburgs.
>
> We do not approve, however, of the proposed general strike as a form of protest, because—and we say so with the traditional sincerity of our party—the country is thirsty for fruitful work, and this deluge of strikes certainly does not help in that.
>
> The Peace of Versailles must be corrected and brought into keeping with the progress of humanity.

This is also our idea. Rather than seek or beg for useless cooperation, let us outline a program of our own of understanding and action. I refuse, after having got rid of the old, to accept the new dogmas. I think that it is possible to create a strong economic organization in Italy based upon these principles:

1. Absolute independence from all parties, groups, and sets.

2. Federation and autonomy.

3. Abolition, as far as possible, of all paid officials.

4. No steps to be taken without having consulted regularly, by means of a referendum, the masses interested.

The means of obtaining this end may be altered according to time and place. The organization will promote at times cooperation, and at times war between the classes and the expropriation of class. It will not always be for cooperation, but neither will it always be in favor of class preservation; and when it expropriates, it will not be to make all poor, but to make all rich. In the conquest of a colonial market and in certain questions connected with the customs, the middle classes and the proletariat can work together. When there is division of booty, then class war; but class war in times of under-production is destructive nonsense.

In the Political Field. The Electoral Reform will pass. The scrutiny of lists and proportional representation will pass. That will determine, for obvious reasons, the great coalitions—the Socialist-Leninist, the Clerical-Popular, and, lastly, ours, which might be called the "Alliance for the Constituent," the Republican Alliance, or the group of the "interveners" of the Left.

Our program is to present candidates who pledge themselves to place the problem of constitutional revision before the new Chamber in the first session.

This is the Constituent as I understand it. This is the lowest denominator to which all of us can pledge ourselves and around which we can all form a union. The moment is particularly propitious for such an organization. I think that all we who are represented in this Milanese Committee of Intesa e Azione can follow this path.

It is a case of "nationalizing" this attempt, of making it general all over Italy. We could, if we wished, number not thousands, but millions of followers. I myself refuse, in the actual delicate economic situation in Italy, to adhere to any movement that makes the path clear for Bolshevism and ruin. The victory cannot and must not be destroyed. I understand a certain impatience, but I beg you to reflect that if the lives of individuals are counted in years, the lives of nations are counted in centuries, and we must not refer egoistically to ourselves that which is of a general nature. Good strategy is calculation and audacity. We do not wish to govern by recourse to the bayonet alone, because that would be dictatorship, which we condemn. We wish first to sound the masses by the coming elections. Once having had our principles accepted, we will spring to action.

The revolution we desired and obtained in 1915 will be ours again by the victorious peace in its conclusive phase, and it will be called "Wellbeing," "Liberty" and, above all, "Italy." (Loud applause.)

Fascism and the Rights of Victory

October 9th, 1919, Florence, first Congress of the Fascists

At Florence was held the first Congress of the Fasci Italiani di Combattimento (Italian Fasces of Combat), which was the name originally given to the Fascist movement. This Congress succeeded the improvised, unorganized meeting of March 19th at Milan, and was held in an atmosphere of isolation and hostility, amid continuous tumult and interruption; so much so, that the members of the Congress were repeatedly obliged to suspend their proceedings and go out into the streets to defend themselves against hostile demonstrations.

At that time, Florence, the cradle of art, and famed for courtesy and hospitality, had been temporarily submerged under waves of Bolshevism; Serrati and Lenin, referring to the Italian situation, could point to the capital of Tuscany as "the most fertile soil for the imminent revolutionary harvest."

But even on that occasion Italian Fascism was able to hold the center successfully, in spite of the numbers of the adversary.

◆ ◆ ◆

Fascist comrades! I do not know if I shall succeed in giving you a very connected speech, as I have not had the opportunity of preparing it, as is my habit. I had intended to make a Fascist speech tomorrow morning for a personal reason which might also interest you, and which gave me the right to ask some hours of rest.

The other day I left Novi Ligure in a "S.V.A." with a magnificent pilot, and, having crossed the Adriatic, came down at Fiume, where d'Annunzio gave us a great welcome. Returning yesterday, we were caught in a storm on the Istrian plateau, and were obliged to go out of our course and to come down at Aiello.

At Fiume I lived in what d'Annunzio justly calls "an atmosphere of miracles and prodigies." In the meantime, I bring you his message; he was thinking of writing one especially for our meeting. (Applause.) My arrival at Fiume coincided with the capture of the ship *Persia*, about which Captain Giulietti of the Federation of the Sea was so agitated.

The situation at Fiume is splendid from every point of view. There are supplies for three months. The Yugoslavs have no intention of moving. Not only that, the Croats, to a certain extent, are supplying the town, which shows how inappropriate and insidious the movement was that tried to stir up the people and make them believe that we were on the verge of a war against the Yugoslavs. Nothing of this exists. D'Annunzio has not, so far, fired a single shot against those who are on the other side of the line of the armistice; on the contrary, he has issued a proclamation to the Croats, which is a magnificent document both from the political and the human point of view. It ends with these words: "Long live the Italian-Croat brotherhood! Long live the brotherhood on the sea!"

Now, as regards international relations, the position of Fiume is perfectly clear. D'Annunzio will not move, because everything is in his favor. What can the plutocratic powers of Western capitalism do against him? Nothing! Absolutely nothing, because to strive against a *fait accompli* would be to let loose a still greater calamity that nobody thinks of either in France or England. In France—and we can say so with tranquility—there is a sacred horror of further bloodshed; and as for the English, they have made war very well and brilliantly, but now all their ideas are contrary to any warlike undertakings and any adventures of even a slightly complicated nature. Tomorrow Fiume would be a *fait accompli* for everybody, because nobody would have the strength to modify it. If the Government had been less cowardly, the problem of Fiume would be settled by now, and the Allies would have had to accept it.

The Forces of the Socialist Party. And now we come to our affairs. We must keep the Socialist Party within sight. Let us look a little closer at their forces. They have had lately to number their forces, and fourteen thousand of its eighty thousand members have disappeared. They are the disbanded. As many as five hundred sections were not represented in what they call the Assizes of the Italian Proletariat. Nothing of very great importance was said or done during the congress. Bordiga is not a great general. He is only a little above mediocrity. What he said to the tribune was what I told the crowd in 1913. Only Turati's speech was of any real significance. All the other unlimited speeches did not, in the end, give practical indications of that which the Socialists wish or ought to do.

Our statements are much more definite than theirs, and we tell you at once that we must present an ultimatum to the Government, saying that, if the censor is not abolished, we Fascists will not take part in the elections. It is necessary to protest against an enforced censorship during the period of the elections; otherwise, we shall seem to show that we are ready to accept an arbitrary act. To this we can add another positive and effective protest. As for the Socialists, the larger part of them are distinguished by physical cowardice. They do not like fighting; they do not wish to fight; fire and steel frighten them.

On the other hand, and I want to draw your attention to this, we must not confuse this creation, which is for the most part artificial, with a party of which the proletariat is a lowest minority, while those members abound who want a seat in Parliament, or in the communal councils and in the organizations. It is really a political clique, which wishes to substitute itself for the ruling clique. We must not confuse this group of mediocre politicians with the immense movement of the proletariat, which has a reason for its existence, development, and brotherhood.

Against Every Idol. I repeat here what I said before. No demagogism. Work-worn hands are not yet enough to show that a man is capable of upholding a State or a family. We must react against these "cajolers" and these new semi-idols, in order to uplift these people from the moral and mental slavery into which they have fallen. We must not approach them in the attitude of partisans. We are syndicalists, because we think that by means of the mass it may be possible to determine an economic readjustment, but this readjustment involves long and complicated consideration. A political revolution is accomplished in twenty-four hours, but the economic constitution of a nation, which forms part of the world system, is not overturned in twenty-four hours.

But we do not, by this, mean to be considered as a kind of "bodyguard" of the bourgeoisie, which, especially where it is composed of the new rich, is simply unworthy and cowardly. If these people do not know how to defend themselves, they must not hope for protection from us. We defend the nation and the people as a whole. We desire the moral and material welfare of the people.

I think that, with this as our attitude, it will be possible to approach the masses. In the meantime, the Federation of Seamen has separated itself from the General Federation of Labor; the railwaymen have proved in the big strike that they are Italian and wish to be Italian; and while the upper bureaucracy of the public administration is, on the whole, in favor of Nitti and Giolitti, the proletariat of the same administration tends to sympathize with us. For fifty years generals, diplomats, and bureaucrats have been taken from the upper classes and from a certain limited number of persons of rank and position. It is time to put an end to all this, if we want to infuse new energy and new blood into the body of the nation.

For the Elections. And now we come to the elections. We must deal with them, because whatever happens it is always a good thing to keep together and not to burn one's boats. It may happen that in this month of October events may be hurried on at such a rate that the elections may be side-tracked. It may be, on the other hand, that they will take place. We must be ready also for the second contingency. And then we Fascists must do our utmost by ourselves, we must come out clearly marked and numbered, and if we are few, we must remember that we have only been in the world six months. Where there is no probability of isolated success, a union with the "interveners" of the Left might possibly be formed, which must vindicate, on the one hand, the utility of the Italian intervention in the name of humanity and the nation against all those who opposed it, whether followers of Giolitti, Socialists, or Clericals. On the other hand, this program cannot exhaust our action, and we shall then have to present to the masses the fundamental principles upon which we wish to build up a new Italy. Where the situation may prove more complicated we might also be able to identify ourselves with a group of "interveners" in a wider and fuller sense of the word.

After Vittorio Veneto. But we wish, above all, to reaffirm solemnly at this meeting of ours the great Italian victory, vindicating it before all those who wish to deny and forget it.

We have subdued an empire which was our enemy, which had

advanced to the Piave, and whose leaders had endeavored to over-throw Italy. We now possess the Brenner, the Julian Alps, and Fiume, and all the Italians of Dalmatia. We can say that between the Piave and the Isonzo we have destroyed that empire and determined the fall of four autocracies. (Enthusiastic applause.)

The Tasks of Fascism

September 20th, 1920, Politeama Rossetti, Trieste

The following speech may be considered as the first of the series of those belonging to the period of elaboration of the Fascist program. The moment chosen was not the most favorable, because it coincided with two manifestations equally critical both with regard to internal and to foreign policy. We refer to the occupation of the factories, then at an acute and threatening stage, and to the Legionary occupation of Fiume, the first anniversary of which was celebrated at this time.

Benito Mussolini, although taking into due account these two important events, destined not to be ignored by history, could and did rise above the circumstances of the moment. As a far-seeing statesman looking forward to resistance and final victory, he drew the attention of his hearers to a sane conception of the problems of foreign policy, not included in the enterprise of Ronchi, and, at the same time, heartening all Italians who were panic-stricken under the arrogant tyranny of Social-Bolshevism.

◈   ◆   ◈

I do not consider you, men of Trieste, as Italians to whom the whole truth cannot yet be spoken, because I think of you as among the best in the country, and your enthusiasm today has confirmed me in my opinion. The event, which had its counterpart in Rome on September 20th, 1870,[34] was a magnificent picture in a poor frame, but upon this I am not going to dwell.

A *Comforting Balance*. After a lapse of fifty years since the breach of Porta Pia, we must undertake the examination of our consciences.

---

[34] The capture of Rome, the final event of the unification of Italy (Risorgimento).

A nation like ours, which had issued from many centuries of disunion, which had barely achieved unity, had not then muscles strong enough to bear the weight of a world policy. A great Italian thinker broke this tradition.[35] In fifty years Italy has made marvelous progress. In the first place she has a sure foundation, and that is the vitality of our race. There are nations which every year scan the birth-rates with a certain preoccupation, because, gentlemen, it is just the want of balance in this sphere that produces the great crises—you know to what I allude. But Italy is not thus preoccupied. Italy had 27 million inhabitants in 1870; she has now 50 million, 40 million of whom live in the Peninsula and represent the most homogeneous block in Europe, because, compared with Bohemia, for instance, where 5 million of the Czecho race govern 7 million of other races, Italy has only 180,000 German subjects in Alto Adige and 360,000 Slavs,[36] all the rest forming one compact whole. And besides these 40 million, there are 10 million who have immigrated to all the continents and beyond all the oceans; there are 700,000 Italians in New York alone, another 400,000 in the state of San Paulo, 900,000 in Argentina, and 120,000 in Tunis.

National Discipline. It is a pity that foreigners know us so little, but it is still more serious that Italians know Italy so little. If they knew her a little better, they would realize that there are peoples beyond her boundaries who are more retrograde than she is; they would learn, for instance, that Italy possesses the most powerful hydro-electric plant in the world.

Do not speak to me of reactionary forces in Italy. Those who talk to me of a reactionary Government make me laugh, especially if they are immigrants or renegades from Trieste. Because if there is a country in the world where liberty is in danger of degenerating into license, and where it is the inviolable patrimony of every citizen, it is Italy. There has not yet been seen in our country that which has been seen in France, where, as the result of a political strike, the Republic dissolved the General Confederation of Labor, locked up the leaders,

---

[35] Francesco Crispi, among the main protagonists of the Risorgimento, a close friend and supporter of Giuseppe Mazzini and Giuseppe Garibaldi. He served as Prime Minister of Italy from 1887 to 1891 and again from 1893 to 1896.

[36] Severino uses the term Upper Adige as a literal translation, but the term Alto Adige is used in both languages. Today, the area is known as South Tyrol or officially as the Autonomous Province of Bolzano, the northern most province in Italy.

and keeps them still in prison. Nor have we seen that which has been witnessed in England, where so-called undesirable elements are sent over to the other side of the Channel; or in the ultra-democratic republic of the United States, where, in one single night, five hundred rebels were seized and sent over the Atlantic. If there is something to say, it is this: it is time to impose an iron discipline upon the individual and upon the masses, because social renovation is one thing—and this we are not against—but the destruction of the country quite another. As long as transformation is spoken of we are all agreed, but when instead it is a question of a leap in the dark, then we put our veto upon it. You will pass, we say, but it will be over our bodies; you will have to overcome our resistance first.

The Greatness of Victory. Now, after this half-century of the life of Italy which I have thus roughly sketched, Trieste is Italian and the tricolor waves over the Brenner. If it were possible to pause one moment to measure the greatness of the event, you would find that the fact of the tricolor on the Brenner is of capital importance, in the history not only of Italy, but also of Europe. The tricolor on the Brenner means that the Germans will no longer descend with impunity upon our lands. Glaciers have now been placed between us and them, and on these glaciers are the magnificent Alpine soldiers who went to the assault of Monte Nero, who were sacrificed at Ortigara, and who have on their flag the motto "No passage this way." (Loud applause.)

Now it is a most important fact that Trieste has come to Italy after a great victory. If we were not so occupied with the daily material necessities of life and the solution of commonplace and banal problems, we should know how to appreciate all that which took place on the banks of the Piave and at Vittorio Veneto. An empire was destroyed in an hour, an empire which had outlasted a century, an empire in which necessity had developed a superfine art of government which consisted in the eternal "Divide et impera" (divide and rule), according to the wisdom of Budapest and Vienna. This empire had an army, a traditional policy, a bureaucracy, and had bound all its citizens together in a universal suffrage. This empire, which seemed so powerful and invincible, fell before the bayonets of the Italian people.

The Italian Risorgimento is only a struggle between a people and a State, between the Italian people on one side and the Hapsburg State on the other, between the live forces of the future and the dead past.

It was inevitable that, having passed the Mincio in 1859, and Alto Adige in 1866, we had, in 1915, to pass the Isonzo and get beyond; it was so far inevitable that the neutralists themselves have had to acknowledge that Italy could not, under pain of death, and what is worse, dishonor, have remained neutral.

This vindication of our intervention is the fact which gives us the greatest satisfaction. And what does it matter if I read in a gloomy and pessimistic book that the acquisition of Trento, Trieste, and Fiume still represents a deficit in the balance of the war? This way of arguing is ridiculous. In the first place, historical events cannot be regulated like a page of book-keeping with receipts and payments, debit, and credit. It is impossible to make out an estimate of historical facts and expect it to agree with the final balance.

All this is the result of a melancholy philosophy which was widespread over Italy after the war. But let us hope it will soon pass to leave room for a little optimism and pride. This after-war period is certainly critical; I fully recognize the fact. But who can expect that a gigantic crisis like that of five years of a world-war will be settled at once, that the world will return to its previous tranquil state in less than two years? The crisis is not limited to Trieste, Milan, or Italy; it is worldwide and is not yet over.

The Necessity of Struggle. Struggle is at the bottom of everything, because life is full of contrasts. There is love and hate, black and white, night and day, good and evil, and until these contrasts are balanced, struggle will always be at the root of human nature, as the supreme fatality. And it is a good thing that it is so. Today there may be war, economic rivalry, and conflicting ideas, but the day in which all struggle will cease will be a day of melancholy, will mean the end of all things, will mean ruin. Now this day will not come, because history presents itself as a changing panorama. An attempt to return to peace and tranquility would mean fighting against the existing dynamic period. It is necessary to prepare ourselves for other surprises and struggles. "There will not be a period of peace," they say, "unless the nations indulge in a dream of universal brotherhood and stretch out their hands beyond the mountains and the oceans." I, for my part, do not put too much faith in these ideals, but I do not exclude them, because I never exclude anything; everything is possible, even the impossible and absurd. But today, being today, it would be fallacious, criminal, and dangerous to build our houses on the quicksands of international Christian-Socialist-Communism. These ideas are very respectable, but a long way from the truth. (Applause.)

The Patriotism of Fascism. What is the position of Fascism in this difficult post-war period? The foundation-stone of Fascism is patriotism; that is to say, we are proud of being Italian. Now it is just this which separates us from a great many other people, who are so ridiculous and small and hide their patriotism, because 80 percent of the Italian population was once illiterate. This does not mean anything, for narrow, poor, elementary education may be worse than pure and simple illiteracy. It is an outworn idea that one who knows how to write must be more intelligent than one who does not know how to.

Now we vindicate the honor of being Italian, because in our wonderful Peninsula—wonderful, although there are inhabitants who are not always wonderful—there has been enacted the most marvelous story of humanity. Do you think that a man who lives in far Japan or in America or in any other far-off spot can be counted educated if he does not know the history of Rome? It is not possible.

Rome. Rome is the name that filled history for twenty centuries. Rome gave the lead to universal civilization, traced the roads, and assigned the boundaries; Rome gave the world the laws of its immutable rights. But if this was the universal task of Rome in ancient times, we have now another universal task. Our destiny cannot become universal unless it is transplanted to the pagan ground of Rome. By means of Paganism, Rome found her form and found the means of upholding herself in the world.

Note that the task of Rome is not yet completed. No! Because the story of Italy of the Middle Ages—the most brilliant story of Venice, which lasted for ten centuries, with her ships in all seas and her ambassadors and her government, the likes of which is no longer to be found today—is not closed. The story of the Italian communes is full of wonders, grandeur, and nobility. Go to Venice, Pisa, Amalfi, Genoa, and Florence, and you will find in the palaces and in the streets the signs and vestiges of this marvelous and not yet decayed civilization.

Now, my friends, after this period, in the beginning of 1800, when Italy was divided into seven little States, there arose a generation of poets. Poetry also has its task to perform in history, in arousing enthusiasm and in kindling faith, and not for nothing the greatest modern Italian poet—whether second-rate writers, who do not know how to express the smallest idea, recognize it or not—Gabriele d'Annunzio, represents in a magnificent union of thought and sentiment, the power of action characteristic of the Italian people.

The Dolomites of Italian Thought. We are proud of being Italians, and not only for reasons of exclusivism. The modern spirit reaches out toward beauty and truth. One cannot think of a modern man who has not read Cervantes, Shakespeare, Goethe, and Tolstoy. But all this must not make us forget that we were great when the others were not yet born, that while German Klopstock was writing his verbose *Messias*, Dante Alighieri had been a giant for centuries. And we have also the sculpture of Michelangelo, the painting of Raffaello, the astronomy of Galileo, and the medicine of Morgagni, and with these the mysterious Leonardo da Vinci who excelled in all fields. And then, if you want to pass to politics and war, there is Napoleon and, above all, Garibaldi, most Italian of all.

These are the Dolomites of Italian thought and spirit, but beside these almost inaccessible peaks are lower summits in great numbers, which show that it is quite impossible to think of human civilization without the gigantic contribution made by Italian thought. And this must be repeated at our boundaries, where there are tribes chattering incomprehensible languages who would pretend, simply on account of their numbers, to supplant our marvelous civilization, which has endured two millennia and is ready for a third.

The Sincerity of Fascism. The second foundation-stone of Fascism is represented by anti-demagogism and pragmatism. We have no preconceived notions, no fixed ideas, and, above all, no stupid pride. Those who say, "You are unhappy, here is the receipt for happiness," make me think of the advertisement "Do you want health?" We do not promise men happiness either here or in the next world, differing thus from the Socialists, who pretend that they can set the Russian mask on the face of the Mediterranean.

Once there were courtiers who burned incense before the king and the popes; now there is a new breed, which burns incense, without sincerity, before the proletariat. Only those who hold Italy in their hands have the right to govern her, they say, while these do not know even how to control their own families. We are different. We use another language, more serious, unprejudiced, and worthy of free men. We do not exclude the possibility that the proletariat may be capable of using its present forces to other ends, but we say that before it tries to govern the nation it must learn to govern itself, must make itself worthy, technically and, still more, morally, because government is a tremendously difficult and complicated task. The nation is composed of millions and millions of individuals whose interests clash, and there are no superior beings who can reconcile all these differences and make a union of life and progress.

Fascism is not Conservative. But we are not, on the other hand, traditionalists, bound hand and foot to the stones and debris. Everything must be changed in the modern city. The ancient streets will no longer stand the wear and tear of the trams and motor traffic, because through them passes the whole of civilization. It is possible to destroy in order to create anew in a form more beautiful and great, for destruction must never be carried out in the method of a savage, who breaks open a machine in order to see what is inside. We do not refuse to make changes in our spiritual life just because the spirit is a delicate matter. No social transformation which is necessary, is repugnant to me. In this way I accept the famous control of the factories and also their cooperative management by companies; I only ask that there shall be a clear conscience and technical capacity, and that there shall be increased production. If this is guaranteed by the workmen's unions, instead of by the employers, I have no hesitation in saying that the former have the right to substitute the latter.

The Bolshevist Mask. That which we Fascists are opposing is the Bolshevist element in Italian Socialism. It is strange that a race that has produced Pisacane and Mazzini should go in search of gospels first to Germany and then to Russia. Pisacane and Mazzini ought to be studied, and then it would be seen that some of the truths pretended to have been revealed in Russia, are only truths already consecrated in the books of our great Italian thinkers.

How can Communism be thought possible in the most individualistic country in the world? It is only possible where every man is a number, not in Italy where every man is an individual, and more, has individuality. But after all, my dear friends, does Bolshevism exist in Russia? It does not any longer. There are no longer councils of the factories, but dictators of the factories; no longer eight hours of work, but twelve; no longer equal salaries, but thirty-five different categories, not according to need, but according to merit. There is not in Russia even that liberty which there is in Italy. Is there a dictatorship of the proletariat? No! Is there a dictatorship of the Socialists? No! There is a dictatorship of a few intelligent men, not workmen, who belong to a section of the Socialist Party, and their dictatorship is opposed by all the other sections.

This dictatorship of a few men is what is called Bolshevism. Now we do not want this in Italy. The Socialists themselves, realizing what they have seen in Russia, recognize, when you question them, that that which has gone badly in Russia cannot be transplanted into Italy. Only they are wrong in not saying so openly; they are wrong in playing with equivocations and deceiving the masses. We repeat, we are not against the working classes, because they are necessary to the nation, sacredly necessary. The 20 million Italians who work with their hands have the right to defend their interests. What we oppose is the deceitful action of politicians to the detriment of the working classes; we fight these new priests who promise, in bad faith, a paradise they do not believe in themselves. Those who are the most ardent advocates of Bolshevism here in Trieste take up this attitude in order to make themselves popular with the Slav masses who live near. And if I have a profound lack of esteem for the Bolshevist leaders in Italy, and despise many of them, it is because I know them all well and have been in contact with them. I know perfectly well that when they play the lion they are rabbits, and that they are like certain monks in Heinrich Heine who openly preach the drinking of water and drink wine themselves in secret. We wish to see this shameful speculation finish, because it is against the interests of the nation.

Always Against Italy. Can you tell me by what curious chance the Socialists are always against Italy in all questions? Can you tell me why they always side with those who are against Italy? With the Albanians, the Croats, the Germans, and others? Can you tell me why they shout "Long live Albania!" who is fighting for Vlorë, which is Albanian, and do not shout "Long live Italy!" who is fighting for Trento and Trieste, which are Italian? By what criterion are they always against Italy, shouting, "Down, down!" Four Arabs revolt in Libya and they shout, "Down with Libya!" Six thousand Albanians attack Vlorë and it is, "Down with Vlorë!" And if tomorrow the Croats of Dalmatia attack us it will be, "Down with Dalmatia!" And if, upon the burning mountain of the Carso, an insurrectional movement develops against Trieste, I am afraid the Italian Socialists would cry, "Down with Trieste!" But there are Italians here and elsewhere who would strangle the fratricidal cry in their throats.

It was the same with their opposition to the war. War is a horrible thing in itself. Those who have been through it know. But it is necessary to explain. If they say, "War in itself and for itself, for whatever reason, in whatever latitude, under whatsoever pretext, must not be made," then I respect these humanitarians and Tolstoyans. If they say, "I abhor that blood shall be spilled under any pretext," then I respect them and admire them, although I find this impracticable. But when they cry, "Down with the war!" when Italy makes it, and "Long live the war!" when Russia makes it, it is a different matter. They had a paper which was very happy when the so-called Bolshevists were marching toward Warsaw, and employed the military style, "While we are writing the cannons. . . ." etc.; we know it all by heart. Is not this war then the same thing? Does not the Russian war make widows and orphans? Is it not made with guns, airplanes, and all the innumerable instruments which tear and kill human bodies? Either they must be contrary to all wars, in which case we can discuss together, or if they make distinctions between war and war, between the war which can be made and the war which cannot—well, we can tell them that their humanitarianism is simply horrible. And if they have reason to make war, we had reason to make it for the destinies of the country in 1915. (Applause.)

The Epic of d'Annunzio. What, then, is to be the task of Fascism? It is this: to bridle demagogism with courage, energy, and impetuosity. Fascism is called the Fascio of Fighters, and the word "fighters" does not leave any doubts about its aims, which are, to fight with peaceful arms, but also with the arms of warriors. And this is normal in Italy, because all the world is arming itself, and so it is absolutely necessary that we Italians arm ourselves in our turn.

But the task of Fascism here is more delicate, more difficult, and more necessary. Fascism here has a reason for existence, and finds a natural field for development. I have unlimited faith in the future of the Italian nation. Crises will succeed crises, there will be pauses and parentheses, but we shall arrive at a settlement, and the history of tomorrow cannot be thought of without the participation of Italy.

There have been many orders of the day, many articles in the papers, much more or less senseless talk, but the only man who has achieved a real revolutionary stroke, the only man who for twelve or thirteen months has held in check all the forces ranged against him is Gabriele d'Annunzio with his legionaries. Against this man, of pure Italian blood, are leagued all the cowards, and it is for this reason that we are proud to be with him, even if all this tribe turn against us too. This man also represents the possibility of victory and resurrection. And this possibility exists because we have made war and won. It is ridiculous that those who most profited by it in wages, votes, and honors are those who, today, turn round and revile it. In any case I think, as indeed this meeting of yours bears witness, that the hour of the vindication of our national efficiency has struck. While on the one hand there is a vast world of wretched, poor creatures, there is also a world which does not forget and does not ignore our victory. (Applause.)

The Rebirth of Ideals. Just as I was leaving Milan, I received from the mayor of Cupra Marittima, a little town of Central Italy, an invitation to be present at their commemoration of the fallen. I did not accept, because I do not like making speeches. But this episode, like the pilgrimage of the Ortigara, the pilgrimage to the Grappa, the pilgrimage of October 24th to the rocky Carso, tells you that all ideals are not lost, but are, on the contrary, being re-born. We wish to assist this spiritual rebirth in every way possible.

Yesterday, I experienced a moment of great emotion when passing over the Isonzo. Every time that I have passed that river with my pack on my back, I have stooped to drink of its crystal waters. If we had not reached the other side of that river, the tricolor would not today be flying from San Giusto.

This is the real and true meaning of the war. If the tricolor flies from San Giusto, it is because twenty years ago a man of Trieste was the forerunner; it is there because in 1915 Italian soldiers threw themselves upon the Austrian defenses, and all Italy took part in that act, from the Alpine detachments of the mountains of Piedmont, Lombardy, and Friuli to the magnificent infantry of the Abruzzi, Puglie, and Sicily and the soldiers of the generous island of Sardinia, too much neglected by the Government! And these generous sons have not yet risen up to take reprisals against the demagogues of Italy, because they are always ready to fulfil their duty.

Men of Trieste! The tricolor of San Giusto is sacred, the tricolor on the Nevoso is sacred, and still more so is that on the Dinaric Alps. The tricolor will be protected by our dead heroes, but let us swear together that it will be defended also by the living. (Prolonged applause.)

Fascism and the Problems of Foreign Policy

February 6th, 1921, Politeama Rossetti, Trieste

Just as, a few months before, at the time of Italy's darkest hour, when the Bolshevist movement was at its zenith, Mussolini had addressed to the people of Trieste wise words of faith, so in the spring of 1921, the spring famous for anti-Socialist reaction, Trieste was once more the city he chose as the place best suited for the exposition of his analysis of the problems of foreign policy. On that occasion the patriotic and liberated town, which gave the first impulse of assault in the energetic offensive against the local Austrian Bolshevists, accorded to the leader of the new Italy hearty manifestations of general assent.

❖　◆　❖

In order to indicate the direction which Italian foreign policy should take in the immediate future, it is a good thing to give a glance first at the general situation in the world, and at the forces and currents which are at work, with a view to finding out what may be the possible developments and results.

All the States of the world are in a condition of fatal interdependence. The period for splendid isolation is passed for everyone. It can well be said, that with the war the story of mankind has acquired a world movement. While Europe, severely weakened, struggles to recover her economic, political, and spiritual balance, already beyond the boundaries of the old Continent a formidable clash of interests is shaping itself. I allude to the conflict between the United States and Japan, and to the accounts of recent episodes, from the Affair of the Cable to the Bill against the Yellow Immigration in California, which have occupied the papers. Japan has a population of 77 million, and the United States 110 million. That it was known that a struggle between these two States was inevitable is proved by the very significant fact that the book which had the widest circulation among all classes in Tokyo was called *Our Next War with the United States*, a book which outlined the war between the continents for the dominion of the Pacific. The center of world civilization is tending to alter its position. Up to about 1500 it was in the Mediterranean; after the discovery of America, it shifted to the Atlantic; today its passage to the biggest ocean of the planet is indicated. I said, last time I spoke here, that we were approaching the "Asiatic" century. Japan is destined to be the fermenting element of all the Yellow world.

As the result of shifting the center of civilization from London to New York (which has already 7 million inhabitants and will soon be the largest agglomeration of human beings on the earth), and from the Atlantic to the Pacific, there are those who foresee a gradual economic and spiritual decay of our old Europe, and of our wonderful little continent, which has been, hitherto, the guiding light of all the world. Shall we live to see the eclipse of the European role in the history of mankind?

The European Situation. To this disquieting and depressing question we answer, "It is possible." The life of Europe, especially that of Central Europe, is at the mercy of the Americans. Europe presents a troubled political and economic panorama, a thorny maze of national and social questions, and it happens that communism is sometimes the mask of nationalism and *vice versa*. European "unity" does not seem to be any nearer realization. Egoism and the interests of nations and classes exist in proud contrast. Russia is no longer an enigma from the economic point of view. In Russia there is neither communism nor socialism, but an agrarian revolution of the democratic lower-middle-class kind. She only remains an enigma from the political point of view. What foreign policy does Russia follow? Is it a policy of peace or war? The variety of facts which reach our ears make us continually waver between one opinion and another. Perhaps under the emblem of the sickle and the hammer is hidden—or not hidden—the old Pan-Slavism, which today is dominated, besides, by the immediate necessity of extending the revolution to the rest of Europe, in order to save the Government of the Soviets in Russia. If Russia adopts a policy of war, the fate of the Baltic States (Lithuania, Latvia, and Estonia) will be sealed. The fate of Poland would also be uncertain, and she might find herself driven against the unfriendly German wall by an eventual breaking loose of the Russian forces. There are serious conflicting interests between the different states of those northeast shores. There is a disagreement between Poland, Lithuania, and Russia as regards Wilna (Vilnius) and Grodno. The rights on the basis of history and statistics are with Poland. There are 263,000 Poles in the district of Wilna as compared with 118,000 Lithuanians, 8,000 White Ruthenians, and 83,000 Jews. The same figures, proportionately, are found in Grodno. As for Upper Silesia, which keeps the Polish and German worlds in a state of continuous agitation, the German statistics give these returns: 1,348,000 Poles; 588,000 Germans. Upper Silesia is, therefore, Polish, but its final destiny will be decided by the plebiscite summoned for March 15th.

The Treaties of Peace. The Great War has resulted in six treaties of peace up to the present: Versailles, St. Germain, Trianon, Neuilly, Sèvres, Rapallo. Not one of these treaties has wholly satisfied the victors; not one, even the Treaty of Rapallo, which was supposed to be a masterpiece of friendly and peaceful negotiation, has been accepted by the vanquished. As far as the Treaty of Versailles, the greatest of all, is concerned, even at this moment the important question of the indemnity that Germany ought to pay is still under discussion. It is a figure that makes us feel giddy, and the last word has not yet been said. All the settlements, especially those made by diplomats, have an ironically provisional character.

The Germans, who have formed the "sacred union" of non-payment, announce that they will make counterproposals by the same representatives who will speak at London in a few weeks' time. Our opinion is, that if the Germans can pay they ought, as far as it is possible, and the experts must ascertain the truth of this possibility. We must not forget, before allowing ourselves to pity the Germans—who had already fixed our indemnity at 500 billion, in the case of their victory—that it was the Germans who began the war, and that the first irredentism was directed against Italy, on account of those minorities which had descended, without right, into Alto Adige.

German Austria, Macedonia, and Smyrna. The present Austrian Republic was the result of the Treaty of St. Germain. Can it continue to live, formed as it is at present? It is generally thought not. There remains the alternative of a Danube Confederation with its center at Vienna and Budapest, but the "Little Entente" sees to it that there shall be no return, under any form, of the old regime. We think that, by the force of events, an economic Danube Confederation will be formed sooner or later, in which case the conditions of Austria, and especially of Vienna, would improve until she had arrived at the point of lessening the pro-German annexationist movement. From the standpoint of justice, and whenever there was a clear manifestation of the will of the people, Austria would have the right of separating herself from Germany. This possible eventuality cannot leave us indifferent, because of the boundaries of the Brenner, which is a question of life or death for the Paduan valley. A hungry and pauper Austria cannot organize a dangerous irredentism against us; but as the result of union with Germany the question of Alto Adige would certainly become more acute.

As for Hungary, she can certainly expect a revision of the treaty that mutilates her on every side. It must be added, however, that the chapter of Fiume is definitely closed in Hungarian history.

Centers of infection for another war exist all over the Balkan world. Let us quote Montenegro and Albania, for example. We are in favor of the independence of both these states, provided that they show themselves capable of enjoying it. Bulgaria has a right to Macedonia,[37] and also to a port on the Aegean. And this is of capital importance for the economic expansion of Italy in Bulgaria. The Treaty of Sèvres crushed Turkey in order to exalt the Greece of Venizelos and Constantine, which gave the European war the sacrifice of 787 Evzones.[38] We consider, as far as the Eastern Mediterranean is concerned, that Italy, on the whole, should follow a pro-Turkish policy.

The Treaty of Rapallo. Immediately after the signing of the Treaty of Rapallo, the Central Committee of the Fascio passed its judgment upon it, finding it "acceptable for the Eastern boundaries, inacceptable and deficient as regards Fiume, and insufficient and to be rejected as regards Zara and Dalmatia." At three months' distance this judgment does not seem to be contradicted by successive events. The Treaty of Rapallo is an unhappy compromise, against which pages of

---

[37] Population: 1,181,000 Bulgarians, 499,000 Turks, and 228,000 Greeks.
[38] Elite light infantry and mountain units of the Greek Army.

criticism were printed in the *Popolo d'Italia*, which it is now useless to repeat.

It must be explained why victorious Italy ever arrived at the point of signing the Peace of Rapallo. And the explanations do not need much mental exertion. Rapallo was the logical consequence of the line of foreign policy followed by us or imposed upon us before, during, and after the war. It is explained by Wilson and his so-called experts and the absolute lack of Italian propaganda abroad and the dead-tiredness of the people. Rapallo is explained by the meeting of the oppressed nationalities held at Rome in April 1918, which meeting can be directly connected with the ill-fated story of Caporetto. Everything is paid for in this life. On November 12th, 1920, we paid at Rapallo for the breakdown of October 24th, 1917. Had there been no Caporetto, there would have been no Pact of Rome. In that congress the Yugoslavs threw dust in our eyes because in reality they did nothing toward breaking up the Dual Monarchy from within, of which they were the faithful slaves to the last, with traditional Croat loyalty. Not for nothing did the Hapsburg monarchy, upon its decease, try to present the Yugoslavs with its navy. But it was in the April of 1918 that the irreparable was committed, with the consent of all currents of Italian public opinion, including ours and the Nationalists—that is to say, our worst enemies were raised to the rank of effectual and powerful allies, and naturally, when the victory was obtained, there was no accepting of the role of vanquished, but they adopted that of cooperators with a relative share in the common booty. After the Pact of Rome it was no longer possible to place our knee on the chest of Yugoslavia—this is the truth. And so it happened that the Italian people—tired, impoverished, and unnerved by two long years of useless negotiations, demoralized by the policy of the Government and the tremendous wave of after-war sabotage (against which only the Fascists reacted powerfully)—accepted, or rather suffered, the Treaty of Rapallo, without manifestations of grief or joy. And, in order to finish it once and for all, many people would also have accepted the terrible line of Montemaggiore. All the parties of all the grades of Left and Right accepted the treaty as a lesser evil. We, too, submitted to it, considering it merely as a transitory and ephemeral act (has there ever been anything definite in the world, much less upon the moving sands of diplomacy?), and with the intention of gathering our forces to be ready for the revision which, sooner or later, would improve the treaty and not make it worse, would carry our boundaries to the Dinaric Alps, but never again allow the boundaries of Yugoslavia to reach the Isonzo.

The fate meted out to Dalmatia makes us very sad. But the fault does not lie wholly with the negotiators of the eleventh hour; the renunciation had already been made in Parliament, in the papers, and in the universities themselves, where a professor printed a book, which was naturally translated at Zagreb, in which he proved, in his own way, that Dalmatia is not Italian. The Dalmatian tragedy lies in this ignorance, bad faith, and want of understanding; faults which we hope to repair with our work by making Dalmatia known, loved, and defended.

The treaty, once signed, could be annulled in one of two ways: by outside war or internal revolution—both equally absurd. You do not make the people throng the squares in order to change a peace treaty after five years of bloodshed. Nobody is capable of working such prodigies. It was possible to cause a revolution in Italy in order to obtain intervention; but to cause a revolution in November 1920, in order to annul a peace treaty which, good or bad, had been accepted by 99 percent of the Italian people, could not be considered. I do not mind much about coherence, but there are stenographic records which bear witness to the fact that I steadily refused to go against the treaty either by promoting outside war or internal revolution. I considered that it was also dangerous to get mixed up in an armed resistance to the treaty.

The Tragedy of Fiume. Two months of polemics and daily articles during November and December bear witness to my support of the cause of Fiume, and my open and strong opposition to the Parliament.

It is a pity that oblivion falls so quickly on the words of a daily paper, and I have not the melancholy habit of unearthing what I publish. But the undeniable truth is this: that day after day I fought so that the Government at Rome should recognize the Government at Fiume; so that the representatives of the regency should be invited to Rapallo; and so that the Government at Rome should avoid any armed attack on Fiume. At the outset I called the attack of Christmas Eve an enormous crime, and I always upheld the spirit of justice, liberty, and free-will which were the inspiration of the legions of Ronchi.

The Audience in the Gallery. It sometimes happens in history as in the theatre, that there is an audience in the gallery, which, having paid for its tickets, demands that the performance shall run to a close at all costs. Thus in Italy today there are two types of individuals: those who blame d'Annunzio for having lived to see the end of the Fiume tragedy, and those who blame Mussolini for not having brought about that easy, pretty little thing which is called a revolution! I have always disdained the cowardly method by which, in Italy, impotence, anger, and misery are laid upon the heads of real or imaginary scapegoats. The Fasci had never promised to bring about revolution in the event of an attack on Fiume, nor have I ever written or made known to d'Annunzio that revolution depended upon my caprice. Revolution is not a Jack-in-the-box which can be worked at will. I do not carry it in my pocket, any more than those who fill their noisy mouths with its name and in practice do not get beyond disorders in the squares after unimportant demonstrations accompanied by a providential arrest to avoid any more serious complications. I know the breed. I have been in politics for twenty years. In the war between Caviglia and Fiume, either great things should have been accomplished, or else, for reasons of self-respect, excessive shouting and raising of smoke, which vanished at once without trace and without bloodshed, should have been avoided.

With Whom and Where? History learned from far-off events teaches men little, but that which we see written daily under our eyes ought to be more successful. Now these chronicles of every day tell us that revolution is made with an army and not against an army; with arms, not without arms; with movements of trained squadrons, not with the untrained masses called to meetings in the squares. They succeed when they are made in an atmosphere of sympathy on the part of the majority; if this is lacking they die down and fail. Now in Fiume the army and navy did not fail. A certain revolutionary spirit of the eleventh hour did not take definite shape; it was the work sometimes of anarchists and sometimes of Nationalists. According to some emissaries it was possible to put the devil and holy water together, the nation and that which was against the nation: Misiano and Del Croix. Now I reject all forms of Bolshevism, but if I were obliged to choose one, I should choose that of Moscow and Lenin, if for no other reason because at least it has gigantic, barbaric, and universal proportions. What revolution was it to be, then? National or Bolshevist?

A great uncertainty, complicated by a great many minor considerations, confused men's minds, while the nation, in a mood of revolt against that which had happened round Fiume, abandoned itself to an attitude of grief, in which the only bright spot was the hope that the episode would retain its local character and come quickly to a peaceful conclusion.

Hypotheses and Certainties. If there had been an insurrection on our part—and this was not possible owing to the armed forces the Government had at its disposal—there must have been one of two results: defeat or victory. In the first case, everything would have been irretrievably lost in the abyss of civil war. Let us, for the sake of argument, presuppose the second hypothesis: that of victory with the fall of the Government and of the regime. After the more or less easy period of demolition, what form would the revolution take? Social, as some Bolshevists wish—those with the motto "Always further Left," the equivalent of the grotesque "Go to the reddest"—or national, Dalmatian, and reactionary, as others desire?

There is no possibility of reconciliation between the two currents. In a revolution of the social order, what importance would the territorial questions, and more precisely that of Dalmatia, have had? In the other event of a national revolution against the Treaty of Rapallo, everything would have been limited to a formal annulment of the treaty and to a substitution of men; to be followed later by another treaty in another Rapallo, in order that one day or another the nation might have her peace. An episode of civil war was not remedied by letting loose a bigger war in times like these through which we are passing, and nobody is capable of prolonging and creating artificially historical situations which are over and done with. Only the man who knows how to lift himself above common passions, who knows how to draw conclusions from conflicting elements and how to distinguish the pure grain from the equivocal chaff, is able to understand that Fiume Christmas,[39] which can be called the tragic crossroads between the reasons of the State and of the ideal: the meeting-place of all our deficiencies and all our greatness.

Suspended Problems. The first is that of Fiume. We do not feel the

---

[39] Bloody Christmas, December 24th–29th, 1920, which led to the conclusion of the Fiume campaign carried out by Gabriele d'Annunzio.

necessity of reaffirming our sympathy for the sacrificed city. We have given the most tangible proofs, recently, of our solidarity with the Fascio of Fiume, in order to put it in a position to undertake the struggle against the Croats, who are now beginning to show signs of life. The action of the Fascists must tend, for the moment, toward economic annexation of Fiume to Italy, to arousing the interest of the Government and private individuals, and at the same time keeping alive, by every means, the torch of Italy, so that in due time economic will be followed by political annexation. We shall achieve this in spite of everything. All the Fascist force, national and parliamentary, must be concentrated on Zara, so that the little city shall be able to accomplish her important and delicate mission in history. There must be efficacious education for the Italians who have remained in the principal cities of Dalmatia, and no separate constituencies for the Slavs in Istria and the Germans in Alto Adige. It is not possible to establish such a precedent, as it would carry us far. The French of the Val d'Aosta, who are in reality excellent Italians, have no special constituencies and privileges of that sort. These duplicate constituencies would be a grave mistake. It is up to the Fascists of Trento and Trieste to prevent this happening at any cost.

Old and New Directions. The lines of the program laid down at the meeting at Milan in May last year have not become out of date or in need of revision. Fascism has the name of being "imperialist." This accusation goes together with that of being reactionary. Fascism is against renunciations when they mean humiliation and diminution.

Given these general premises—*first*, that Fascism does not believe in the principles of the so-called League of Nations nor in its vitality; *secondly*, that Fascism does not believe in the Red Internationals, which die, reproduce themselves, multiply, and die again: for they are small, artificial organizations, small minorities compared to the masses of the population, which, living, dying, progressing, or retrogressing, finishes by deciding those changes of interests before which the international organizations of the first, second, and third order crumble to pieces; *thirdly*, that Fascism does not believe in the immediate possibility of general disarmament; and *fourthly*, considers that Italy, in the present historical period, should follow a policy of European equilibrium and conciliation—it follows that the Italian Fascio of Fighters demands:

1. That the treaties of peace shall be revised and modified in those parts which have proved inapplicable, or which might prove in application the cause of formidable hatred and new wars.

2. The economic annexation of Fiume to Italy, or the care of the Italians resident in Dalmatia.

3. The gradual economic emancipation of Italy from abroad by the development of her productive forces.

4. The renewal of relations with the enemy countries—Austria, Germany, Bulgaria, Turkey, and Hungary—but with dignity and holding fast to the supreme necessity of maintaining our northern and eastern boundaries.

5. The creation and intensification of friendly relations with the peoples of the East, not excluding those governed by the Soviets and Southeastern Europe.

6. The vindication of the rights and interests of the nation as regards the colonies.

7. The abandonment of the old systems and the replacement of all our diplomatic representatives with others from the special university faculties.

8. The furtherance of the Italian colonies in the Mediterranean and beyond the Atlantic by economic and educational means and by rapid communications.

Toward a New Italy. I have enormous faith in the future greatness of the Italian people. Ours is the most numerous and homogeneous of the peoples of Europe.

The war has enormously increased the prestige of Italy. "Long live Italy!" is now cried in far-off Latvia and still more distant Georgia.

Italy is the tricolor wing of Ferrarin, the magnetic wave of Marconi, the baton of Toscanini, the revival of Dante, in the sixth centenary of his departure. Let us prepare ourselves by energetic everyday work for the Italy of tomorrow of which we dream, an Italy free and rich, resounding with song, with her skies and seas populated with her fleets, and her earth fruitful beneath her ploughs. And may the coming citizens be able to say what Virgil said of ancient Rome: "Imperium oceano, famam terminavit astris" (The Empire was bound by the ocean, but her fame reached the stars.)

How Fascism Was Created: Its Evolution and Essence

April 3rd, 1921, Teatro Comunale, Bologna

Bologna, the capital of the so-called Red region of Emilia, a region thought to be lost to the Italian State as far as laws and authority were concerned, from April 2nd to the 4th passed through truly memorable days.

The learned and noble city, with its fine patriotic traditions, whose very walls recall the popular and patrician insurrection against the Austrians, welcomed Benito Mussolini with manifestations of solidarity and veneration such as were accorded to Giuseppe Garibaldi. For if the latter was a liberator from foreign tyranny, the former had been no less a liberator from an equal tyranny, arising from similar causes, although materialized through different means and by different agents living in our midst.

All who witnessed those enthusiastic manifestations instantly perceived that the problem of Italian internal politics was now solved by the definite defeat of that parasitic, anti-National Socialism, the enemy of liberty, which had chosen the Po Valley as the most suitable experimental field for the fecundation of the microbes of Collectivist Utopia, and incidentally for the exploitation of the masses of the proletariat.

◆ ◆ ◆

Fascists of Emilia and Romagna—Citizens of Bologna! I feel that I might be carried out of that sphere of eloquence that is mine by all the circumstances of this meeting, beginning with the welcomes of yesterday evening and the songs of last night, and ending with this magnificent sea of heads and the greeting I received with the greatest veneration from the widow of our unforgettable Giulio Giordani, and the presence of two heroic women, the widows of the two heroes,

Battisti and Venezian. (Applause.) But as I hope, and am almost certain, that you do not expect eloquence from me, but a short abrupt speech as is my habit, I will proceed to speak clearly in the Fascist manner. **How Fascism Was Born.** I thank my friend Grandi for having presented me to you and with such flattering words. I do not think, however, that I am guilty of the sin of pride if I accept them. I think I may say, in accordance with Socrates, that I know myself. (Applause.)

How then was this Fascism born; amid what conflicting passions, sympathy, hatred, and lack of comprehension? It was not only born in my mind and heart, in that meeting held in March 1919 in the little hall at Milan, it was born of the profound and perennial need of this our Mediterranean and Aryan race, which felt the essential foundations of its existence threatened by a tragic folly, which will crumble to pieces, today, upon the ground on which it was raised.

We felt then—we, who were not penitent Magdalens; we, who had always had the courage to uphold intervention and reason in those days of 1915; we, who were not ashamed of having barred the way to Austria on the Piave and having crushed her at Vittorio Veneto; we, who wished for a victorious peace, felt at once, almost before the exultation of victory had passed, that our task was not ended, and I, myself, felt that my work was not done. As a matter of fact, at every turn of events it was said that my task and the task of the forces I lead was accomplished. In May 1915, when the Fasci d'Azione Rivoluzionaria had swept away all neutralists from the streets and squares of Italy, even in the smallest villages, it was said: "Mussolini has no more to say to the nation." But when the tragic days of Caporetto came and Milan was gray and ghastly for those who felt that if the Austrians passed and came to the city of the Cinque Giornate it would be the end of Italy, then we felt that we still had a word to say. And again, after victory, when there arose the more or less democratic school of renunciation that was intent upon mutilating the victory, we Fascists had the supreme and unprejudiced courage to proclaim ourselves imperialists and against all renunciation.

That was the first battle, fought in the theatre of La Scala in January 1919. But how did it happen? We had won, we had sacrificed the flower of our youth, and they came to us with bills of usury and extortion! They disputed with us the sacred boundaries of the country, and there were Democrats in Italy, whose democracy consisted in imperialism for others and no imperialism for us, who threw this ridiculous accusation at us, because we intended that Italy should be bounded on the north by the Brenner, as she shall be while there is Italian blood in Italy! We intended that the eastern boundaries should be at the Nevoso, because that is the just and natural confine of our country; and they accused us because we did not turn deaf ears to the appeal of Fiume, because we feel in our hearts the sufferings of our brothers in Dalmatia, because, in fact, we feel those bonds of race to be alive and vital which bind us, not only to the Italians of Zara, Ragusa, and Cattaro, but also to those of the Canton Ticino and Corsica, to those beyond the oceans, to all that great family of 50 million men whom we wish to unite in the same pride of race. (Applause.)

Already we have noticed the first signs of the Socialist offensive. On February 16th, Milan was the witness—to the fear and terror of the trembling middle classes—of a procession of twenty thousand Bolshevists, who, after having hymned Lenin from the top of the castle towers, proclaimed that the Bolshevist revolution was imminent.

The Pride of Victory. The following day, I issued an article, which made an impression also among some friends, and which was entitled, "The Return of the Triumphant Beast."[40] In it was said: "We are ready to dig trenches in the squares of Italy and set up barbed wire, in order to win and fight to the last against the enemy." And the sabotage, begun with that parade, lasted all the summer.

Also, in those days, we Fascists had the courage to defend certain actions which, measured by the standard of current morals, perhaps were indefensible. But, gentlemen, war is like revolution: it must be taken as a whole; detail cannot and must not be gone into. But, meanwhile, the campaign had its results upon the elections. One million eight hundred and fifty thousand electors registered their vote with the symbol of the sickle and the hammer. One hundred and fifty-six deputies were returned to the Chamber. The catastrophe seemed imminent. Then I was fished out, a suicide of the waters—not by any means too limpid—of the old Naviglio!

But one thing had been forgotten—our tenacious spirit and sometimes indomitable will. I, proud of my four thousand votes—and those

---

[40] In *Popolo d'Italia*, February 17th, 1919.

who saw me in those days know how immovably I accepted that electoral response—said, "The battle goes on!" Because I firmly believed that the day would come in which the Italians would be ashamed of the elections of November 16th, that the day would come in which the Italians would no longer elect in two cities that ignoble deserter whom I do not wish to name. And it has proved true, because this man today, not being able to maintain his part in the drama, has descended from the stage and, having despised the Guardie Regie, now asks them for protection.

But has the growth of this movement of Fascism, this young ardent and heroic movement, finished yet? I, who vindicate the paternity of this, my creature so overflowing with life, feel sometimes that it has already overstepped the modest boundaries I laid down for it. Now we Fascists have a clear program; we must move on led by a pillar of fire, because we are slandered and not understood. And, however much violence may be deplored, it is evident that we, in order to make our ideas understood, must beat refractory skulls with resounding blows.

Necessary Violence. But we do not make a school, a system or, worse still, an aesthetic of violence. We are violent when it is necessary to be so. But I tell you at once that this necessary violence on the part of the Fascists must have a character and style of its own, definitely aristocratic, or, if you prefer, surgical.

Our punitive expeditions, all those acts of violence which figure in the papers, must always have the character of a just retort and legitimate reprisal, because we are the first to recognize that it is sad, after having fought the external enemy, to have to fight the enemy within, who, whether they like it or not, are Italians. But it is necessary, and as long as it is necessary, we shall continue to carry out this hard and thankless task.

Now the Democrats, the Republicans, and the Socialists accuse us of various things. The Socialists, hitherto, have said that we were sold to the profiteers and the agrarians. Now there are not enough profiteers in the whole of Italy to support a movement like ours, and in any case I must say that they would be rather stupid profiteers, because from March 1919 we, in our Fascist programs, have laid down fiscal provisions that are pretty heavy and in any case anti-profiteer. The accusations of the Democrats are equally ridiculous, and also those of the Republicans. I cannot explain to myself why the Republicans are against a movement that has republican tendencies like ours. I could understand them being against us if we were in favor of the monarchy. They say to us, "You have no preconceptions." We have not, and we are proud of it. But you must explain the phenomenon of the anger and the incomprehension of the Socialists. The Socialists had formed a State within a State. If this new State had been more liberal, more modern, nearer the old type, there would have been nothing against it. But this State, and you know it by direct experience, is more tyrannical, illiberal, and overbearing than the old one; and for this reason that which we are causing today is a revolution to break up the Bolshevist State, while waiting to settle our accounts with the Liberal State that remains. (Applause.)

The Socialist Crisis and the Fascist Attitude toward the Elections. There are those who think that the Socialist crisis is only a crisis limited to a few men, but it goes deeper, my dear friends, and it represents a general upheaval.

Among other absurd things, there has been that of baptizing Socialism as scientific. Now there is nothing scientific in the world. Science explains the "how" of things, but does not explain the "why." If, then, there is nothing scientific in what are called the exact sciences, what is more absurd than to try and pass off as scientific a vast, uncertain, underground, and dark movement such as Socialism has been, even though it may have had a useful function at first, when it directed the oppressed peoples toward new ways of life, because you will agree with me that there is no turning back? Foolish reactionary and Conservative contraband practices must not be carried on under the Fascist flag. To wrench from the masses the conquests they have obtained through sacrifice would be impossible. We are the first to recognize that a state law should grant the eight-hour work day, and that there should be a social legislation corresponding to the exigencies of the new times. And this is not because we recognize the importance of the proletariat. We look at the question from another point of view. We realize that there cannot be a great nation, capable of doing great things, if the working masses are constrained to live under brutalizing conditions. It is necessary, then, that by preaching and practicing the reconciliation of right and duty, which I call Mazzinian, this enormous mass of tens of millions of people who work shall be raised to an ever-higher level of life.

Brothers, not Enemies! It is absurd to depict us as the enemies of the working classes. We feel ourselves to be brothers in spirit of all those who work, but we do not make distinctions, we do not put work-worn hands into the first rank. We do not place the new divinity, manual labor, upon the altar. For us, all work: the astronomer who in his observatory consults the trajectory of the stars; the lawyer; the archaeologist; the student of religion; and the artist, if they are increasing by their work the sum total of spiritual wealth at the disposal of mankind. We wish to see the realization of a communion between spirit and matter, between the arm and the brain, the realization of the solidarity of the race.

Fascism is then the blast of heresy which beats at the doors of all the churches and says to the old and more or less tearful priest, "Get out of the way of these temples which threaten ruin to you, for our triumphant heresy is destined to bring light to all brains and all souls!" And we say to all men, great and small, upon the national political scene, "Make way for the youth of Italy which wishes to affirm its faith and passion. And if you do not make way spontaneously, you will be overwhelmed in our universal punitive expedition, which is to collect all the free spirits of Italy and bind them together in a Fascio." (Applause.)

We are now face to face with a fact, which is that of the elections. The Chamber being old, and more than old, worn out, the protagonists of this semi-tragedy being tired and misled, it is time to make that new appeal to the electors which is imperative. Do you not feel that, if the elections of 1919 had the character of sabotage, the elections of 1921 will be definitely Fascist? Do you not feel that the helm of State will never return to the old men of the old Italy?

I received a message today on the strength of which I feel I can state that the difference, more or less artificially created, which existed between the defenders of Fiume—to whom we pay the homage of our gratitude—and us, her defenders at home, has no more *raison d'être*. And this difference, which, rather than by the legionaries, was created by certain politicians who were not even at Fiume when it was attacked seriously, will be put an end to by Gabriele d'Annunzio.

The Day Consecrated to Fascism. Another characteristic of Fascism is pride of nationality. And, in connection with this, I am pleased to tell you that we have already decided the Fascist day. If the Socialists have May Day, if the Popular Party have May 15th, and other parties other days, we Fascists will have one, too, and it shall be the day of the birth of Rome, April 21st. Upon that day, in token of the eternity of Rome, in memory of that city which gave two civilizations to the world and will give a third, we Fascists will gather together, and the regional legions will file past in the Fascist order, which is neither military nor German, but simply Roman. We have abolished the procession and substituted this ancient form of manifestation, which imposes individual control on each participator and order and discipline upon all. For we wish to introduce strict national discipline, without which Italy cannot become the Mediterranean and world nation of which we dream. And those who blame us for marching like the Germans must remember that it is not we who imitate the Germans, but they who imitate the Romans, for which reason it is we who go back to the original, who return to the Roman style, the Latin and Mediterranean style.

We have no prejudices, because we are not a church, we are a movement. We are not a party; we are a band of free men. If anyone is tired of being Fascist, there are twenty shops, twenty churches at whose doors to knock and ask for hospitality. We have not institutions either; we consider them superfluous. Ours is an army characterized by enthusiasm and voluntary discipline, and known, above all, not in the light of guardian of some party or faction, but as guardian of the nation. We are known for the love we bear to Italy, to her history and her civilization, as well as to her inhabitants and geographical constitution.

Yesterday, while the train carried me to Bologna, I felt myself in harmony with all things and all men. I felt bound to this earth; I felt myself an infinitesimal part of that great river which flows from the Alps to the Adriatic; I recognized my brothers in the peasants, those peasants with the grave attitudes of those who work the soil; I saw myself in the blue sky, which awakened my inextinguishable passion for flight; I recognized myself in all the aspects of nature and man. And a profound prayer arose in my heart. It is the prayer that every Italian should make, when the sunrise illumines the sky and the twilight descends over the earth. "We, Italians of the twentieth century, who have witnessed the great tragedy which has brought about the fulfilment of our nationality; we, who carry in the depths of our souls the memory of the dead, who are our religion; we, citizens of Italy, shall make one oath, one single resolution: that we only shall be the modest but persevering builders of her present and future fortunes." (Applause.)

The Italy We Want Within, and Her Foreign Relations

September 20th, 1922, Udine

The four following speeches are undoubtedly the most important of this collection, because they depict Mussolini as the polemic, the agitator, the warrior, the leader, traveling to his political maturity. In reading them one recognizes the *condottiero* who is quite sure of himself, who is near the end of his march, and is certain of reaching his final goal.

Except for a gradually accelerated rhythm, proportionate to the precipitation of events, the tone of the four speeches is almost the same. There is no pause, no perplexity, nothing which might induce the reader to think of a change of direction, of a truce, of the relinquishing of the struggle. But rather one notices the close march of a compact and well-equipped army, determined to struggle on and to win at whatever cost.

At Udine, that strong old town, the sentinel of the country, dear to the heart of all Italian soldiers, the leader of Fascism initiates the spiritual and physical mobilization of the Blackshirts, while he hurls the first challenge at the old political caste and lays down the fundamental points of the imminent national revolution.

◆　◆　◆

The speech I intend to make today is going to be an exception to the rule which I have imposed upon myself of limiting my speeches, as far as I can. Oh! if it were only possible to do as the poets advise and strangle the verbose, inconclusive oratory which has side-tracked us for so long! I am certain, or at any rate I hope, that you do not expect anything from me in a speech which is not eminently Fascist, that is to say straightforward, hard, bare facts.

The Unity of the Country. Do not expect a commemoration of

September 20th. Certainly the subject would be tempting and there would be ample material for reflection in reexamining by what prodigies of immeasurable force, and through how many and how great sacrifices, Italy has been able to achieve her not yet complete unity. I say not yet complete, because perfect unity cannot be spoken of until Fiume and Dalmatia and the other territories have come back to us, thus fulfilling the proud dream we carry in our hearts. Instead, I ask you to consider that throughout the Risorgimento—which began with the first attempt at rebellion on the part of a small section of a cavalry regiment at Nola, and ended with the breach of Porta Pia in '70—two forces were brought into play: one, the traditional and conservative force, of necessity rather stationary and sluggish, the force of the Savoy and Piedmont tradition; the other, the rebellious and revolutionary force, which sprang from the best elements among the bourgeoisie especially. And it was only as the result of the reconciliation and balancing of these two forces that we were able to realize the unity of the country. Perhaps something of the sort can be found today, and of this I shall go on to speak later.

Rome! Have you ever asked yourselves why the unity of the country is summed up in the symbol and the name of Rome? We Fascists must forget the more or less ungrateful welcome we received at Rome in the October of last year, otherwise we should show ourselves to be mean-spirited, and we must have the courage to own that part of the responsibility for what happened belongs to us, on account of some elements among us which were not on the high level the situation required.

And Rome must not be confused with the Romans, with those hundreds of so-called "fugitives of Fascism" who are to be found at Rome, Milan, and other centers in Italy, who effectively arouse harmful anti-Fascist feeling in the country. But if Mazzini and Garibaldi tried three times to arrive at Rome, and if Garibaldi gave his "red shirts" the tragic and inexorable alternative of "Rome or death," this means that, to the best men of the Risorgimento, Rome already had an essential function of the first importance to perform in the new history of the Italian nation.

Let us then, with minds pure and free from animosity, lift up our thoughts toward Rome, which is one of the few spiritual cities that exists in the world, because at Rome, among those seven hills so pregnant with history, occurred one of the greatest spiritual miracles which have ever taken place—that is, the transformation of an Eastern religion, not understood by us, into a universal one, and which has succeeded, under another form, to the Empire that the Roman legions had carried to the extreme ends of the earth. And we want to make Rome the city of our ideals, a city cleaned and purified of all those elements that corrupt and defile her; we wish to make Rome the throbbing heart, the living spirit of the Italy of which we dream.

Somebody might object, saying, "Are you worthy of Rome? Are you capable of inheriting and transmitting the ideals and glories of an empire?" And then surly critics busy themselves with trying to find signs of uncertainty in our young, exuberant organization!

Fascist Discipline. People speak to us of Fascist *autonomy*. I tell the Fascists and citizens that this autonomy has no importance whatsoever. It is not an autonomy of ideas and prejudice. Fascism has no prejudices; they are the sad privilege of the old parties, associations scattered over all countries, whose members, having nothing better to do or to say, end by imitating those sordid priests of the East who discussed all the questions of the world while the Byzantine Empire perished. The few and sporadic attempts on the part of Fascists to establish autonomy are either frustrated or nearly so, because they represent only revenge of a personal nature.

We come to another question: *discipline*. I am in favor of the most rigid discipline. We must first sternly discipline ourselves, otherwise we shall not have the right to discipline the nation. And it is only by the discipline of the nation that Italy can make herself heard in the councils of the other countries. Discipline must be accepted. If it is not, it must be imposed. We put aside the democratic dogma that one must forever proceed by sermonizing and lecturing in a more or less liberal manner. At a given moment discipline must show itself under the form of a command or of an act of force.

I exact discipline, and I do not speak to the men of the Friulian district, who are—let me say—perfect as regards sobriety and correctness, austerity, and quiet living, but I speak to the Fascists of all Italy, who, if they must have a dogma, must have one which bears the clear name of discipline. Only by obedience, by the humble and sacred pride in obedience, can the right to command be conquered. And only when it is conquered can it be imposed upon others; otherwise, no!

The Fascists of Italy must take note of this. They must not interpret discipline as a call to order of the administrative kind or as the fear of shepherds who foresee the scattering of their flock. This cannot be, because we are not shepherds and our forces cannot be called, by any means, a flock. We are an army, and it is just because we have this special organization that we must make discipline the supreme pivot of our life and action.

Violence! I come now to the question of violence. Violence is not immoral. On the contrary it is sometimes moral. We dispute the right of our enemies to bewail our violence, because, compared with that which was committed in the unlucky years of '19 and '20 and with that of the Bolshevists in Russia—where 2 million people have been executed and another 2 million still pine in prison—our violence is child's play. On the other hand violence is decisive, because at the end of July and August, after having made use of it systematically for forty-eight hours, we got results which we should not have obtained in forty-eight years of sermons and propaganda. When, therefore, violence removes a gangrene of this sort, it is morally sacred and necessary.

But, my Fascist friends, and I speak to the Fascists of all Italy, our violence must have certain Fascist characteristics. The violence of ten to one is to be disowned and condemned. There is a violence that frees and a violence that binds; there is moral violence and stupid, immoral violence. Violence must be proportionate to the necessities of the moment, and not made a school, a doctrine, or a sport. The Fascists must be careful not to spoil with sporadic, individual, and unjustifiable acts of violence, the brilliant and splendid victories of August.

This is what our enemies are waiting for. As the result of certain episodes—let us frankly admit disagreeable episodes—such as that at Taranto, they have been led to believe and to hope that violence has become a sort of second habit, and that when we no longer have a target upon which to practice, we shall turn against ourselves and against each other, or the Nationalists. Now the Nationalists differ from us on certain questions, but the truth is this, that in all the battles we have fought we have had them by our side. It may well be that among them there are leaders who do not see Fascism as we see it, but it must be recognized and proclaimed that the "blue shirts" (Nationalists) at Genoa, Bologna, and Milan, and in another hundred centers, were with the Blackshirts. In consequence the occurrence at Taranto was most displeasing, and I hope that the leaders of Fascism will act in such a way that it remains an isolated incident to be forgotten in a local reconciliation and in a national manifestation of sympathy and solidarity.

Our Syndicalism. Another argument which raises the hopes of our enemies is the existence of the masses. You know that I do not worship the new divinity, the masses. It is a creation of democracy and Socialism. Just because they are numerous, they must be right. Not a bit of it, the opposite has often proved to be true that the masses are against the right. In any case history proves that it has always been the minorities, a handful from the first, that have produced profound changes in human society. We do not adore the masses, even if they have got work-worn hands and brains. We shall bring, instead, into our examination of social life, ideas and elements new at any rate in Italian circles. We could not turn away the masses; they came to us. Ought we to have received them with kicks on the shins? Are they sincere? Do they come to us as the result of conviction or fear, or because they hope to get from us what they failed to obtain from the Socialists? These questions are really superfluous, as no one yet has found the way to penetrate into their inmost minds.

We have, therefore, had to adopt syndicalism, and we are doing so. They say, "Your syndicalism will end by being in every way exactly like that of the Socialists, and you will have, of necessity, to promote class war." The democracy, or a section of them, that section which does not seem to have any better object than stirring up the mud, continues from Rome (where they print too many papers, many of which do not represent anybody or anything) to work in this direction. But our syndicalism differs from that of the others, because we do not allow strikes in public services under any pretext, and we are in favor of cooperation among the classes, especially in a period like the present one of acute economic crisis. We try to make this conception penetrate the brains of our syndicates. But it must be made equally clear that the industrial workers and their employers must not blackmail us, because there is a limit which must not be passed; and these workers and their masters—the bourgeoisie in a word—must take into account that the nation also consists of the people, a mass which labors, and one cannot think of the greatness of the nation if this portion is restless and idle. The task of Fascism is to make the people organically one with the nation, so that they may be ready to-morrow when the nation has need of them, as the artist takes his raw material in order to create his masterpiece. Only with the masses forming an intimate part of the life and history of the nation can we have a foreign policy.

Foreign Policy. And now I come to the subject which, at the present moment, is of the greatest positive importance. It is evident that at the end of the war it was not understood how to make peace. There were two alternatives: the peace of the sword, and the peace of approximate justice. But, under the influence of a pernicious democratic mentality, the peace of the sword was not made by occupying Berlin, Vienna, and Budapest, and neither has the approximate peace of justice been accomplished.

Men, many of whom were ignorant of history and geography (and it seems that these famous experts who thus disarrange and rearrange the map of Europe at their will really know as little about it as their masters), have said, "The moment the Turks give trouble to the English, we will suppress Turkey; but the moment that Italy, in order to become a Mediterranean power, ought to have the Adriatic as her inland gulf, we deny Italy her Adriatic rights." What is the result? The result is that this kind of treaty naturally falls to pieces before the others. But, since everything depends upon the making up of these treaties, since they are all connected with each other, so the failure of the Treaty of Sèvres may possibly involve the failure of all the others. Moreover, if the position becomes more involved, you will see the indestructible Russian Cossack, who changes his name but not his nature, coming forward again. Who armed the Turkey of Kemal Pasha? France and Russia. Who may possibly arm Germany tomorrow? Russia. Considering what we aim at in our foreign policy, it is very fortunate that besides our national army, of glorious tradition, there is the Fascist army.

Our ministers for foreign affairs ought to know how to play this card too, with the warning, "Be careful; Italy no longer follows a policy of renunciation and cowardice, cost what it may!" So it has come about that while in other countries men are beginning to realize the force represented by Italian Fascism, in the field of foreign policy our ministers still remain in a yielding attitude. We are asked what is our program. I have already answered this question, which was meant to be insidious, at a little meeting held at Levanto in the presence of thirty or forty Fascists, and I did not think that a little homely speech would have such a vast echo.

Our Program: The Crisis of the Liberal State. Our program is simple: we wish to govern Italy. They ask us for programs, but there are already too many. It is not programs that are wanting for the salvation of Italy, but men and willpower.

There is not an Italian who does not think that he possesses the one sure method by which the most acute problems of our national life may be solved. But I think you are all convinced that our political class is deficient. The crisis of the Liberal State has proved it. We have made a splendid war from the point of view of collective and individual acts of heroism. From having been soldiers, the Italians, in 1918, became warriors. I beg you to note the essential difference. But our political class carried on the war as if it had been work of ordinary administration. These men whom we all know, and whose very features are familiar to every one of us, now appear men of the past, ruined, tired, and beaten.

I do not deny, in my absolute objectivity, that this middle class, which might, with a worldwide title, be called Giolittian, has its merits. It certainly has. But today, when Italy is still under the influence of Vittorio Veneto—today, when Italy is bursting with life, vigor, and passion, these men, who are above all accustomed to Parliamentary mystification, do not appear to us to be big enough for the situation. It is necessary, therefore, to consider how to replace this political class, which has of late consistently surrendered to that swollen-headed puppet, Italian Socialism.

I think that this replacement has become necessary, and that the more complete it is the better. Certainly Fascism, in taking the entire 47 million Italians under its care, will assume a great responsibility. It is to be foreseen that many will be disappointed, because, in any case, there is always disappointment sooner or later, whether things are accomplished or not.

Friends! Like the life of the individual, the life of the nation brings with it a certain amount of risk. One cannot hope to run forever on the Decauville track of daily regularity. At a given moment both men and parties must have the courage to shoulder heavy responsibility and to adopt a daring policy. They may succeed; they may fail. But there are also unsuccessful attempts that suffice to ennoble and uplift for all time the soul of a movement such as Italian Fascism.

The Question of Regime: The Monarchy and Fascism. I had intended to repeat this speech at Naples, but I think that I shall have other things to deal with there. Do not let us delay, therefore, about entering on the delicate subject of regime.

Many of the controversies raised by the question of the nature of my tendencies are forgotten, and everybody is convinced that they were not formed suddenly, but represented a settled idea. It is always like that. Certain attitudes appear improvised to the general public, which is neither fitted nor obliged to follow the slow changes that take place in a restless spirit desirous of making a profound examination of certain problems. But there is inward pain and toil, which is sometimes tragic. You must not think that the heads of Fascism do not know what this individual, and above all national, travail is.

The much-talked-of republican tendency had to be a kind of attempt at separation from the many elements that had come to us simply because we had won. These elements do not please us. These people who always side with the victor, and who are ready to change their flag with a change of fortune, must be looked upon with suspicion and carefully watched by the Fascists. Is it possible—here is the question—to bring about a profound transformation in our political regime and to create a new Italy without touching the monarchic system? What is the general attitude of the Fascists as regards political institutions? Our attitude does not commit us in any sense. In truth, perfect regimes are only to be found in books of philosophy. I think that it would have been disastrous for the Greek city if the theories of Plato had been literally applied. A people content under a republic never dreams of having a king. A people not accustomed to a republic longs to return to a monarchy.

It was in vain that the Germans tried to make the Phrygian cap fit their square heads. The Germans hate a republic, and the fact that it was imposed by the Entente, and that it has been a kind of *ersatz*, is another reason for their hating it. So that, generally speaking, political forms cannot be approved of or condemned forever, but must be examined from the point of view of their direct relation with the mentality, the economic condition, and the spiritual force of any particular people. (A voice cries, "Long live Mazzini!")

Now, I think that the regime can be largely modified without interfering with the monarchy. In reality—and I refer to the cry of my friend—the same Mazzini, republican and advocate of republicanism, did not consider his doctrines incompatible with the monarchic aspect of Italian unity. He resigned himself to it and accepted it. It was not his ideal, but the ideal cannot always be realized.

We shall, then, leave the monarchic institution outside our field of action, which will have other great objects, because we think that a great part of Italy would regard with suspicion a change in the regime which was carried thus far. We should have regional separatism, perhaps, because it is always so. Today there are many indifferent to the monarchy who tomorrow would be its supporters, and who would find highly respectable and sentimental reasons for attacking Fascism, if it had dared to aim at this target.

I do not think that the monarchy has really any object in opposing what must now be called the Fascist revolution. It is not in its interests, because by doing so it would immediately make itself an object of attack, in which case we could not spare it, because it would be a question of life or death for us.

Those who sympathize with us must not withdraw into the shade; they must stay in the light. They must have the courage to remain monarchists. The monarchy would represent the historical continuity of the nation, a splendid task and one of incalculable importance.

On the other hand, the Fascist revolution must also avoid risking everything. Some firm ground must be left, so that the people shall not feel that everything is falling to pieces, that everything must be begun again, because in that case the first wave of enthusiasm would be followed by a wave of panic. Now everything is very plain. The social-democratic superstructure must be destroyed.

The State We Want. We must have a State which will simply say, "The State does not represent a party, it represents the nation as a whole, it includes all, is over all, protects all, and fights any attempt made against her inviolable sovereignty."

This is the State which must arise from the Italy of Vittorio Veneto: a State which does not acknowledge that the strongest power is right; which is not like the Liberal State, which, after fifty years of life, was unable to install a temporary printing press so as to issue its paper when there was a general strike of printers; a State which does not fall under the power of the Socialists; which does not think that problems can be settled only from the political point of view, as machine-guns do not suffice if there is not the spirit behind to keep them going. The whole armory of the State falls to pieces like the old scenery in an operatic theatre when it is not inspired by the most deep-rooted sense of the necessity of the fulfilment of duty—nay, of a mission.

That is why we want to remove from the State all its economic attributes. We have had enough of the State railwayman, the State postman, and the State insurance official. We have had enough of the State administration at the expense of Italian taxpayers, which has done nothing but aggravate the exhausted financial condition of the country. It still controls the police, who protect honest men from the attacks of thieves, the masters responsible for the education of the rising generations, the army which must guarantee the inviolability of the country and our foreign policy.

It must not be said that the State thus shorn will remain very small. No! It will remain very great, because it will still have all the spiritual dominion, having given up only material power.

Citizens, I have placed my ideas before you as a whole; it is enough, to my mind, for you to individualize them.

To Friends and Enemies. If this mentality of ours was not sufficient, there are our methods, there is our daily activity, which we do not mean to give up, though watching at the same time that it is not carried to extremes, that it does not overreach itself and so harm Fascism. But when I say these words, I say them with intention, because if Fascism was a movement like all the rest, the attitude of the individual or of the group would have a relative importance. But blood has been shed for our movement, and this must be remembered when there are attempts at autonomy and lack of discipline. The recent dead must be thought of before all things. It must be remembered that such autonomy and lack of discipline serve to arouse the miserable instincts of the Socialists, who, though subdued, still secretly hatch plots for revenge, a revenge which we shall prevent by collective action and the avoidance of bloodshed.

After all, the Romans were really right: if you want peace you must show yourself prepared for war. Those who are not prepared for war do not have peace, and are defeated into the bargain. So we say to all our enemies: "It is not enough for you to go planting the tricolor all over the place. We wish to see you put to the proof. You will have for a little while to undergo a sort of spiritual and political quarantine. Your leaders, who might again infect us, must be sent where they can do no harm." Only by thus avoiding the lure of the mistaken idea of quantity shall we succeed in saving the quality and the spirit of our movement, which is no ephemeral one, since it has already lasted four years, equal in this tempestuous century to forty. Our movement is still in its prehistoric period and process of formation; its real history begins tomorrow. All that Fascism has accomplished thus far has been negative. Now it must begin to reconstruct. In this way its force, its spirit, and its nobility will appear.

Friends, I am sure that the Fascist officers will do their duty. I am sure, too, that the men will do theirs. Before proceeding to the great task we must make an inexorable selection from the rank and file. We cannot carry useless impedimenta; we are an army of *velites*, with a rearguard of solid territorials. We do not wish to have untrustworthy elements among us.

I salute Udine, this dear old Udine to which I am bound by so many memories. Many generations of Italians who were the flower of our race have passed by its broad ways. Many of its young men now sleep their last sleep in the little isolated cemeteries of the Alps or beside the Isonzo, now once again the sacred river of Italy.

Men of Udine! Fascists! Italians! Take upon yourselves the spirit of these our unforgettable dead and make of it the burning emblem of our immortal country! (Loud applause.)

The Piave and Vittorio Veneto Mark
the Beginning of New Italy

September 25th, 1922, Cremona

Before forty thousand *contadini* set free from the Social-Clerical yoke, who march past in military order in closely-following battalions, the leader's eloquence is roused and elated, so that one seems to hear the very sound of joy bells ringing in his speech.

❖　◆　❖

Fascists and working men of Cremona and the provinces! As so often happens, reality has surpassed the most brilliant expectations. Your meeting, Fascists of Cremona, is the most impressive that I have yet attended. I have come among you to tell you how completely I am with you, from your fine leader Roberto Farinacci to the last man in your ranks. (Prolonged applause.)

Here in times long past great ideas were conceived. This was the birthplace of democracy, which had a period of glory before it became crippled and enfeebled by the influence of socialism. And in spite of the profound differences of opinion that divided us after the war, I must call to remembrance another noble figure of your fruitful land— I speak of Leonida Bissolati. (Frantic applause.)

Those who, as the result of being led into false ideas by incorrect information, talk about agrarian slavery, ought to come here and see with their own eyes this crowd of genuine workers, people with shoulders broad enough and arms strong enough to bear the weight of the increasing fortunes of the nation. (Applause.)

Only the rabble could accuse us of being the enemies of the

people, for we are the sons of the people; we have known what manual labor is; we have always lived among the working classes, who are infinitely superior to the false prophets who pretend to represent them. (Unanimous and prolonged applause.) But just because we are the sons of the people, we do not wish to deceive them, we do not wish to mystify them or promise them the unattainable, although we solemnly and formally pledge ourselves to protect them and to vindicate their just rights and their legitimate interests.

As I watched your procession passing—disciplined, ardent, and exulting—as I watched the little Balillas,[41] who represent the still immature spring of life, followed by the squadrons in the full flush of youth, and finally the men in the vigor of manhood and even old men, I said to myself that the series was complete since all phases of life, from the first to the last, were represented.

Fascists! Great tasks await us. That which we have accomplished is nothing compared to that which awaits us. There is already a strong and manifest contrast between the Italy of the cowardly politicians and the vigorous healthy Italy who is preparing to give the deathblow to all inefficiency and egoism and to clear away the infected strata of the Italian community. (Loud applause, and cries of "Rome! Rome!")

Our adversaries must not delude themselves. They thought in the unfortunate year of 1919, when we here in Cremona and all over Italy were no more than a handful of men, that Fascism would only be a passing phenomenon. Fascism has now been alive four years, and it has tasks enough to fill a century. Nor must our enemies deceive themselves by thinking that they can break up our organization, because we intend to make it more compact, more solid, better equipped against all emergencies; since, my friends, if a decisive blow is necessary, every man from the first to the last will do his exact duty. In a word, we want Italy to become Fascist. (Clamorous applause.)

That is simple and clear. We want Italy to become Fascist, because we are tired of seeing her governed by men whose principles are

---

[41] Fascist youths who at this time were not organized officially, but became the Opera Nazionale Balilla (ONB) in 1926, operating until 1937 when they were absorbed by Gioventù Italiana del Littorio (GIL), a youth section of the National Fascist Party. Balilla, meaning "little boy," was the nickname of Giovanni Battista Perasso (1735–1781), a Genoese boy who, according to tradition, started the revolt of 1746 against the Habsburg forces that occupied the city in the War of the Austrian Succession by throwing a stone at an Austrian official.

continually wavering between indifference and cowardice. And, above all, we are tired of seeing her looked upon abroad as a negligible quantity.

What is that feeling which stirs you when you hear the song of the Piave? It is that the Piave does not mark an end, it marks a beginning. (Hear, hear!) It is from the Piave, it is from Vittorio Veneto, it is from our victory—even if it was mutilated by a mistaken diplomacy—that our standards move on!

It was on the banks of the Piave that the march was begun that cannot stop until Rome is reached. (Enthusiastic applause.) And there are no obstacles, either of men or things, that can prevent us from arriving there.

I wish to thank you, Fascists of Cremona and people of this city, for your reception. I know and like to think that it is not to me personally that you pay this honor, but to the ideal, our cause, which has been sanctified by so much blood shed by the flower of Italian youth. And embracing my old friend Farinacci I mean to embrace all the Fascists of Cremona, to the cry of Long live Italy! Long live Fascism! (Enthusiastic applause.)

The Fascist Dawning of New Italy

October 6th, 1922, "Sciesa," Milan

At the seat of the local Fascist group "Antonio Sciesa," Mussolini pays his tribute to the memory of her two dead who fell, as Garibaldi fell, during the days of August, and then devotes himself to the analysis of a well-matured plan, strategic and tactical, for the coming battle.

◆　　◆　　◆

I agreed to come and speak to the Sciesa group this evening for three reasons—first sentimental, second personal, and third political. For the sentimental reason, because I wished to pay the tribute of my admiration and profound devotion to our unforgettable and magnificent fallen—Melloni, Tonoli, and Crespi; the first two of your squad and the last of the Sauro. I remember them perfectly. Then I agreed also because of the way in which this group has interpreted this meeting. Lastly, in view of the general attitude of suspense all over Italy at this moment, I did not wish to let the opportunity slip for defining certain points, a definition which is necessary in these difficult times through which we are passing.

You feel, to judge from your silent and austere bearing, that if the flesh is corruptible, the spirit is immortal. You feel that here in this little hall this evening the spirits of our fallen are still with us. We feel their presence, because the soul cannot die, and they fell in the most heroic action yet accomplished by Fascism in the four years of its history. Many times when the Fascists have gone forth to destroy with fire and sword the haunts of the cowardly Social-Communist delinquents, they have only seen the backs of the flying enemy, but the members of the Sciesa squad and the two fallen, whom we remember, and all the squadrons of the Milanese Fascio, went to the assault of the offices of the *Avanti!* as they would have attacked an Austrian trench. They had to scale the walls, break through barbed wire, burst open doors, and face the leaden hail which the enemy poured forth from their weapons. This is heroism. This is violence. This is the violence of which I approve and which I uphold, and which Fascism—and I speak to the Fascists of all Italy—ought to make hers. Not little, individual, sporadic acts of violence, but the great, wonderful, relentless violence of the decisive hour. It is necessary, when the moment comes, to strike with the utmost decision and without pity. You must not think that I wish to hide the very strong sympathy I have for the Milanese Fascio, because my love, above all, is for the cause. When a cause has been sanctified by so much pure young blood, it must not, at any cost, become defiled in any way. Our friends have been heroes, their action has been that of warriors, their violence saintly and moral. We exalt them, we remember them, and we will avenge them. We cannot accept the humanitarian, Tolstoyan moral standard, the moral standard of slavery. In times of war we adopt the formula of Socrates: "Overcome friends with kindness, overcome enemies with evil."

Nation and State. Our line of conduct is perfectly correct. Those who do good to us will have good; those who do ill, ill. Our enemies cannot complain, if being such, they are treated hardly, as enemies must be treated. We are in a historical period of crisis which every day becomes more acute. The general strike, which was averted by the sacrifice of blood of the Fascists, was an episode in this crisis. Dissension lies between the State and the nation. Italy is not a State, she is a nation, because from the Alps to Sicily there is the fundamental unity of our race, our customs, our language, and our religion. The war fought from 1915 to 1918 consecrates this unity, and if this is enough to characterize the nation, the Italian nation exists, full of power and resource and impelled toward a glorious destiny.

But the nation must create for itself the State. And there is no State. Today the paper that represents Liberalism in Italy, the paper with the largest circulation—and which, for this reason, by upholding absurd arguments has done a great deal of harm at times—stated that there are two Governments in Italy, and if there are two, there is one too many. There is the Liberal Government and the Fascist Government, the State of today and the State of tomorrow. "Wanted, a Government," said the *Corriere della Sera*. We agree, a Government is wanted.

The Lesson of Two Episodes. Two occurrences during these last days—one characteristic of our activity in the cause of humanity, the other of our activity in the cause of national rights—have proved the superiority of the Fascist over the Liberal State, and have shown that Fascism is capable and worthy to succeed that State.

At San Terenzo of La Spezia, if all the dead were buried and the wounded taken to the hospital, if the country was cleared of debris, and the furniture and belongings safeguarded from the base attempts of human jackals, if the soldiers had their supplies in good time, it was by the activity of the Fascist State.[42] And the mayor of Lerici—who is not a Fascist—telegraphed his great gratitude, not to the Prime Minister, but to us, as you learned in the *Popolo d'Italia.*

This is a question of mercy, humanity, and national solidarity. Let us transfer our attention to Bolzano. Here it is a question of our rights and the Italian law. Who stood up for those rights and imposed the Italian nationality in a city which ought to be Italian? Fascism. Who banished Perathoner who for five years held in check five Italian Ministers? Fascism. It has been Fascism that has given a school and a church to the Italians in Alto Adige and inspired them with the sense of their own dignity. Who placed the bust of the king in the Council Hall? The Fascists. The Germans are astonished at seeing before them all these young Fascists, splendid physically and morally. Inhabiting as they do without right our Italian soil, they seem to wonder, "What Italy is this?" And we answer, "By the action of the defeatist ministers and as a result of the unfortunate peace, you Germans are accustomed to the Italy of Abba Garima; now you must accustom yourselves to the Italy of Vittorio Veneto, which has force and energy, and which says, 'We are at the Brenner, and there we mean to stay! We do not wish to go to Innsbruck, but do not imagine that Germany and Austria can ever return to Bolzano!'"

---

[42] On September 28th, 1922, a bolt of lightening struck an arsenal of explosives at the Falconara Fort in San Terenzo. The blast killed 144 people and injured hundreds, causing damage within a ten-mile radius, including in nearby Lerici.

This is the Fascist State which reveals itself to Italian eyes in two typical moments of everyday history, the disaster of San Terenzo and the occupation of Bolzano.

For the Italy of Tomorrow. The citizens wonder which State will end by dictating its law upon the nation. We have no hesitation in answering that it will be the Fascist State. The *Corriere della Sera* says that something must be done quickly, and we agree. A nation cannot live nursing in its bosom two States, two Governments, one in action and the other in power. But what is the way to give the nation a Government? I say Government, because when we say State we mean something more. We mean the spirit and not merely the inert and transitory form. There are two ways, gentlemen. If the whole of Rome was not suffering from softening of the brain, they would summon Parliament at the beginning of November, and having passed the Bill for Electoral Reform, make an appeal to the electors in December. Because the crisis for which the *Corriere* asks could not alter the situation. Thirty crises in the Italian Parliament as it is today would mean thirty reincarnations of Signor Facta.[43] If the Government does not follow this path, gentlemen, we shall be obliged to take the other. You see our tactics are now clear. When it is a question of assaulting the State it is no longer possible to have recourse to little plots, of which the "to be or not to be" remains a secret to the last. We must give orders to hundreds and thousands of men, and it would be merely absurd to try to keep it secret. We play an open game. We leave our cards on the table until it is necessary to lift them, and we say, "There is an Italy that you, Liberal leaders, no longer understand. You do not understand it because your mind works on old-fashioned lines; you do not understand it because Parliamentary policy has killed your spirit. The Italy which has come from the trenches is strong and full of life."

Fascism, the Bourgeoisie, and the Proletariat. It is an Italy which deserves to begin a new period of history. There exists, therefore, a dramatic contrast between the Italy of yesterday and our Italy. The conflict appears inevitable. It is a question now of developing our forces, summoning all our energies and strength, so that the conflict

---

[43] Luigi Facta, the Prime Minister of Itay before Mussolini and at the time of this speech, serving from February 26th to October 31st, 1922. He was a member of the Liberal Union and then the Italian Liberal Party.

shall end in victory for us—and, as a matter of fact, upon that score there can be no doubt.

Now the Liberal State is a mask behind which there is no face; it is a scaffolding behind which there is no building. There is force but there is no spirit behind them. All those who ought to uphold it feel that it is approaching the extreme limits of incompetence, impotence, and absurdity.

On the other hand, as I said at Udine, we do not wish to stake everything on the game, because we do not present ourselves as the saviors of humanity, nor do we promise anything special to the people. We may even impose greater discipline and more sacrifices upon them. And we shall make no difference between the proletariat and the bourgeoisie, because there is an infected proletariat just as there is a bourgeoisie still more infected. There is a part of the proletariat that must be chastised in order that it may be redeemed afterwards, and there is a part of the middle class that detests us and tries to throw our lines into confusion, which finances anti-Fascist slander, which has hitherto ignobly courted the anti-national forces, and for which I do not feel one ounce of pity. We are surrounded by enemies, and those who are our open foes, and who belong to the Bolshevist parties, have now perfected themselves in the art of ambush and assassination.

A Warning! But there are other insidious enemies who try to harm Fascism under cover of the tricolor and other similar emblems, who try to insinuate themselves into our movement and to create simulacra of organizations in order to weaken us just at the time when it is most necessary for us to remain united. Now I must say that if we do not have mercy upon those who attack us from behind hedges, neither shall we have mercy upon those who attack us thus insidiously. When the clock of history strikes the hours, we must speak as the peasants do, simply, sincerely, and loyally.

We have no great obstacles to overcome, as the nation is waiting for us, the nation hopes in us and feels itself represented in us. Certainly we cannot promise to plant the tree of liberty in the squares. We cannot give liberty to those who would profit by it to assassinate us. The shortsightedness of the Free State lies in this, that it gives freedom to all, including those who use this freedom to overthrow it. We shall not give this universal liberty, not even if it assumes the garb of immortal principles. Finally, it is not electoral subterfuges that divide us from democracy. If people wish to vote, let them vote. Let us all vote until we are sick of it! Nobody wants to suppress universal suffrage.

Policy Needed. But we shall carry out a severe and reactionary policy; we are not afraid of doing so. If the representative organs of democracy say that we are reactionary, it does not offend us, because what distinguishes us from the Democrats is mentality and spirit. History does not follow a given itinerary; it is made up of contrasts and all kinds of vicissitudes; there are no centuries that are all light and no centuries that are all darkness. It is not possible to transport Fascism out of Italy, as Bolshevism has been transported out of Russia.

The Italians can be divided into three categories: the indifferent, who will stay at home; the sympathetic, who will have freedom of movement; and the antagonistic, who will have their freedom restricted. We shall make no promises. We shall not give ourselves out as missionaries who bring the revealed truth.

But I do not think that our enemies will place serious obstacles in our way. Bolshevism is defeated. Look at the Congress of Rome. What a pitiful sight! When the leader of a congress behaves like the lawyer of Busto, then you understand that we are upon the bottom rung of the ladder. There was one Socialism, today there are four, and there is a tendency toward further divisions. And not only this, but each of these divisions claims to represent the authentic party. It is no wonder that the proletariat scatters, discouraged and disgusted by the attitude of Socialism. As I have already said, the day of Socialism is not only past as a party; its philosophies and doctrines no longer stand. The Italians and the Western peoples in general must burst with logical criticism the grotesque bubble of international Socialism. Perhaps, looking at things from a historical point of view, it is a struggle between the East and the West, between the chaotic, fatalistic East (look at Russia) and us, we people of the West, who cannot be carried away by flights of metaphysics and require hard concrete realities.

Let Us Flee from Imitations. Italians cannot be mystified for long by Asiatic doctrines, which are absurd and criminal in their practical application. This is the essence of Italian Fascism, which represents a reaction against the Democrats who would have made everything mediocre and uniform and tried every way to conceal and to render transitory the authority of the State, from the supreme head to the last usher in the law courts; consequently everybody from the king to the lowest official has suffered from this false conception of life. Democracy thought to make itself indispensable to the masses, and did not understand that the masses despise those who have not the courage to be what they ought to be. Democracy has taken "elegance" from the lives of the people, but Fascism brings it back; that is to say, it brings back color, force, picturesqueness, the unexpected, mysticism, and in fact all that counts in the souls of the multitude. We play upon every cord of the lyre, from violence to religion, from art to politics. We are politicians and we are warriors. We are syndicalists and we also fight battles in the streets and the squares. That is Fascism as it was conceived at Milan, and as it was and is realized. And, my friends, we must maintain this privilege, and Fascism must be kept up to this level of strength and wisdom. We must not abandon ourselves to imitations, because that which is possible in a particular agricultural region in a given time and place is not possible here in Milan. Here the situation has been dominated more by the spontaneous maturing of events than by men's violence or by circumstances. Here our domination becomes more and more decided.

But, my friends, we must prepare ourselves with hearts free from preoccupation for the tasks that await us. Tomorrow it is probable, almost certain, that the formidable burden of the direction of a modern State will be on our shoulders. And it will be on the shoulders not only of a few men; it will be on the shoulders of the whole of Fascism.

Toward a More Glorious Destiny. And millions of eyes, many of them malicious, and millions of men, many of them beyond our frontiers, will be looking at us. They will want to see how we are organized, how justice is administered in the Fascist State, how honest people are protected, how we deal with the problems of the school and the army. And the wrongdoing of any man, his error, and his shame will react upon the whole organization of the State and of necessity upon Fascism. Have you, my friends, realized how formidable is the task that awaits you? Are you spiritually prepared for it? Do you think that enthusiasm alone is enough?—because it is not enough. It is necessary, because it is a primitive and fundamental force in human nature; it is impossible to do anything not inspired by intense passion or religious mysticism, but that is not enough. Together with these must work the reasoning forces of the brain. I think that in the case of a general crisis Fascism would have all that was necessary to impose itself and to govern, not according to the ideas of demagogism, but according to the ideas of justice. And then, by ruling the nation well, by leading her toward a more glorious destiny, by conciliating the interests of all classes without increasing the hatred of one and the selfishness of another, by uniting the Italian people to face the world-task, by fulfilling with patience this hard and cyclopean task, we shall inaugurate, thus, a really great period in Italian history. Thus will our dead be made immortal and their names written in the gold book of the Fascist aristocracy. We shall point them out to the rising generation, to the children who are growing up and who represent the eternal spring of life. We shall say, "Great was the effort and hard the sacrifice, and pure was the blood that was shed; and it was not shed to safeguard the interests of individuals, class, or caste; it was not shed in the name of materialism; it was shed in the name of an ideal, of all that is most noble, beautiful, and generous in the human soul." With the example of our dead before you, I ask you to remember to be worthy of their sacrifice and to examine daily your own activity. Friends, I have faith in you. You have faith in me. In this mutual trust is the guarantee and certainty of our victory. Long live Italy! Long live Fascism! Honor and glory to the martyrs of our cause! (Loud applause.)

The Moment Has Arrived When the Arrow Must Leave the Bow or the Cord Will Break!

October 24th, 1922, Naples

At this, the final stage of the pilgrimage of the ever-swelling ranks of Italian youth, where the first trench is dug in preparation for the imminent assault of the Blackshirts, Mussolini in the morning, as politician, hurls his vehement reproach against "the three black souls," the ministerial exponents of anti-Fascist reaction. In the afternoon he shows himself in the guise of a warrior, and, wearing the colors of Rome on his breast, contemplates thoughtfully his fifty thousand faithful crusaders in Piazza del Plebiscito, who shout with one insistent voice, "To Rome! To Rome!"

◆ ◆ ◆

Fascists and citizens! It may be, or rather it is almost certain, that my eloquence will disappoint you, accustomed as you are to the impetuosity and rich imagery of your own orators. But since I realize my incapacity for rhetoric, I have decided to limit myself, when speaking, to plain necessity.

We have gathered together here at Naples from every part of Italy to perform an act of brotherhood and love. We have with us our brothers from the borderland of betrayed Dalmatia, men who do not mean to yield. (Applause, and cries of "Long live Italian Dalmatia!") There are also the Fascists from Trieste, Istria, and Venezia Tridentina, Fascists from all parts of Northern Italy, even from the islands, from Sicily and Sardinia, all come together to affirm quietly and positively the indestructibility of our united faith, which means to oppose strongly every more or less masked attempt at autonomy or separatism.

Four years ago the Italian infantry, made great through twenty years of work and hardship, the Italian infantry in which the sons of your country were so largely represented, burst from the Piave and, having defeated the Austrians, surged on toward the Isonzo, and only the foolish democratic conception of the war prevented our victorious battalions from marching through the streets of Vienna and the highways of Budapest. (Applause.)

From Rome to Naples. A year ago at Rome, at one time, we found ourselves surrounded by a secret hostility, which had its origin in the misunderstandings and infamies characteristic of the uncertain political world of the capital. (Hear, hear!) We have not forgotten all this.

Today we are happy that all Naples—this city which I call the big safety-reserve of the nation—(Applause)—welcomes us with a sincere and frank enthusiasm, which does our hearts good, both as men and Italians. For this reason I request that not the smallest incident of any kind shall disturb this meeting, for that would be a mistake, and a foolish one. I demand also, as soon as the meeting is over, that every Fascist not belonging to Naples shall leave the town immediately.

All Italy is watching this meeting, because—and let me say this without false modesty—there is not a post-war phenomenon of greater interest and originality in Europe or the world than Italian Fascism.

You certainly cannot expect from me what is usually called a big speech. I made one at Udine, another at Cremona, a third at Milan, and I am almost ashamed to speak again. But in view of the extremely grave situation in which we find ourselves today, I consider this an appropriate opportunity to establish the different points of the problem in order that individual responsibilities may be settled. The moment has arrived, in fact, when the arrow must leave the bow, or the cord, too far stretched, will break. (Applause.)

The Solving of the Problem. You remember that my friend Lupi and I placed before the Chamber the alternatives of this dilemma, which is not only Fascist but also national, that is to say, legality or illegality, Parliamentary conquest or revolution. By which means is Fascism to become the State? For we wish to become the State! Well! By October 3rd I had already settled the question.

When I ask for the elections, when I ask that they shall take place soon, and be regulated by a reformed electoral law, it is clear to everyone that I have chosen my path. The very urgency of my request shows that the tension of my spirit has arrived at the breaking point. To have, or not to have; understood this means to hold, or not to hold, the key to the solution of the whole Italian political crisis.

The request came from me, but it also came from a party consisting of a formidably organized mass, which includes the rising generations in Italy and all the best, physically and morally, of the youth of the country, and from a party, too, which had a tremendous following among the vague and unstable public.

But, gentlemen, there is more. This request was made after the incidents of Bolzano and Trento, which had made plain to all eyes the complete paralysis of the Italian State, and revealed, at the same time, the no less complete efficiency of the Fascist State.

Well! In spite of all this, the inadequate Government at Rome puts the question on the footing of public safety and public order!

What We Have Asked the Government. The whole question has been approached in a fatally mistaken manner. Politicians ask what we want. We are not people who beat about the bush. We speak clearly. We do good to those who do good to us, and evil to those who do evil. What do we want, Fascists? We have answered quite simply: the dissolution of the present Chamber, electoral reform, and elections within a short time from now. We have demanded that the State shall abandon the ridiculous neutral position that it occupies between the national and the anti-national forces. We have asked for severe financial measures and the postponement of the evacuation of the third Dalmatic zone; we have asked for five portfolios as well as for the Commission of Aviation. We have, in fact, asked for the Ministry of Foreign Affairs, the War Office, the Admiralty, the Ministries of Labor and of Public Works. I am sure none of you will find our requests excessive. But to complete the picture, I will add that I shall not take part with the Government in this legal solution of the problem, and the reason is obvious when you remember that to keep Fascism still under my control I must of necessity have an unrestricted sphere of action both for journalistic and polemic purposes.

A Ridiculous Answer. And what has been the Government's reply? Nothing! No, worse than that, it has given a ridiculous answer. In spite of everything, not one of the politicians has known how to pass the threshold of Montecitorio in order to look the problem of the country in the face. A miserable calculation of our strength has been made; there has been talk of ministers without portfolios, as if this, after the more or less miserable experiences of the war, was not the culmination of human and political absurdity. There has been talk of subportfolios, too, but that is simply laughable! We Fascists do not intend to arrive at government by the window; we do not intend to give up this magnificent spiritual birthright for a miserable mess of ministerial stew. (Loud and prolonged applause.) Because we have what might be called the historical vision of the question as opposed to the merely political and Parliamentary view.

It is not a question of patching together a Government with a certain amount of life, but of including in the Liberal State—which has accomplished a considerable task which we shall not forget—all the forces of the rising generation of Italians who issued victorious from the war. This is essential to the welfare of the State, and not of the State only, but to the history of the nation. And then . . . ?

A Question of Strength. Then, gentlemen, the question, not being understood within its historical limits, asserts itself and becomes a question of strength. As a matter of fact, at turning points of history force always decides when it is a question of opposing interests and ideas. This is why we have gathered, firmly organized and strongly disciplined our legions, because thus, if the question must be settled by a recourse to force, we shall win. We are worthy of it. It is the right and duty of the Italian people to liberate their political and spiritual life from the parasitic incrustation of the past, which cannot be prolonged indefinitely in the present, as it would mean the death of the future. (Applause.)

It is then quite natural that the Government at Rome should try to divert and counteract the movement, that it should try to break up the Fascist organization, and to surround us with problems.

These problems have the names of the Monarchy, the Army, and Pacification.

The Acceptance of the Monarchy. I have already said that the discussion, abstract or concrete, of the good and evil of the monarchy as an institution is perfectly absurd. Every people in every epoch of history, given the time, place, and conditions necessary, has had its regime. There is no doubt that the unity of Italy is soundly based upon the House of Savoy. (Loud applause.) There is equally no doubt that the Italian Monarchy, both by reason of its origin, development, and history, cannot put itself in opposition to the new national forces. It did not manifest any opposition upon the occasion of the concession of the Charter, nor when the Italian people—who, even if they were a minority, were a determined and intelligent minority—asked and obtained their country's participation in the war. Would it then have reason to be in opposition today, when Fascism does not intend to attack the regime, but rather to free it from all those superstructures that overshadow its historical position and limit the expansion of our national spirit? Our enemies in vain try to keep this alleged misunderstanding alive.

Fascism and Democracy. The Parliament, gentlemen, and all the paraphernalia of democracy have nothing in common with the monarchy. Not only this, but neither do we want to take away the people's toy—the Parliament. We say "toy" because a great part of the people seem to think of it in this way. Can you tell me else why, out of 11 million voters, 6 million do not trouble themselves to vote? It might be, however, that if tomorrow you took their "toy" away from them, they would be aggrieved. But we will not take it away. After all, it is our mentality and our methods that distinguish us from democracy. Democracy thinks that principles are unchangeable when they can be applied at any time or in any place and situation.

We do not believe that history repeats itself, that it follows a given path, that after democracy must come super-democracy. If democracy had its uses and served the nation in the nineteenth century, it may be that some other political form would be best for the welfare of the nation in the twentieth. (Well said!) So that not even fear of our anti-democratic policy can influence the decision in favor of that continuity of which I spoke just now.

The Army. As regards the other institution in which the regime is personified—the army—the army knows that when the Ministry advised the officers to go about in civilian clothes to escape attack, we, then a mere handful of bold spirits, forbade it. (Prolonged applause.) We have created our ideal. It is faith and ardent love. It is not necessary for it to be brought into the sphere of reality. It is reality in so far as it is a stimulus for faith, hope, and courage. Our ideal is the nation. Our ideal is the greatness of the nation, and we subordinate all the rest to this.

For us the nation has a soul and does not consist only in so much territory. There are nations that have had immense possessions and have left no traces in the history of humanity in spite of them. It is not only size that counts, because, on the other hand, there have been tiny, microscopic States that have left indelible marks in the history of art and philosophy. The greatness of a nation lies in the aggregation of all these virtues and all these conditions. A nation is great when its spiritual force is transferred into reality. Rome was great when, from her small rural democracy, little by little, her influence spread over the whole of Italy. Then she met the warriors of Carthage and fought them. It was one of the first wars in history. Then, bit by bit, she extended the dominion of the Eagle to the furthermost boundaries of the known world, but still, as ever, the Roman Empire is a creation of the spirit, as it was the spirit which first inspired the Roman legions to fight. (Applause.)

Our Syndicalism. What we want now is the greatness of the nation, both materially and spiritually. That is why we have become syndicalist, and not because we think that the masses by reason of their number can create in history something that will last. These myths of the lower kind of Socialist literature we reject. But the working people form a part of the nation, and they are a great part of the nation, necessary to its existence both in peace and in war. They neither can nor ought to be repulsed. They can and must be educated and their legitimate interests protected. (Applause.) We ask them, "Do you wish this state of civil war to continue to disturb the country?" No! For we are the first to suffer from the ceaseless Sunday wrangling with its list of dead and wounded. I was the first to try to bridge over the gap that exists between us and what is called the Italian Bolshevist world.

How Peace Can Be Obtained. To prove this, I have just recently signed an agreement most gladly; in the first place because it was Gabriele d'Annunzio who asked me to, and in the second place because it was, as I thought, another step toward a national peace.

But we are no hysterical women who continually worry themselves by thinking of what might happen. We have not the catastrophic, apocalyptic view of history. The financial problem so much talked about is a question of willpower. Millions and millions would be saved if there were men in the Government who had the courage to say "No" to the different requests. But until the financial question is brought on to a political basis, it will not be solved. We are all for pacification, and we should like to see all Italians find the common ground upon which it is possible for them to live together in a civilized way. But, on the other hand, we cannot give up our rights and the interests and the future of the nation for the sake of measures of pacification that we propose with loyalty but which are not accepted in the same spirit by the other side. We are at peace with those who ask for peace, but for those who ensnare us and, above all, ensnare the nation, there can be no peace until after victory.

A Hymn to the Queen of the Mediterranean. And now, Fascists and citizens of Naples, I thank you for the attention with which you have listened to me.

Naples gives a fine display of strength, discipline, and austerity. It was a happy idea that led to our coming here from all parts of Italy, that has allowed us to see you as you are, to see your people who face the struggle for life like Romans, and who, with the desire to rebuild their lives and to gain wealth through hard work, carry ever in their hearts the love of this their wonderful town, which is destined to a great future, especially if Fascism does not deviate from its path.

Nor must the Democrats say that there is no need for Fascism here, as there has been no Bolshevism, for here there are other political movements no less dangerous than Bolshevism and no less likely to hinder the development of the public conscience.

I already see the Naples of the future endowed with an even greater splendor as the metropolis of the Mediterranean; and I see it together with Bari (which in 1805 had sixteen thousand inhabitants and now has one hundred and fifty thousand) and Palermo forming a powerful triangle. And I see Fascism concentrating all these energies, purifying certain circles, and removing certain members of society, gathering others under its standards.

And now, members of the Fascio of all Italy, lift up your flags and salute Naples, the capital of Southern Italy and the Queen of the Mediterranean.

PART V

MUSSOLINI THE FASCIST MEMBER OF PARLIAMENT

Fascism and the New Provinces[44]

June 21st, 1921, Chamber of Deputies,[45] Rome

❖ ◆ ❖

I am not displeased, gentlemen, to make my speech from the benches of the Extreme Right, where formerly no one dared to sit.

I may say at once, with the supreme contempt I have for all nominalism, that I shall adopt a reactionary line throughout my speech, which will be, I do not know how Parliamentary in form, but anti-Socialist and anti-Democratic in substance. (Approval.) In spite of this I am audacious enough to affirm that I shall be listened to with advantage by all sections of the Chamber. In the first place by the Government, which will notice our position with regard to it. In the second place by the Socialists, who, after seven years of changing fortunes, see before them, in the proud attitude of a heretic, the man they excommunicated from their orthodox church.[46] They will listen to me, too, because, having held their fortunes in the palm of my hand for two years, there may still be some secret longings for me in the depths of their hearts!

I may also be listened to with interest by the Popular Party and the other groups and sections. In fact, since I hope to define some

---

[44] The general election of May 15th, 1921 was the first election in which the recently acquired regions of Trentino-Alto Adige, Venezia Giulia, Zara, and Lagosta island elected deputies. These are the new provinces.

[45] The following speeches of Part V are all part of one speech delivered June 21st, 1921. On May 15th, 1921, Mussolini was elected to the lower chamber of the Italian Parliament, the Chamber of Deputies.

[46] Referring to Mussolini being expelled from the Italian Socialist Party in 1914 for his support of Italian intervention in the First World War.

political aspects, and I may add some historical ones, of this extremely powerful and complicated movement Fascism, perhaps what I have to say may have political consequences worthy of note.

I beg you not to interrupt me, because I shall never interrupt anybody, and I add that from this moment I shall make sparing use of my freedom of speech in this Assembly.

And now to the argument.

Italophobia in Alto Adige. In the speech from the throne, the Hon. Giolitti made the Sovereign say that the barrier of the Alps was entirely in our hands. I dispute the geographical and political exactness of this statement. We have not yet, at a few miles from Milan, the barrier of the Alps as the defense of Lombardy and the Po Valley.

I am touching on a delicate subject, but it is well known, both in this Chamber and elsewhere, that in the Canton Ticino,[47] which is being Germanized and bastardized, there is springing up a nationalist vanguard whom the Fascists look on with favor.

What is the present Government doing to defend the Alpine barrier of the Brenner and the Nevoso? Its policy, as regards Alto Adige, is simply lamentable and, though its representatives would doubtless be extremely capable of running a kindergarten, I absolutely deny that they have the necessary qualifications for governing a region where several languages are spoken and the rivalry between the races is very bitter. The governor of Venezia Tridentina, for instance, has made a present of the constituency of Gorizia to the Slovaks and of four German deputies to the Italian Chamber, while the other belongs to that category of more or less respectable people who are slaves to one so-called immortal principle, which consists in maintaining that there is only one form of good government in the world, and that it is applicable to all peoples, at all times, and in all quarters of the globe.

Allow me to put before the Chamber the results of a few personal enquiries I have made into the situation in Alto Adige.

The political anti-Italian movement in Alto Adige is monopolized by the Deutscher Verband,[48] an offspring of the Andreas Hofer Bund,

---

[47] An Italian-speaking region of southern Switzerland.
[48] A coalition of bourgeois German-speaking political parties formed in Alto Adige (South Tyrol) in 1919 after the region was annexed by Italy. The coalition won 90 percent of the vote in the 1921 election and elected all four of the deputies allotted to the region.

which has its center at Munich, and claims that the German frontier is not at the Pass of Salorno but at the Bern Clause or Chiusa di Verona.

Now the representative of whom I have just spoken is responsible for this German propaganda, because he has written the preface to a book that states that the natural boundaries of Germany are at the foot of the Alps toward the Po Valley. In the first days of the military occupation, immediately after the Armistice, this Italophobia was not possible; but when, by a great misfortune, this governor was appointed, the attitude of the people changed immediately and the submission previously shown was succeeded by an insolent arrogance, which denied the Austrian reverses and kept alive the desire for the return of the Hapsburgs.

At the sample fair organized by the Chamber of Commerce of Bolzano, a nest of Pan-Germanism, all Italian firms were excluded, so much so that the invitations were issued in German, and a Bavarian band played for the whole duration of the fair!

I come now to the events of April 24th, when a Fascist bomb, justly administered by way of reprisal, and for which I take upon myself the moral responsibility—(Loud applause and comments)—marked the limit to which Fascism intended that the German movement should go.

The demonstration of April 24th in Tyrol was only a simultaneous manifestation to the plebiscite which had been summoned that day beyond the Brenner, because the Germans in Alto Adige (South Tyrol) resort to these subtle tricks of making the same manifestations under different guises. In this way, when they publicly mourned the loss of Alto Adige on this side of the Brenner, on the other they did the same for the fallen Austrian soldiers. When the Fascists presented themselves at Bolzano, they found the police helmeted and tasseled, and when they were arrested, the enquiry was entrusted to Count Breitemburg, a notorious member of the Deutscher Verband.

I will not linger over the cases of Malmeter, because they are more like the chapters of a novel. But I cannot help mentioning one most curious episode.

The commissioner of Merano went to the commune of Maja Alta and was received, not in the town hall, but in an old mansion house, where were gathered the mayor and the councilors. The commissioner read the form of the oath, and the mayor and the councilors, sitting down immediately, put on their hats and burst out laughing. The commissioner had hardly recovered from his surprise when the mayor rose to his feet and began a storm of abuse against the King, Italy, and the commissioner, who, returning to Merano, requested the dismissal of this council. But the Deutscher Verband interceded with the governor, who returned the commissioner's report, writing at the same time that it was not a good thing to practice irredentism. And the representatives of the commune remained as they were!

Since the period of mismanagement, Alto Adige is no longer bilingual. The mayor himself refused to accept the evidence he had asked for concerning the events of April 24th, because they were written in Italian. These are small individual cases, but they serve to give an idea of the whole situation.

At Megré the Italophobic president of the Young Catholics' Club turned out two young men because they presented their demands in Italian, saying that that language would not do for his office and telling them to keep it for themselves. And among all those competing for the office of President of the Court of Appeal of redeemed Italian Trento, the one selected was a man who in 1915 had resigned his magistracy in order to serve as a Kaiserjäger volunteer under the Austrian flag. Today this man administers justice in the name of Italy! (Comments.)

If you imagine that the postal and telegraphic services in Alto Adige are in Italian hands, you are much mistaken. The Deutscher Verband has control of all the communications and disposes of them at its pleasure. Although April 24th was a holiday, the Pan-Germans and the heads of the movement at Innsbruck were kept informed all along of the development of events at Bolzano, while all communications with the civil and military authorities were cut and the town completely isolated from Trento and the rest of Italy for twenty-four hours. This is the situation.

What the Fascists Ask as Regards Alto Adige. Gentlemen of the Government, as regards Alto Adige, we ask you for these immediate measures:

1. The abolition of everything which reminds us of the Austro-Hungarian Monarchy, even in outward form. Because I wish to say to the House that it is useless to make compacts to prevent the return

of the Hapsburgs with the Austrian heirs, who are more Austrian than Austria, when we leave a great part of Austria intact within our own boundaries.

2. The dissolution of the Deutscher Verband.

3. The immediate dismissal of the two Italian governors.

4. The formation of a united province of Trento with the administration at Trento, and the strictest observance of the use of the two languages in every act of public administration.

I do not know what measures will be adopted by the Government in these cases, but I hereby declare, and I do so before the four German deputies that they may repeat it and make it known beyond the Brenner, that there we are and there we mean to stay at all costs. (Applause.)

(Giolitti, Prime Minister and Minister of the Interior: "Upon this we are all agreed.") (Applause.)

I note with pleasure the explicit declaration the Prime Minister has just made.

The Question of Montenegro's Independence

◆　◆　◆

What is going to be our line of policy in view of the vast field for dis-agreement which has been left by the peace treaty, or rather peace treaties, all over the world?

I shall not touch upon the quarrel between Greece and Turkey, alt-hough inconceivable complications may result if it is true, as is said, that Lenin is an ally of Kemal Pasha and has already dispatched the advance guard of the Red army to Asia Minor. Neither shall I speak of Upper Silesia, as I have not yet succeeded in defining the attitude of the Government on this question. Egypt, again, I shall leave un-touched. But I cannot hold my peace about the fate prepared for Mon-tenegro.

How is it that Montenegro has lost her independence? In theory she has not lost it, but actually she lost it in October 1918. And yet Count Sforza said that the independence of Montenegro was com-pletely guaranteed, first by the Treaty of London of 1915, which pre-supposed her aggrandizement at the expense of Austria and the res-titution of Scutari; secondly, by the conditions laid down by Wilson for the Allies, which safeguarded her existence with that of Belgium and Serbia; and thirdly, by the decision of the Supreme Council of the Conference of January 1919, in which the right of Montenegro to be represented by a Delegate at the Paris Peace Conference was recog-nized. Not only this, but when Franchet d'Espèrey entered Montene-gro with Serb and French elements, he gave out that he was governing in the name of King Nicholas.

When, however, King Nicholas, the Court, and the Government wished to return to Cetinje,[49] France, in whose interest it was to create a powerful Yugoslavia to counterbalance Italy in the Adriatic, informed the Montenegrin Government that she would have broken off all diplomatic relations had they done so.

What attitude did Italy adopt in this difficult situation? The Hon. Federzoni spoke yesterday of a Convention that became a scrap of paper; and it was this Convention of April 30th, 1919. In it the relations between Italy and Montenegro are clearly established. And this is what it says:

> Following upon the agreement made between the Italian Minister for Foreign Affairs and the Government of Montenegro [so there was a Government still in 1919], represented by their Consul General at Rome, Commander Ramanadovich, the Montenegrin Government will form a nucleus of officers and troops, drawn from the Montenegrin refugees, and will receive from the Italian Government the necessary funds in money for the payment of the allowances of the officers and men.

Other conditions follow, the last being, "The present Convention cannot be altered without the common consent of both the Italian and Montenegrin Governments."

Now this Convention was destroyed after the death of King Nicholas.[50] Signs of disaffection were noticed among the Montenegrin troops, and the commander asked for military aid from our Government, in order to proceed to the work of elimination. A Commission was appointed, presided over by Colonel Vigevano. This commission, which was to save the Montenegrin army, was the chief cause of its disbandment. And not only this—on May 27th the Italian Minister for Foreign Affairs told the Montenegrin Government that the troops must be disbanded or no more funds would be forthcoming from Italy. And in this way the Convention of April 30th, 1919 was violated, because in it, it had been said that no alteration was to be made without the common consent of the two Governments, and this decision had never been accepted by the consul general at Rome, who represented the Montenegrin Government. The fact is that the Italian Minister had

---

[49] The former (1878–1918) royal capital of Montenegro.
[50] March 1st, 1921.

made use of the presence of the Montenegrin army in Italy for political purposes, thinking thereby to obtain better terms with Yugoslavia. This expectation not being realized, the Montenegrin army, at a given moment, was cast aside like a worn-out coat. The fact of the election of the Constituent does not justify the tragic state of abandonment in which Italy left Montenegro, because only 20 percent of the electors voted, and of those only 9 percent in favor of annexation by Serbia. The Serbian authorities have introduced a real reign of terror in Montenegro and have prevented the presentation of lists which might contain the names of candidates favorable to the independence of the country.

But I hope Count Sforza will not think that the question of Montenegro is a thing of the past. First, as he knows, the Montenegrin people are still in arms against the Serbs, and secondly, the Italian people are unanimous as regards this question. Even the Socialists, and I say it to their honor, have several times declared in their papers that the independence of Montenegro is sacred. The Universities of Padua and Bologna have pronounced in favor of her independence, while the Fascists have presented a motion to this effect.

The shameful page which signs the death warrant of the Montenegrin people must be redeemed by the adoption of our motion, because if you bring the question once more before the Great Powers, so that another plebiscite be summoned, I am certain that, under conditions of liberty, anti-Serbian results will be returned.

D'Annunzio and Fiume

♦   ◆   ♦

In the speech from the throne, the Alps which go down to the Brenner were spoken of. Now we wish to know if these Alps include Fiume or not. I deplore the fact that in this speech no notice was given to the action of Gabriele d'Annunzio and his legionaries—(Applause)—without whom our boundaries today would be at Monte Maggiore instead of at the Nevoso. Such a reference would have been generous, as well as politically opportune.

I do not intend to enlarge upon the sacrifice of Dalmatia. My honorable friend Federzoni spoke very eloquently on the subject yesterday. But I was surprised when in that same speech from the throne it was affirmed that Zara must be the advance guard of Italy on the opposite shores, because Zara is crushed between the Slav sea and the Slav hinterland.

While upon the subject of the Adriatic, gentlemen, we Fascists cannot forget, we who speak for the first time in this hall, the attitude that you adopted in the affair of Fiume. We cannot forget that you attacked Fiume, and that when on December 28th General Ferrario said that he could not suspend the order for the bombardment that would have leveled that town to the ground, that general and the Government that gave him the order compromised our national dignity more than a little. (Approval on the Right.)

You put a knife to the throat of Fiume, but you did not solve the problem. You sent a commander there with an amazing scheme for the formation of a Government, which was to accept the conditions agreed upon at Belgrade—accept, that is to say, the Consortium, which means the near, if not immediate, destruction of the port of Fiume. Because you are well aware that after the lapse of twelve years

Porto Barro and the Delta ought to go to Yugoslavia, and you have already handed them over, because, if you had not done so, you would have been obliged to make statements which have not been made.

Italy, Zionism, and the English Mandate in Palestine

◆

I come now to another very delicate question that must be faced, because it is historically necessary and because, in view of the recent Pontifical Allocution before the Secret Consistory, it can no longer be put off.

We must choose: the Government must decide what line it is going to take up. Either it must adopt the English attitude in favor of the Zionists, or that of Benedict XV. I do not think that I shall be boring the Chamber if I run over the antecedents of this question.

On November 2nd, 1917, the English Government declared itself in favor of the creation in Palestine of a national center for the Jewish race, it being clearly understood that nothing would be done to offend the rights, civil or religious, of the non-Jewish communities already existing in Palestine or of the Jews in the rest of the world. Later the Allied Powers agreed to this, and finally, in Article No. 222 of the Peace Treaty, confirmed on August 20th at Sèvres, Turkey renounced all her rights in Palestine, and the Allied Powers chose England as mandatory.

Now it has come about, that while the civilized nations of the West have not altered the common regime of liberty for the different religions, in Palestine just the reverse has happened, and this in particular because the administration of the State in embryo has been entrusted to the political organization of the Zionists.

But there have been Arabs in Palestine for ten centuries. There are 600,000 now, and 70,000 Christians, while the Jews only number 50,000. In this way an extraordinarily interesting situation has been created.

The native Jews, who have lived for years under the shadow of the mosque of Jerusalem, cordially dislike those immigrant elements from Poland, Ukraine, and Russia, on account of their extremely emancipated ideas. They have already divided into three sections, one of which, commonly known by its abbreviated name "Mopsy," being already inscribed in the Third International at Moscow as Communist Section.

I wish to say, however, that no anti-Semitism, which would be new in this hall, must be read into my words.

I recognize the fact that the sacrifices made by the Italian Jews during the war were considerable and generous, but now it is a question of examining certain political positions and of indicating what line the Government might eventually adopt.

An alliance between the Arabs and the Christians has now been established in Palestine, and a party formed at the Conference of Jaffa, which opposes by civil war all Jewish immigration. On May 1st and 14th, serious disturbances occurred which resulted in some hundreds of wounded and several deaths, including a writer of note.

Now, according to the *Bulletin du Comité des Délégations Juives*, page 19, it appears that the text of the English Mandate for Palestine must be submitted to the Council of the Society of the League of Nations in the next meeting at Geneva. I should wish the Government, in this delicate situation, to accept the point of view of the Vatican.

This is in the interest of the Jews, who, having fled from the pogroms of Ukraine and Poland, must not meet Arab pogroms in Palestine; moreover, it is advisable that the Western nations should refrain from creating a painful legal position for the Jews, since tomorrow those same Jews, becoming citizen-subjects of those States, might immediately form foreign colonies within them.

The Attitude of Fascism Toward
Communism and Socialism

◆

I do not wish to enlarge upon the question of foreign policy, as I should then find myself out in the open, and I might ask the Minister for Foreign Affairs what Italy's position exactly is in the face of the formidable conflicts that loom upon the horizon of international politics. While Count Sforza is at the head of Foreign Affairs in Giolitti's Cabinet, we Fascists cannot but find ourselves among the opposition. (Comments.)

I shall pass now to an examination of the position of Fascism with regard to the various parties—(Signs of attention)—and I shall begin with the Communists.

Communism, the Hon. Graziadei teaches me, springs up in times of misery and despair. When the total sum of the wealth of the world is much reduced, the first idea that enters men's minds is to put it all together so that everyone may have a little. But this is only the first phase of Communism, the phase of consumption. Afterwards comes the phase of production, which is very much more difficult, so difficult, indeed, that that great and formidable man (not yet legislator) who answers to the name of Vladimir Ulyanov Lenin, when he came to shaping human material, became aware that it was a good deal harder than bronze or marble. (Approval and comments.)

I know the Communists. I know them, because a great many of them are my sons—I mean, of course, spiritually—(Laughter)—and I recognize with a sincerity that might appear cynical, that it was I who first inoculated these people, when I put into circulation among the Italian Socialists a little Bergson mingled with much Blanqui.

There is a philosopher sitting among the ministers who certainly teaches me that the neo-spiritualistic philosophies continually oscillating between the metaphysical and the lyrical are very dangerous for small minds.[51] (Laughter.) The neo-spiritualistic philosophies are like oysters—they are palatable, but they have to be digested. (Laughter.)

These, my friends or enemies. . . .

(Voices from the Extreme Left: "Enemies, enemies!")

Very well, then—enemies, swallowed Bergson when they were twenty-five and have not digested him at thirty. I am very surprised to see among the Communists an economist of the standing of Antonio Graziadei, with whom I had great battles when he was a reformer and had thrown aside Marx and his doctrines. While the Communists speak of the dictatorship of the proletariat, of republics more or less united with the Soviet, and other far-fetched absurdities of that kind, between them and us there cannot be other than war. (Interruptions from the Extreme Left. Comments.)

Our position is different as regards the Socialist Party. In the first place we are careful to make a distinction between party Socialism and the Socialism of Labor. (Comments on the Extreme Left.)

I am not here to overrate the importance of the syndicalist movement. When you think that there are 16 million working men in Italy and of these hardly 3 million belong to the syndicates, whether the General Conference of Workmen, the National Italian Syndicate, the Italian Workmen's Union, the Confederation of Italian Economic Syndicates, the White Federation, or other organizations which do not concern us, and that their membership increases and diminishes according to the times; when you think that the really advanced and scrupulous thinkers are a scanty minority, you will realize at once that we are right when we do not overrate the historical importance of this movement of the working classes.

But we recognize the fact that the General Federation of Workers did not manifest the attitude of hostility at the time of the war which was shown by a great part of the Official Socialist Party. We recognize, also, that through the General Federation of Workers technical forces have come to the front which, in view of the fact that the organizers are in direct and daily contact with the complex economic reality, are

---

[51] Benedetto Croce, Minister of Public Instruction.

reasonable enough. (Interruptions from the Extreme Left and comments.)

We—and there are witnesses here who can prove the truth of my words—have never taken up *a priori* an attitude of opposition to the General Federation of Workers. I add also that our attitude might be altered later if the Confederation detached itself—and the political directors have for some time considered the possibility of this being done—from the political Socialist Party—(Comments)—which is only a fraction of political Socialism, and is formed of those people who, in order to act, have need of the big forces represented by the working-class organizations.

Listen to what I am going to say. When you present the Bill for the Eight-Hour Day, we will vote in favor of it. We shall not oppose this or any other measures destined to perfect our special legislation. We shall not even oppose experiments of cooperation; but I tell you at once that we shall resist with all our strength attempts at State Socialism, Collectivism, and the like. We have had enough of State Socialism, and we shall never cease to fight your doctrines as a whole, for we deny their truth and oppose their fatalism.

We deny the existence of only two classes, because there are many more. (Comments.) We deny the possibility of explaining the story of humanity in terms of economics. We deny your internationalism, because it is a luxury only the upper classes can afford; the working people are hopelessly bound to their native shores.

Not only this, but we affirm, and on the strength of recent Socialist literature which you ought not to repudiate, that the real history of capitalism is beginning now, because capitalism is not only a system of oppression, but a selection of that which is of most worth, a coordination of hierarchies, a more strongly developed sense of individual responsibility. (Applause.) So true is this that Lenin, after having instituted the building councils, abolished them and put in dictators; so true is it that, after having nationalized commerce, he reintroduced the regime of liberty; and, as you who have been in Russia well know, after having suppressed—even physically—the bourgeoisie, today he summons it back, because without capitalism and its technical system of production Russia could never rise again. (Applause from the Right. Comments.)

Let me speak to you frankly and tell you the mistakes you made after the Armistice, fundamental mistakes which are destined to influence the history of your politics.

First of all you ignored or underrated the survival of those forces which had been the cause of intervention in the war. Your paper went to ridiculous lengths, never mentioning my name for months, as if by that you could eliminate a man from life and history. You showed yourselves worse scoundrels than ever by libelling the war and victory. (Loud approval on the Right.) You wildly propagated the Russian myth, awakening almost messianic expectation; and only afterwards, when you realized the truth, did you change your position by executing a more or less prudent strategic retreat. (Laughter.) Only after two years did you remember, beside the sickle—a noble tool—and the hammer—no less noble—to place the book—(Bravo!)—which represents the rights of the spirit over matter, rights which cannot be suppressed or denied—(Bravo!)—rights which you, who consider yourselves the heralds of a new humanity, ought to be the first to inscribe upon your banners. (Great applause from the Extreme Right.)

The Attitude of Fascism Toward the Popular Party, The Vatican, and Social Democracy

◆

I come now to the Popular Party, and I wish to remind it first that in the history of Fascism there are no invasions of churches, and not even the assassination of the monk Angelico Galassi, who was killed by revolver shots at the foot of the altar.[52] I confess to you that there have been some chastisements and the sacred burning of the offices of a newspaper which called the Fascists a band of criminals. (Comments; interruptions from the Center.)

Fascism neither practices nor preaches anti-Clericalism. It can also be said that it is not in any way tied to Freemasonry; this, however, should not be the cause of alarm which it is to some members of the Popular Party, as to my mind Freemasonry is an enormous screen behind which there are generally small things and small men. (Comments and laughter.) But let us come to concrete problems.

The question of divorce has been touched on here. I am not, at bottom, in favor of divorce, because I do not believe that questions of the sentimental order can be settled by juridical formula, but I ask the Popular Party to consider if it is just that the rich can obtain divorce by going into Hungary, while the poor are sometimes obliged to be tied all their lives.

We are one with the Popular Party as regards the liberty of schools. We are very near them as regards the agrarian problem, for we think that where small properties exist it is useless to destroy them; that where it is possible to create them, they ought to be

---

[52] Murdered by Socialists during a riot in Abbadia San Salvatore in Siena, Tuscany on August 15th, 1920.

created; that where they cannot be created, because they would be unproductive, other methods must be adopted, not excluding more or less collective cooperation. We agree about administrative decentralization, provided, necessarily, that autonomy and federation are not spoken of, because regional federation would lead to provincial federation, and so on till Italy returned to what she was a century ago.

But there is another problem more important than these incidental questions to which I wish to draw the attention of the Popular Party, and that is the historical problem of the relations between Italy and the Vatican. (Signs of attention.)

All of us, who from fifteen to twenty-five drank deep at the fountain of Carduccian literature, learned to hate "una vecchia vaticana lupa cruenta" of which Carducci speaks,[53] I think, in the ode *To Ferrara*; we heard talk of "a pontificate dark with mystery" on the one hand, and on the other of the sublime truth and the future in the words of the poet-prophet. Now all this, confined to literature, may be most brilliant, but to us Fascists, who are eminently practical, it seems today more than a little out of date.

I maintain that the Imperial and Latin tradition of Rome is represented today by Catholicism. If, as Mommsen said thirty years ago, one could not stay in Rome without being impressed by the idea of universality, I both think and maintain that the only universal idea at Rome today is that which radiates from the Vatican. I am very disturbed when I see national churches being formed, because I think of the millions and millions of men who will no longer look toward Italy and Rome. For this reason I advance this hypothesis, that if the Vatican should definitely renounce its temporal ambitions—and I think it is already on that road—Italy ought to furnish it with the necessary material help for the schools, churches, hospitals, etc., that a temporal power has at its disposal. Because the increase of Catholicism in the world, the addition of 400 million men who from all quarters of the globe look toward Rome, is a source of pride and of special interest to us Italians.

The Popular Party must choose: either it is going to be our friend, our enemy, or neutral. Now that I have spoken clearly, I hope that some member of the party will do likewise.

---

[53] "The Vatican, the old bloody wolf."

Social Democracy seems to have a very ambiguous position. First of all one wonders why it is called Social Democracy. A democracy is already necessarily social; we think, however, that this Social Democracy is a kind of Trojan horse, which holds within it an army against whom we shall always be at war.

PART VI

Mussolini the Fascist Prime Minister

Mussolini the Fascist Prime Minister

◆

We deem it superfluous to linger over a detailed analysis of the separate speeches delivered by Benito Mussolini after November 1st, 1922, the day on which, by the will of the people, he rose fully equipped to the dignities and responsibilities of power.

Foreigners are to a great extent ignorant of the origin, the character, and the evolution of the Fascist movement, owing to the lack of literature on the subject outside Italy. They have, however, already had the means of appreciating the qualities of strength, balance of mind, and foresight revealed from the very first by the Italian Fascist Premier. Although European public opinion may be logically entitled to an attitude of reserve in the face of the crisis of evolution and renovation through which Italy is passing, it is certain that the young President of the Council—of humble birth, and risen to power by a remarkable combination of circumstances—romantic, daring, ingenious, tempestuous—stands now the principal figure in the arena of world politics.

A New Cromwell in the Parliament

November 16th, 1922, Chamber of Deputies, Rome

◆ ◆ ◆

Honorable Members,—(Signs of great attention)—I perform today in this hall an act of formal deference toward you for which I do not expect any special gratitude.

I have the honor of announcing to the Chamber that His Majesty the King, by a Decree of October 31st, has accepted the resignations of the Hon. Luigi Facta from the office of President of the Council and of his colleagues, Minister, and Undersecretaries of State, and has asked me to form the new Ministry. On the same day His Majesty has appointed me President of the Council of Ministers and Minister of the Interior and of Foreign Affairs, etc.

For many years—for too many years—crises in the Government took place and were solved by more or less tortuous and underhand maneuvers, so much so that a crisis came to be regarded as a regular scramble for portfolios, and the Ministry was caricatured in the comic papers.

Now, for the second time in the brief space of seven years, the Italian people, or rather the best part of it, has overthrown a Ministry and formed for itself an entirely new Government from outside, regardless of every parliamentary designation.

The seven years of which I speak lie between May 1915 and October 1922. I shall leave to the gloomy partisans of super-constitutionalism the task of discoursing, more or less plaintively, about all this. I maintain that revolution has its rights; and I may add, so that everyone may know, that I am here to defend and give the greatest value to the revolution of the Blackshirts, inserting it intrinsically in the history of the nation as an active force in development, progress, and the restoration of equilibrium. (Loud applause from the Left.) I could have carried our victory much further, and I refused to do so. I imposed limits upon my action and told myself that the truest wisdom is that which does not forsake one after victory. With three hundred thousand young men, fully armed, ready for anything and almost religiously prompt to obey any command of mine, I could have punished all those who have slandered the Fascists and thrown mud at them. (Approval on the Right.) I could have made a bivouac of this gloomy gray hall; I could have shut up Parliament and formed a Government of Fascists exclusively; I could have done so, but I did not wish to do so, at any rate at the moment. Our adversaries remained in their shelters and then quietly issued forth and obtained their freedom, of which they are already taking advantage to set traps for us and slander us, as at Carate, Bergamo, Udine, and Muggia.

I have formed a coalition Government, not with the intention of obtaining a Parliamentary majority, with which at the moment I can perfectly well dispense, but in order to gather together in support of the suffering nation all those who, over and above questions of party and section, wish to save her.

From the bottom of my heart I thank all those who have worked with me, both Ministers and Undersecretaries; I thank my colleagues in the Government, who wished to share with me the heavy responsibilities of this hour; and I cannot remember without pleasure the attitude of the Italian working classes, who indirectly encouraged and strengthened the Fascists by their solidarity, active or passive. I believe also that I shall be giving expression to the thoughts of a large part of this assembly, and certainly of the majority of the Italian people, if I pay a warm tribute to our Sovereign, who, by refusing to permit the useless reactionary attempts made at the eleventh hour to proclaim martial law, has avoided civil war and allowed the fresh and ardent Fascist current, newly arisen out of the war and exalted by victory, to pour itself into the sluggish mainstream of the State. (Cries of "Long live the King!" The Ministers and a great many deputies rise to their feet and applaud.)

Before arriving here we were asked on all sides for a program. It is not—alas!—programs that are wanting in Italy, but men to carry them out. All the problems of Italian life—all, I say—have long since been solved on paper, but the will to put these solutions into practice has been lacking. The Government today represents that firm and decisive will.

The Foreign Policy of the Fascist Government

November 16th, 1922, Chamber of Deputies, same speech

◊ ◆ ◊

Honorable Members, our foreign policy is the business which chiefly concerns us at the present moment. I shall speak of it at once, as I think that what I am going to say will dispel many apprehensions. I shall not touch upon all the questions connected with the subject, because, in this sphere as in all others, I prefer actions to words.

The fundamental principle upon which our foreign policy is based is that treaties of peace, once signed and ratified, must be carried out, no matter whether they are good or bad. A self-respecting nation cannot follow another course. Treaties are not eternal or irreparable; they are chapters and not epilogues in history; to put them into practice means to try them. If in the course of execution they are proved to be absurd, that in itself constitutes the possibility of a further examination of the respective positions.

I shall bring before the consideration of Parliament both the Treaty of Rapallo and the Agreements of Santa Margherita, which are derived from it.

Agreed that treaties, when once perfected and ratified, must be loyally carried out, I go on to establish another fundamental principle, which is the rejection of all the famous "reconstructive" ideology. We admit that there is a kind of economic union or interdependence among European countries. We admit that this economic life must be reconstructed, but we refuse to think that the methods hitherto adopted will succeed in doing so. Commercial treaties concluded between two Powers—the basis of the closest economic relations between nations—are of more value in the reconstruction of the European economic world than all the complicated and confused general plenary conferences, whose lamentable history everybody knows.

As far as Italy is concerned, we intend to follow a policy which will be dignified and at the same time compatible with our national interests. (Loud applause.) We cannot allow ourselves the luxury of a policy of foolish altruism, or of complete surrender to the desires of others. *Do ut des.* For Italy today has a new importance which must be reckoned with adequately, and this fact is beginning to be recognized beyond her boundaries. We have not the bad taste to exaggerate our powers, but neither do we wish to belittle them with excessive and useless modesty.

My formula is simple: "Nothing for nothing." Those who wish to have concrete proofs of friendship from us must give us the same. Fascist Italy, just as she does not intend to repudiate treaties for many reasons, political, moral and economic, does not intend, either, to abandon the Allies—Rome is in line with London and Paris; but Italy must assert herself and impose upon the Allies that strict and courageous examination of conscience which has not been faced by them from the time of the Armistice up to the present day.

Does an Entente still exist in the full sense of the word? What is the position of the Entente with regard to Germany and Russia? with regard to an alliance between these two countries? What is the position of Italy in the Entente, of the Italy who, not solely by reason of the weakness of her governors, lost strong positions in the Adriatic and the Mediterranean, who did not obtain any colonies or raw materials, who is literally crushed under the load of debts incurred in order to obtain victory, and whose most sacred rights, even, were held in question? In the conversations I intend to have with the Prime Ministers of England and France, I mean to face clearly and in its entirety the question of the Entente and Italy's position within it.

As a result of this, alternatives will arise; either the Entente, finding a way of settling her inward perplexities and contradictions, will become a really solid homogeneous body, with evenly distributed forces, with equal rights and equal duties, or her hour will have struck, and Italy, regaining her freedom of action, will turn loyally with a new policy to the work of safeguarding her interests.

I hope that the first eventuality will be realized, particularly in view of the new uprising in the East and the growing intimacy between Russia, Turkey and Germany. But, however it may be, we must get beyond conventional phrases. It is time, in fact, to abandon diplomatic expedients, which are renewed and repeated at every conference, in order to deal directly with historical fact, by which alone it is possible to decide one way or another the trend of events. Our foreign policy, which aims at protection of our interests, respect of treaties and the settling of our position in the Entente, cannot be described as adventurous and imperialist, in the vulgar sense of the word. We want to follow a policy of peace that will not, however, be at the same time suicidal.

In order to refute the pessimists who expected catastrophic results to follow upon the advent of the Fascists to power, it is enough to remind them that our relations with the Swiss are perfectly friendly, and that a commercial treaty, already in the process of formation, will further contribute toward strengthening them when it is completed; that they are perfectly correct as regards Yugoslavia and Greece; we are on good terms with Spain, Czechoslovakia, Poland and Romania, and the other Baltic States, where of late Italy has gained a great deal of sympathy, and where we are trying to make commercial agreements; and on equally good terms with the other States.

As far as Austria is concerned, Italy will keep faith as regards her promises, and will not neglect to enter into economic relations with her as well as with Hungary and Bulgaria.

We maintain, as regards Turkey, that what is now an accomplished fact ought to be recognized as such at Lausanne, with the necessary guarantees as to trade in the Straits, European interests and the interests of the small Christian communities. The situation which has arisen in Islam is going to be carefully watched. When Turkey has got what belongs to her she must not try to obtain more. There will come a day when it will be necessary to say, "Thus far and no further!" The danger of complications in the Balkans, and in consequence in Europe in general, can be avoided by firmness, which will have an increased effect in proportion to the loyalty of the Allies' conduct. We do not forget that there are 44,000 Mohammedans in Romania, 600,000 in Bulgaria, 400,000 in Albania, and 1,500,000 in Yugoslavia; a world which the recent victory of the Crescent has exalted, at any rate secretly.

As far as Russia is concerned, Italy believes that the moment has come to face the question of her relations with that country in their actual reality; but this apart from internal conditions in that country, with which we, as a Government, do not wish to interfere, since in our turn we shall admit of no interference in our home affairs. In consequence we are disposed to consider the possibility of a definite solution of the situation. As regards the presence of Russia at Lausanne, Italy has supported the most liberal point of view and does not despair of its eventual triumph, although thus far she has only been invited to discuss the single question of the Dardanelles.

Our relations with the United States are very good, and I shall make it my care to see that they are improved, especially as regards a close economic cooperation. A commercial treaty with Canada is on the point of being signed. We are on cordial terms with the republics of Central and South America, and especially with Brazil and Argentina, where millions of Italians live. They must not be denied the possibility of taking part in the local political life around them, which will not estrange them from, but rather bind them all the closer to their Mother Country.

As for economic and financial problems, Italy will maintain in the approaching conference at Brussels that debts and reparations form an indivisible binomial.

In order to carry out this policy of dignity and regard for our national interests, we need to have at the Ministry for Foreign Affairs a central staff competent to deal with the new necessities of the national life and of the increased prestige of Italy in the world. (Applause.)

The Policy of Fascism for Italy:
Economy, Work, and Discipline

November 16th, 1922, Chamber of Deputies, same speech

◆   ◆   ◆

Honorable Members, the policy we shall follow as regards the country itself can be summed up in three words: economy, work and discipline. The financial problem is a fundamental one, the balancing of the State Budget must be accomplished as soon as possible by a regime of careful administration, intelligence in the use of money, the utilization of all the productive forces of the nation and the removal of the trappings of war. (Loud applause.) For further information as regards the financial question, which, though serious, is open to rapid improvement, I refer you to my colleague Tangorra,[54] who will give you information when the financial measures are discussed.

He who talks of work, talks of the productive middle classes in the towns and in the country. It is not a question of privileges for the first or for privileges for the second, but of the safeguarding of all the interests which are in accordance with national production. The proletariat which works, and whose well-being concerns us, though not from weak demagogic motives, has nothing to fear, nothing to lose and everything to gain from a financial policy which preserves the balance of the State and prevents bankruptcy, which would have a disastrous effect, especially among the humbler classes.

---

[54] Vincenzo Tangorra (December 10th, 1866–December 21st, 1922), the Minister of Finance.

Our policy as regards emigration must free itself of an excessive "paternalism," while, at the same time, an Italian who emigrates must know that his interests will be securely guarded by the representatives of his country abroad. The growth of the prestige of a nation in the world is in proportion to the discipline it shows at home. There is no doubt that the internal condition of the country has improved, but it is not yet as I should like to see it. I do not intend to indulge myself in easy optimism. I am no lover of Pangloss.[55] In the big cities, and in all the towns in general, there is peace; instances of violence are sporadic and peripheral; but, at the same time, these also must cease. The citizens, no matter to what party they belong, shall have freedom of movement; all religions shall be respected, with particular regard to the dominant faith, Catholicism; statutory liberty shall not be infringed and the law shall be made to be respected at all costs!

The State is strong and will prove its power equally where all classes of citizens are concerned, including illegal Fascism, because it would now be irresponsible illegality and without any justification. I must add, however, that almost all the Fascists have submitted to the new order of things. The State does not mean to abdicate for anyone, and whoever opposes it must be punished. This explicit statement is a warning to all citizens, and I know will be particularly pleasing to the Fascists, who have fought and won in order to have a State which would make itself felt in every direction with inexhaustible energy. It must not be forgotten that, besides the minority that represent actual militant politics, there are 40 million excellent Italians who work, by their splendid birthrate perpetuate our race, and who ask, and have the right to obtain, freedom from the chronic state of disorder which is the sure prelude to general ruin. Since sermons, evidently, are not enough, the State will put the army it has at its disposal in order by a process of selection and improvement. The Fascist State will form a perfectly organized and united police force, of great mobility and with a high moral standard; while the army and navy—glorious and dear to every Italian heart—withdrawn from the vicissitudes of Parliamentary politics, reorganized and strengthened, will represent the last reserve of the nation both at home and abroad.

---

[55] Pangloss, a fictional character, the pedantic and unfailingly optimistic tutor of Candide, the protagonist of Voltaire's novel *Candide* (1759), a satire on philosophical optimism.

Gentlemen, from the last communication issued you will learn what the Fascist program is in detail with regard to each individual Ministry. I do not wish, as long as it is possible to avoid it, to govern against the wishes of the Chamber; but the Chamber must understand the peculiar position it holds, which makes it liable to dismissal in two days or in two years. (Laughter.) We ask for full powers, because we wish to take full responsibility. Without full powers you know perfectly well that not a penny—a penny I say—would be saved. By this we do not intend to exclude the possibility of voluntary cooperation, which we shall cordially accept, whether it be from deputies, senators or single competent citizens. We have, every one of us, a religious sense of the difficulty of our task. The country encourages us and waits. We shall not give you further words but facts. Let us solemnly and formally pledge ourselves to balance the Budget, and we shall do it. We wish to have a foreign policy of peace, but, at the same time, it must be dignified and firm; and we shall have it. None of our enemies, past or present, need deceive themselves about the rapidity of our advent to power. (Laughter; comments.) Our Government has a formidable hold upon the hearts of the people and is supported by the best elements in the country. There is no doubt that in these last days an enormous step has been taken toward spiritual unity. The Italian nation has found herself again, from the north to the south, from the Continent to those generous islands which shall no more be forgotten—(Applause)—from Rome to the industrious colonies of the Mediterranean and the Atlantic. Gentlemen, do not throw useless words at the nation; fifty-two requests to speak on my lists is too much. Let us work, rather, with pure hearts and ready brains to assure the prosperity and the greatness of the country.

And may God help me to carry my arduous task to a victorious end. (Loud applause. Many deputies come down to congratulate the President.)

Conscientious General Diagnosis of the Conditions of the Country and Its Foreign Policy

November 27th, 1922, Senate, Rome

◆　◆　◆

Honorable Senators, I have listened with deep interest and attention to all the speeches touching upon various subjects which have been delivered in this hall. The Ministers directly concerned can answer to the different individual questions. I shall limit myself to confuting some of the statements which can be said to be of a general order. Of course if the vote of the Senate be unanimous, it will please me— (Laughter)—but you must not believe that unanimity flatters me excessively. I entertain a thorough contempt for those who have more or less clamorously sided with me in these last days. They are so often the kind of people who follow the fair wind and are ready to tumble headlong over to the other side when the wind changes direction. (Laughter.) I prefer sincere enemies to doubtful friends.

Of the speeches delivered in this hall some have a particular importance, as for instance that, generally optimistic, of Senator Conti, which reminded me of the analogous speech, also optimistic, delivered in the Chamber by the Hon. Buozzi. This favorable view of economic conditions in Italy, coming thus from a head of the proletariat and a head of the great Italian industries, is a curious coincidence and certainly of good omen.

A Neat Surgical Operation. I owe a special answer to Senator Albertini. I admire his firm faith in pure Liberalism, but I take the liberty to remind him that Constitutionalism in England, Liberalism in France, in fact all the ideas and doctrines which have in common the name of Liberalism, spring out of a fierce revolutionary travail without which, today, Senator Albertini would not, very probably, have been able to pay these tributes to pure Liberalism.

How was it possible to find a way out of this internal crisis, which every day was becoming more alarming and distressing? A temporary and transitional Ministry was no longer possible. It did not solve the problem; it hardly delayed it. Consequently in two-, three- or six-months' time at the most, with that mobility of opinions and desires that characterized certain Parliamentary circles, we should have found ourselves where we were at the beginning, with nothing gained but the failure which would have aggravated the crisis. (Hear, hear!)

After having thought over the matter deeply, therefore, and having clearly realized the ironic paradox, becoming every day more manifest, of the existence of two States—one the actual State itself and the other which nobody succeeded in defining—I said to myself at a certain moment that only a neat surgical operation could make one compact State of the two and save the fortunes of the nation.

Senator Albertini must not think that this decision was other than the result of long meditation; he must not think that I had not well considered all the dangers and risks of this illegal action. I willed it deliberately. I dare to say more than this—I forced it on. To my mind there was no other way except by revolution to revive a political class grown enormously tired and discouraged in all its sections; and since experience teaches something, or ought to teach something, to intelligent men, I at once set limits and established rules for my action. I have not gone beyond a certain point, I did not in the least become intoxicated by victory, nor did I take advantage of it. Who could have prevented me from closing Parliament? Who could have prevented me from proclaiming a Dictatorship with two or three men? Who could withstand me? Who could have withstood a movement which consisted not only in 300,000 membership cards but in 300,000 rifles? Nobody. It was I who, for love of our country, said that it was necessary to subordinate impulse, sentiment and personal ambition to the supreme interests of the nation; and it was I who put the movement at once on constitutional lines.

I have formed a Ministry with men from all parties in the House. I did not hesitate to include a member of the old Cabinet. I gave importance to technical efficiency and paid no attention to political labels. I formed a Coalition Ministry, and I presented it to the Chamber. I asked for its judgment and its vote, and I found that Chamber a little changed. But when I found out that not less than thirty-three orators had presented thirty-six orders of the day, I said to myself that perhaps it was not necessary to abolish Parliament, but that the country would be glad to see it enjoying a holiday for a certain period. (Laughter.) I have, therefore, no intention of dismissing the Chamber, of destroying all the fruits of the Liberal revolution. I can boast of all this philosophically from a point of view which might almost be called negative. But philosophy must be silent in the face of political necessity. Let us speak frankly! What is this Liberalism, this Liberalism put into practice? Because if there is anyone who believes that, to be a true Liberal, it is necessary to give some hundreds of irresponsible people, fanatics and scoundrels, the power of ruining 40 million Italians, I refuse absolutely to give them this power. (Applause.) Gentlemen, I have no fetishes, and where the interests of the country are concerned the Government has the right to intervene. If it did not do so, it would be inadequate the first time and the next time suicidal.

Respect for the Constitution. I do not intend to deviate from the Constitution or to improvise. The example of other revolutions has shown me that there are some fundamental principles in the life of the people that must be respected. (Hear, hear!) I do not intend that national discipline shall be any longer merely a word. I do not intend that the law shall be any longer a blunt weapon. (Hear, hear!) I do not intend that liberty shall degenerate into license. I do not intend, either, to remain above the fray among those who love, who work for, and who are ready to sacrifice themselves for the nation, or, on the other hand, among those who are ready to do the reverse.

It was for just such a foolish "Rolandism" that this last Government failed. One cannot remain above the fray when the moral forces which are the foundation of the national community are at stake; and nobody can say that a national policy, understood thus, is reactionary. For me all these names of Left and Right, of Conservative, Aristocracy and Democracy are so many empty academic terms. They serve occasionally to distinguish, but more often to confuse.

I shall not follow an anti-proletariat policy, for reasons national, and other than national. We do not want to oppress the proletariat; we do not want to drive it back into humiliating conditions of life. On the contrary we want to elevate it materially and spiritually; but not because we think that the masses, the populace, could create a special type of civilization in the future. Let us leave this kind of ideology to those who profess themselves to be ministers of this mysterious religion. The reasons for which we wish to follow a policy of proletarian welfare are quite different. They lie in the interests of the nation; they are dictated by the reality of facts, by the conviction that no nation can be united and at peace if 20 million workmen are condemned to live in humiliating and inadequate conditions of life. And it may be, nay, it is certain, that our labor policy—or rather anti-demagogic policy, because we cannot promise the paradise we do not possess—will ultimately prove to be much more useful to those same working classes than the other policy which, like an oriental mirage, has hypnotized and mystified them into a vain attitude of waiting. (Approval.)

The Military Organization of Fascism. "What will you do with the military organization of Fascism?" I have been asked. This military organization gave Rome an imposing spectacle. There were 52,000 Blackshirts, and they left Rome within the twenty-four hours prescribed by me. They obey. I dare even to go further and to say that they have the mysticism of obedience! I do not intend to disperse these exuberant forces, not only for the sake of Fascism itself, but in the interests of the nation. What I shall impose upon Fascism is the discontinuance of all the acts for which there is now no necessity— (Hear, hear!)—those small, individual and collective acts of violence which are rather humiliating to everyone, which are often the result of local situations and could with difficulty be associated with the big problems of the different Italian parties. I am sure that what might be called "illegal Fascism," now happily on the decline, will soon end altogether. This is one of the conditions of that pacification to which my friend Senator Bellini alluded; but in order that this pacification may succeed, the other side must also cease their ambushes and acts of violence.

Foreign Policy. I thank the Senate for not having dwelt too much on foreign policy. I am particularly glad that Fascism has universally accepted with enthusiasm my firm decision as regards the application of treaties, because if I do not allow illegality in internal policy, still less shall I allow it in foreign affairs. (Hear, hear!) So let it be clear to all inside this hall and out. Foreign policy will be in the hands of one

man alone, of the man who has the honor of representing and direct-
ing it; because there cannot be an unlimited division and diffusion of
responsibility, and foreign policy is too difficult and delicate a matter
to be thrown as occupation to those who have nothing better to do.
(Laughter.)

I can then tell the Hon. Barzilai that I shall keep the Ministry for
Foreign Affairs for myself. At bottom the Ministry of the Interior is a
Ministry of Police, and I am glad to be the head of the police. I am not
in the least ashamed of it. On the contrary, I hope that all Italian citizens, forgetting certain atavisms, will recognize in the police one of
the most necessary forces for the welfare of our social existence. But,
above all, I intend to follow a line of foreign policy which will not be
adventurous, while, at the same time, it will not be characterized by
self-sacrifice. (Strong approval.) Certainly miracles are not to be expected in this field, as it is impossible to cancel in a conversation, even
in a dramatic one of half an hour, a policy which has been the result
of other conditions and of another period of time.

I think that foreign policy should have as its supreme aim the
maintenance of peace. This is a fine ideal, especially after a war that
has lasted four years. Our policy, therefore, will not be that of the Imperialists who seek the impossible, while, at the same time, it will not
necessarily rest upon the negative formula according to which one
should never have recourse to force. It is well to keep the possibility
of war in sight; it cannot be discarded *a priori*, because in that case
we should find ourselves disarmed with the other nations in arms.
(Great applause.)

But I have no illusions, for, in accordance with my temperament, I
disdain all easy optimism. People who see things through rose-colored glasses make me laugh; I often pity them. I think, however, I have
already succeeded in something, and in no small thing either, which
will have no small results. That is to say, I think I have succeeded in
making the Allies and other peoples of Europe, who had not yet attained a true vision of Italy, see her as she really is. Not as something
vaguely prehistoric, not the Italy of monuments and libraries—all
most respectable things—but Italy as I see her born under my eyes,
the Italy of today, overflowing with vitality, prepared to give herself a
new lease of life, pregnant with serenity and beauty; an Italy which
does not live like a parasite on the past, but is prepared to build up

her own future with her own forces and through her own work and martyrdom.

This is the Italy which has now flashed, be it ever so vaguely, before the eyes of the representatives of other nations, who henceforward must be convinced, whether they wish it or not, that Italy does not intend to follow in the wake of others, but intends to vindicate her rights with dignity, and with no less dignity to protect her interests. (Approval.)

God and the People. I have been admonished in turn by all those who have spoken in this hall. They have said to me: "The responsibility which you take is enormously heavy." Yes! I know it and I feel it. Sometimes, intensified by a deep and vibrating expectancy, it almost crushes me. At these times I have to gather all my force, to arm myself with all my determination, in order to keep before me the interests and the future of our country. Well I know that it is not my interests that are at stake. Certainly, if I do not succeed I am a broken man. These are not experiments that can be tried twice in a lifetime. But my person is of little value. Not to succeed would not mean much to me personally, but it would be infinitely serious for the nation. (Hear, hear!) I intend to take the helm of the ship, and I do not intend to yield it to anybody. But I shall not refuse to take on board all those who wish to form my crew, all those who wish to work with me, who will give me advice and suggestions, who will, in a word, give me their invaluable and indispensable cooperation.

In the other Chamber I invoked the help of God. In this—and I hope my words will not be taken as mere rhetoric—I shall invoke the Italian people. In doing this I might feel that I was walking in the steps of Mazzini, who made a union between God and the people. But if, as I hope and earnestly desire, the people will be disciplined, laborious, and proud of this their glorious country, I feel I shall not fail to arrive at my goal! (Ovation; the Ministers and many Senators advance to congratulate the orator.)

I Remain the Head of Fascism, Although the Head of the Italian Government

December 12th, 1922, before the Fascists in London

◆　◆　◆

Fascists! You must feel that in this last month the Italian people have raised themselves considerably in the eyes of all the other nations. Everybody knows now that a new and vigorous Italy was born in those historic days of October. Remember that the revolution was great, but that it is not over, indeed that it has hardly begun. Hard tasks and heavy responsibilities await us. I remain the head of Fascism, although the head of the Government. Beneath these official clothes, which I wear as a duty, I shall keep the Fascist uniform, just as I wore it before His Majesty when he summoned me to form a new Cabinet.

Fascist Italy, I assure you, is in very strong hands. All our enemies know that every attempt at revolt will be inexorably crushed. The old Italy is dead and will not come to life again. The men who gave their lives in the war will prevent it; those who fell in the Fascist war, no less sacred and necessary, will prevent it; the living will prevent it. We, here and everywhere, are ready for any battle so that we may uphold the foundations of our race and of our history. The time has come to face serenely the sons of other nations. The era of renunciations and obligations is past; the head of the Government tells you this. You asked me to come here upon this occasion of the inauguration of the London section of the Fascist Party. I present you with your banner; keep it as you keep alive the flame of that faith for which so many fine young men have died, keep it for the fortunes of Italy and Fascism.

Our Task in History Is to Make a United State of the Italian Nation

January 2nd, 1923, Ministerial Reception in Chigi Palace, Rome

In answer to the Hon. Teofilo Rossi, Minister of Industry and Commerce, who had concluded his address to the President by saying: "The victorious Greeks returning from Troy through the storm cried: 'Nil desperandum Teucro duce et auspice Teucro.'[56] We in our turn will say: 'Nil desperandum while at the helm of the State there is a man like Benito Mussolini.'"

◆　◆　◆

Dear colleagues, let me first of all say how happy I am that we should have met in these magnificent rooms, which furnish evidence of the strength and beauty of our race, and are also a testimony of our victory, as, if I am not mistaken, these were the apartments of an enemy's Embassy.[57]

I was very much touched by the words spoken just now by our colleague Rossi. The nation as a whole is not deceived, and follows with brotherly sympathy the work of our Government. It is aware of the difficulties we have to overcome: difficulties which arise from the double work of demolition and reconstruction which we have undertaken simultaneously. The nation, little by little, is being restored to order. There are more than ten thousand communes in Italy, and

---

[56] "There is no need to despair with Teucer as our leader and protector."
[57] At the time, Chigi Palace (Palazzo Chigi) was the residence of the Italian Minister for Foreign Affairs, but from 1878 to 1916, it was the residence of the Austro-Hungarian Ambassador to Italy.

there is no reason to fear a catastrophe because there is a quarrel, without any particular positive importance, in one of them during the critical days of Saturday and Sunday.

All this does preoccupy me, however, and I intend by every means possible to get the nation back into a state of general discipline that will be above all sects, factions and parties.

There was an Italian people who had not yet become a nation; the travail of fifty years of history and, above all, the last war has made them a nation. The task in history which awaits us is this: to make a State of this nation, that is to say, a moral idea which is personified and expressed in a system of individual, responsible hierarchies composed of men who, from the first to the last, feel it a pride and a privilege to fulfil their duty.

This work, seen from the standpoint of historical development, cannot be completed in two months and probably not even in two years. But this is the direction in which our Government is working, and every decision we make and every act we achieve is guided by the necessity of establishing one united State, which will be the only depositary of our history and of the future and the strength of the Italian nation.

It is a difficult and arduous undertaking. But life would not be worth living if we did not face these tasks, and if we had not the satisfaction of having met them all the more serenely for their difficulty.

No! I am certain that we shall not frustrate the legitimate hopes of the Italian people. We can and we will adopt a policy of wisdom and severity toward the people and toward ourselves. We must foster the ideals of the nation, and deal relentlessly with the slightest manifestation of lack of discipline.

I, too, should like to quote from the tales of ancient Greece. When the Spartan mothers presented their departing sons with their shields, it was with these words: "Either with this or on it." Now I should like our program to be inspired by this idea, for with this program, and with this only, shall we win.

Through our efforts, our work and our suffering will rise that powerful, prosperous and peaceful Italy of which we dream, which we long for and desire to see! Long live Italy!

The Advance in the Ruhr District

January 15th, 1923, Cabinet, Rome

◆　◆　◆

Honorable Colleagues, the most important event of these last few days in the international world has been the French advance on the Ruhr. It is well to establish clearly the attitude of Italy with regard to this advance, since, for political reasons and also for reasons connected with the Stock Exchange, it has purposely not been properly estimated.

It is necessary to go back to the Conference of Paris, and the rejection of Bonar Law's proposals on the part of Italy, France and Belgium, in order to understand the line of conduct adopted by the Italian Government. It is a fact that each one of the Powers in the Entente has taken up an attitude of its own, due to its own particular conditions. Without taking into consideration the Americans, who have withdrawn their troops from the Rhine, this is the position of the Powers.

England has not joined with France, but has not decided, at any rate up to the present, to recall her troops from German soil, nor has she changed in her friendly attitude toward France, as was set forth by the most recent communications from the Foreign Office.

France, interested in the problem of reparations, has, upon the basis of the deliberations of the Commission appointed to enquire into this question, sent into the Ruhr a Board of Control for the production of coal and, later, troops for the purpose of protection.

Belgium has afforded France some military cooperation and undivided political support.

Italy has only given political and technical support, sending her engineers to the Ruhr. Our country could not isolate herself without committing a very grave mistake. She could not exclude herself entirely from any operation of control taking place in a region of coalfields, and, therefore, of fundamental importance in European and Italian economics.

As regards the project for a continental alliance directed against England, such an idea simply does not exist. The Italian Government never suggested such a thing, and, in any case, would never have been able to consider the possibility of a continental union against England, both on account of her importance in the economic life of the Continent and of existing relations between Italy and that country.

It is true, on the contrary, that the Italian Government had advised France to limit, as far as possible, the military character of the advance in the Ruhr district, and not to reject all possibilities of agreement in this burning question. But if this understanding, which would give peace to Europe, were to be realized, it is the opinion of Italy that it could not come about without the cooperation of England. Italy, which has no coal, cannot afford the luxury of renunciations and isolation, but it is as well to make it clear—because it is the truth—that Italian policy upon this occasion, as upon all others, is inspired by considerations of a general nature, as decided in the Memorandum of London, for the protection of Italian interests and of European economics generally. The Italian Government thinks that if there is a possibility of agreement—and it works in this direction—it would be a grave mistake on the part of Germany to refuse it.

It seems as if a detente between the French command and some of the industrial magnates of the Ruhr district has already taken place. As for the mass of the workmen, it appears as if they do not intend to put insuperable difficulties in the way of the work of control.

The payment of the quota for January 15th is postponed until the end of the month. There are, therefore, fifteen days of useful time, sufficient to mend the situation. It does not seem improbable that the French will support the Italian project presented at London upon the subject of reparations.

As for the attitude of the Soviet Government, it appears to be very circumspect, and has not changed from that previously manifested, though only in words, toward the German proletariat.

From Lausanne comes satisfactory news. I have the pleasure of announcing that, in some of the very delicate questions which seemed to be leading to a rupture, such as that of minorities, if an agreement has been reached, it has been due to the wise and level-headed work of the Italian Delegation.

(Without discussion, the declarations of the Prime Minister are unanimously approved.)

The Grand Council of Fascism. My colleagues in the Cabinet will certainly have read with attention the deliberations of the Grand Council of Fascism, and have noticed the importance of their character.

It is an essentially political organization, which, however, does not encroach in any way upon the sphere of action of the Government, represented by the Cabinet. In fact none of the legislative measures passed or to be passed by the Cabinet were made the subject of discussion by the Grand Council of Fascism. All its decisions are of a purely political nature. Thus they have definitely settled the character of the national militia. They have constituted the organization which is to establish relations between Fascists and Nationalists, as well as those between Fascism and the other parties which loyally co-operate with the Government and the organizations of employers already in existence before the formation of the analogous Fascist groups.

Important also is the vote by which the associations of ex-soldiers (including the disabled) who have entered the sphere of the State have been asked to give men for the purposes of administration. The declaration of loyal devotion to the Monarchy is both magnificent and solemn, and dispels every little misunderstanding of interested dabblers in politics on that score, for whom the warning that closed the proceedings of the Great Council came opportunely—the warning, that is to say, that the Government—note, the Government—will inexorably crush every attempt at direct or indirect opposition to its authority.

The Grand Council of Fascism has also sent messages to the working people of Italy, who are in the process of re-establishing active discipline among themselves, and who accept the provisions of the Government, even the hardest, because they are sure that they are inspired by purely national necessity.

Thus the essentially historic function of the Grand Council of

Fascism at this moment is clearly outlined. The Council will support and safeguard the action of the Government, and perform in the party and in the nation the work of general political orientation which must serve as a base for the work of the Government itself. (The Council of Ministers approves the declarations of the Prime Minister.)

The Government of Speed

January 19th, 1923, Motor Transport Company Headquarters, Rome

◆

I warmly thank Commendatore De Cupis and all the workmen—I was going to say my colleagues—for the warm welcome I have received. If my minutes were not numbered, I should like, here in the presence of the "controllers of the steering wheel," to sing the praises of speed, in this the epoch of speed. The times in which we live no longer allow of a sedentary egoistical life; everything must be on the go, everybody must raise the standard of his activity, both in the offices and in the factories where the work is done—(Applause)—and the Government, which I have the honor to represent, is the Government of speed, that is to say, we get rid of all that is stagnant in our national life.

Formerly the bureaucracy dozed over deferred decisions, today it must proceed with the maximum of rapidity. (Applause.) If we all go ahead with this energy, good-will and cheerfulness we shall surmount the crisis, which for that matter is already partly overcome.

I am pleased to see that Rome also is waking up and can offer us sights such as these works. I maintain that Rome can become an industrial center. The Romans must be the first to disdain to live solely upon their memories. The Coliseum and the Forum are glories of the past, but we must build up the glories of today and of tomorrow. We belong to the generation of builders who, by work and discipline, with hands and brains, desire to reach the ultimate and longed-for goal, the greatness of the future nation, which will be a nation of producers and not of parasites.

The March of Events on the Ruhr: The Position of Italy

January 23rd, 1923, Cabinet, Rome

◆　◆　◆

Honorable Colleagues, since the last meeting of the Cabinet, the situation on the Ruhr has become more complicated, and this also from the social point of view, as the result of the closing down of the factories and the outbreak of strikes in the mines and public services of the occupied zones.

In order to understand the attitudes of the different Powers and the fact that these attitudes have not undergone any changes worthy of note, it is necessary to summarize briefly the events of these last few days of high tension, political and economic.

The period of time granted for the Moratorium having elapsed on January 15th, France and Belgium have caused a Mission of Control to be sent to the mines in the Ruhr district, escorted by protecting troops, and have extended the area of territory occupied in the Ruhr district as far as Dortmund. On January 16th, the French Government gave notice that the industrial magnates on the Ruhr had declared that they had received orders from the German Government not to hand over any more coal. The German Minister for Foreign Affairs himself communicated these instructions to our Ambassador at Berlin.

France and Belgium were not, therefore, receiving any more coal, even when payment was made in advance. In the face of the German resistance, the French and Belgian troops have proceeded to requisition the coal deposits at the pitheads, the factories and the railway stations, and have also taken other serious steps of a political and military order. Italian experts, sent only to take part in economic operations of control, received orders to limit their cooperation to that which concerned coercive measures of a political nature.

Such an attitude was clearly faced and decided in Paris. On the strength of the decision made on December 26th by the Commission of Reparations, which reported the failure of Germany, as regards Italy also, to supply wood, France and Belgium decided to proceed to the exploitation of the Crown and Communal forests in the Rhine territory. Germany had, besides, made it known that coal supplies and cattle would be refused to France and Belgium, by way both of reparation and restitution.

The Commission of Reparations in its decision of January 16th verified this intentional failure on the part of Germany from January 12th, and notified it to the Government. As a result of this, France and Belgium decided to take possession of the west customs frontier of Germany in the occupied zone. The Italian Government took over control of the customs and also of the forests, this being included among the measures which the Italian Memorandum had reserved as a security in the case of the concession of the Moratorium; but it asked the French Government what was going to be the extent to which the action was to be carried. The French Government replied that the occupation of the Ruhr was not of a military character, but was for the protection of French technical bodies, which were very numerous in the occupied area. The Italian Delegate, who was already on the High Commission of the Rhine, which directs the exploitation and also the control of the mines, has received orders to take part in those deliberations which have an economic and financial character, and to abstain from attending those which are political.

As I said before, the attitudes of the Great Powers have not altered to any great extent. England seems officially uninterested in what happens on the Ruhr, but this has not prevented the English Representative on the Rhine High Commission from declaring in the name of his Government that he will be present at the deliberations, abstaining from recording his vote when he thinks it best; but he adds, also, that his Government will not oppose the carrying out of the provisions in the zone occupied by the English troops which still remain on the Rhine. As you see, it is not England's intention to accentuate the difference between her policy and that which is, at present, adopted by France.

Mediation on the part of Italy was spoken of, which might have led later to a direct Anglo-Italian intervention, both at Berlin and Paris. An offer of real mediation does not exist, and could not be made without the certainty that it would be accepted with a certain favor. It would be a grave mistake to expose Italian policy to a failure of this sort. It is a fact that the Italian Government did warn the Germans of the danger of the blind-alley situation in which she has voluntarily placed herself, and in which she seems determined to stay. She also called the attention of France, in a friendly manner, to the complications, not only economic but also political and social, which might arise from the occupation of the Ruhr.

The Work of the Italian Government. Matters standing thus, the Italian Government cannot at present change its attitude, because no step it took now would alter the general situation or exercise a preponderating influence in the decisions of the Governments most involved. The opinion of the Italian Government is that the situation on the Ruhr has not yet reached the stage at which a solution must necessarily be found, and only when that moment arrives will it be able, perhaps, to have an influence on the situation itself.

As for the Moratorium which President Poincaré has decided to propose to the Germans, in view of the fast-approaching date of payment, January 31st, it is worthy of note that it will include some of the points made in the Italian Memorandum of London, namely the two years' Moratorium and the German internal loan.

As far as America is concerned, having once withdrawn her troops from the Rhine, she has not altered her policy of neutral inactivity.

One understands that the events in the Ruhr district have caused a general uneasiness over the whole of Europe, especially in the countries which form the Little Entente. Rumors which spoke of mobilization and the concentration of troops upon some of the frontiers have proved unfounded and exaggerated. As regards Russia, beyond reports of certain political activities on the part of the Third International, carried on with a view to taking advantage socially of the events on the Ruhr, there is no definite news of serious preparations for military intervention on a large scale. At Lausanne, the reaction of the situation on the Ruhr is being felt, and is arousing an increased intransigence on the part of Turkey.

To sum up: The policy of Italy must be inspired first of all by the defense of her own interests, though, at the same time, due note must be taken of considerations and needs of a general order. It is a question whether, by a more exact valuation of the conditions put forward in the Italian Memorandum of London, the grave complications which exist today would not have been avoided. At any rate the Italian Government will take careful and speedy measures to avoid any further difficulties and re-establish as soon as possible a release of tension throughout Europe, which might make it possible to face the problem of reparations and debts under other conditions.

(The Cabinet at the end express entire approval of the line of foreign policy adopted by the Prime Minister.)

The Ruhr, the Conference of Lausanne,
and the Port of Memel

February 1st, 1923, Cabinet, Rome

◆ ◆ ◆

With reference to foreign affairs, the situation, as far as Italy is concerned, cannot be said to have altered much in the interval which has elapsed between the last Cabinet meeting and today.

The German resistance on economic grounds has provoked aggravation of the measures—both military and political—which are being taken by France and Belgium, but from which Italy, following her previous line of conduct, has kept apart.

The complications which were—or could have been—feared, so far have not occurred. Fresh factors have not entered into the close duel which is being fought on the Ruhr. Russia has not altered her attitude as a State, although the dominating party continues to give clamorous verbal demonstrations of solidarity with the German proletariat.

The serious disquietude which had been manifested by the Powers of the Little Entente is diminishing. There had been rumors—more or less without foundation and spread, perhaps, with the object of producing complications—of plans for repeating in Hungary what France had done on the Ruhr, which were attributed to one State or another. These have given Italy the opportunity of confirming and clearly establishing her attitude of opposition to any movement which could extend the conflict to other zones or give the opportunity of attacking the validity of the treaties of peace already concluded.

The Italian Government has been and is following attentively the coal situation on the Ruhr, above all as regards its reaction on other events. I can say that all internal measures, reduction of the train services, including those from abroad, and contracts for fresh supplies, have been quickly and diligently carried through, because, whatever may happen, no paralysis of our industrial activity or of our communications must result. In connection with the supplies of raw materials, I have the pleasure to announce to the Cabinet that the Italian Government has succeeded in concluding a favorable agreement with the Polish Government for oil.

As I said last time, the events on the Ruhr have had the most serious consequences in the developments at the Conference of Lausanne, which has now arrived at its last stage. The Italian Delegation has carried out successful work there with the object of obtaining peace in the East.

The Italian Government has not been among the last to recognize the legitimate rights of Turkey, and thinks today that it would not be in her interests to entrench herself in a position of absolute intransigence. It may be that Turkey has not realized the extensive program that was laid down by the Grand National Assembly of Angora, but it cannot be denied that a great part of that program has been put into execution, since the Turks from Angora have returned not only to Smyrna but to Constantinople and Adrianople, and have got their way, it can be said, in questions of the highest importance, such as that of the domination of the Straits and that of Capitulations.

Taken as a whole, although the general situation continues to be very critical, there seems to be a small ray of light upon the horizon. The action of the Italian Government is directed decidedly toward a policy of general peace.

As regards the question of Memel, the Italian Government has pursued a temperate policy, inspired by principles of equity and justice. It is not possible to do less than recognize the rights of Lithuania over that port, but the Lithuanian Government cannot be allowed to substitute itself for the Allied Powers in deciding its fate.

We, then, have remained in an attitude of solidarity with the Allies in the measures taken for facing the situation there. But we have, on the other hand, tried effectively to reduce those measures to the necessary minimum, avoiding those of such a nature as to provoke further complications.

Ratification of the Washington Treaty of Naval Disarmament

February 6th, 1923, Chamber of Deputies, Rome

◆ ◆ ◆

Honorable Members, I do not think that it is worthwhile losing time in a general discussion upon the qualities of men, good and bad, and upon the question as to whether the war of 1914 will be the last or the one before the last. That would be perfectly idle and would only lead to academic discussions. Let us, instead, turn our attention more practically to the Project of Law which I have presented.

The Convention of Washington was closed a year ago. Now the delay in the ratification of the treaty on the part of Italy has already had ambiguous and, I should almost say, unfavorable consequences in the international world. It will be a good thing, then, to proceed at once to complete this act.

The Conference at Washington shared the fate of all the conferences. It opened with great hopes, flashing before our eyes the possibility of eternal peace. Then the concrete results frustrated these hopes. I confess that I do not believe in perpetual and universal peace. In the life of the peoples, notwithstanding ideals—noble and worthy of respect—there exist the permanent factors of race, and the greatness and decadence of nations, which lead to differences often only settled by a recourse to arms. Now it is not a case of weighing these conventions with a view to peace; they represent a breath, a pause, and it is useless to enquire if they have been laid down for idealistic or for business reasons. In any case I declare that Italy did well to adhere to this Convention. If she had not done so, we should have appeared in the eyes of the world as Imperialists and jingoists, which is far from what we have in our hearts and minds. The fact that the Government asks the Chamber for this ratification gives an idea of the general trend of the Fascist foreign policy. (Applause.)

(The ratification of the Treaty is approved of without discussion, only the Communists being against it.)

Message to the Italians in America Upon the Occasion of the Signing of the Convention for the Laying of Cables Between Italy and the American Continent

February 6th, 1923, Rome

◆ ◆ ◆

The National Government, which has worked indefatigably for three months to set the country going upon the path to better fortunes, has in these days signed the Convention for the laying of cables which are to put our country into communication with you, who represent it in the numerous, rich and patriotic colonies beyond the Atlantic.

The enthusiasm for this work, so necessary to our life as a great nation, seemed at one time to have died down, but today with the rise of youth upon the scenes of Italian politics, that which it seemed would be relegated to some remote future has been transformed into a concrete and almost immediate reality. It is not you, who suffer almost more than any the pangs of homesickness for our adored country, who need to be shown the usefulness and necessity of this undertaking, which will be carried through in the shortest space of time possible. It will render frequent, daily and, above all, free the communications between the 40 million Italians who live in our beautiful peninsula and the 6 million who live beyond the ocean. All the Italians who can give financial and moral support must co-operate so that the undertaking may succeed. The Italian Government does not appeal in vain to its emigrant citizens, because it knows that distance makes the love of their country stronger and more intense.

The cables, which in two or three years will bind together Italy and the Americas across the boundless ocean, are like a gigantic arm which the country stretches out to her distant sons to draw them to her and to make them share more intimately her griefs and her joys, her work, her greatness and her glory.

For the Carrying Out of the Treaty of Rapallo

February 8th, 1923, Prefatory remarks to the Deputies,
accompanying the Project of Law presented by the Hon.
Mussolini, Minister for Foreign Affairs and Prime Minister

◆　◆　◆

Honorable Members, last November I began my statement to Parliament of the program of the National Government as regards foreign policy with the following words:

> The fundamental principle upon which our foreign policy is based is that treaties of peace, once signed and ratified, must be carried out whether they are good or bad. A self-respecting nation cannot follow another course. Treaties are not eternal or irreparable; they are chapters and not epilogues in history; to put them into practice means to try them. If in the course of execution they are proved to be absurd, this in itself may constitute the new element which may open the possibility of a further examination of the respective positions.

The preceding Government had undertaken to present to Parliament the Agreements concluded at Santa Margherita, and signed at Rome on last October 23rd. This undertaking I now fulfil.

These Agreements, contrary to what has been stated by someone, do not contain any new political pledges on the part of Italy, but regulate the relations between the Commune of Zara and the surrounding territory of Dalmatia, make clear some recognized rights on the part of citizens who are Italian by option, and endeavor, by means of friendly agreements, to find a possibility of giving and assuring a peaceful and industrious life to the troubled city of Fiume.

Owing to the way in which it is drawn up—whether on account of its diffuseness in those clauses which touch upon territorial questions, and its brevity in others, or whether on account of the seeming precedence given to the task of the commissions which ought, according to the letter of the treaty itself, to proceed exclusively to the settlement of territorial questions, while for the commissions to which were entrusted the settlement of other questions, limits were established, *a priori*, of a certain amplitude (Article VI)—the Treaty of Rapallo has given Yugoslavia the opportunity of maintaining that it was necessary first to effect the evacuation of the territories over which the sovereignty of the Serbo-Croat-Slovak Kingdom had been recognized, and then of proceeding to the stipulations of the agreements for the regulation of the new relations between the two countries.

They tried to justify this with arguments of a political nature. That is to say, they saw, in the first place, that the opposition met with in various Italian political spheres to the transactions concluded at Rapallo had stirred up the discontent and opposition of the Yugoslavs to the treaty; secondly, that the suspended execution of the Territorial Clauses, evidently attributed to some Italian parties, had given the impression to the Yugoslavs that Italy did not want to proceed to the carrying out of the treaty; thirdly, that, in consequence, the parliamentary opposition to a policy of friendliness toward Italy had become very marked, and rendered extremely difficult the adoption of direct provisions for the favorable regulation of these relations; and lastly, that if, instead, the prearranged course had been followed—that of proceeding, say, first to the evacuation of the territories—a radical change of position would have been realized, which would have allowed of the conclusion of more favorable agreements.

In Italy, on the other hand, the discontent was increased by an idea, entertained by many, that the new State, which had also arisen as the result of Italy's victorious war, ought to give to the citizens, and in Italian interests, privileges no less great than those granted by the Austro-Hungarian Monarchy, not taking into account that a national State, newly formed, may have particular exigencies and susceptibilities. The contrast of such opposite tendencies ended by creating in the relations between the two countries an atmosphere of uneasiness, which has at times reached an acute stage. And in Italy, the intransigence of some circles found justification, above all, in the weakness of the Governments, inasmuch as they had ground for fearing that all our rights would be trodden underfoot the moment we no longer had tangible securities in our hands. By the Agreements which are now handed to us, the Government of Belgrade has recognized the necessity of determining the regime which will have to regulate the reciprocal relations of the new boundaries before passing to the definite execution of the Territorial Clauses.

As for the substance of the Agreements, it is my conviction that their greater or less efficacy will depend upon the spirit in which they are carried out, because never, perhaps, has it been so true, as in this case, that the most perfect pacts become empty formulas if a doubtful or hostile spirit is brought to their execution.

I observe, in conclusion, that the uncertainty which has been manifested in the foreign policy of Italy as regards the Treaty of Rapallo has created a situation unfavorable to her, often preventing her from taking a decided attitude, which would have been in her interest, in most essential questions of a general nature, and making her appear in a light contradictory to her position as a Great Power.

My intense, though brief, experience of Government has shown me that it is not possible to carry out a strong foreign policy without having decisive and clearly defined attitudes as regards the other States.

Italy must get away from this weak situation, must regain her full liberty and efficiency of action also in this sphere. We shall, therefore, carry out the treaty resolutely and loyally, exacting its scrupulous observance. We shall watch over this as is our right and duty. And we wait for time to pass definite judgment upon the soundness and the fate of today's Conventions.

With this understanding, I ask you, Honorable Members, to approve of the following Project of Law:

> Full and entire execution is given to the Agreements and Conventions signed at Rome on October 23rd, 1921, between the Kingdom of Italy and the Kingdom of the Serbs, the Croats and the Slovenes for the execution of the Treaty of Rapallo of November 12th, 1920.

The Agreements of Santa Margherita, Italy, and Yugoslavia

February 10th, 1923, Chamber of Deputies, Rome

◆ ◆ ◆

Honorable Members, with the approval of the Agreements of Santa Margherita, there came to an end what might be called "the Foreign Policy week" of the Italian Government; a week that might also be called pacific, since it began with the ratification of the Convention of Washington, which represents a pause in the great naval armament, and ends with the approval of the Agreements of Santa Margherita, which are the consequence of the Treaty of Rapallo already ratified and partly carried out.

In closing this week of the life of Parliament, I realize that the Chamber has done good work, and that it has during this session undoubtedly raised, in some ways, its prestige in the country. (Comments.) The questions with which the Chamber has dealt are large; they are not concerned with treaties and bills of minor importance, as some have said.

I refuse to embark, as was attempted on the Left, upon the usual discussions of a general character which do not conclude anything. While I am on this bench, the Chamber will not be changed into an electoral meeting.

No Discussion. There is nothing to discuss as regards home policy; that which happens, happens because it is my direct and clear desire and in accordance with my precise orders, and for which I naturally assume full personal responsibility. (Comments.)

It is useless, therefore, to go to the police officials, because the orders are mine. It does not affect me to know of the existence of a plot, in the sense usually attributed to that word; this will be settled by competent authorities. But there are those who thought that they would fight with impunity against the State and Fascism. By now they must be disillusioned; and they will be more so in the future. The difference between the Liberal and Fascist States consists precisely in this: that the Fascist State does not defend itself only, but attacks, and those who intend to slander it abroad and to undermine its authority at home must be warned that their maneuvers bring with them unforeseen consequences. The enemies of the Fascists must not be surprised if I treat them severely as enemies.

As regards the speech of Filippo Turati, my old fighting scent did not deceive me when a few days ago I refused the advances which came to me from that quarter through Gregorio Nofri, who, having been in Russia, felt the overpowering necessity of becoming anti-Bolshevist. Strayed sheep do not enter my fold. I am still faithful to my old tactics. I do not seek anybody. I do not refuse anybody. I put faith above all in my own forces. This is why, lately—after the meeting of the Grand Council of Fascism—I desired that there should be a closer union with those parties with which, fighting on national ground, friendly relations can be established for common work. But all this, let it be said at once, has not been done for parliamentary purposes, but for the sake of cohesion, unity and the pacification of the country.

I agree wholly with that which the Hon. Cavazzoni said yesterday with regard to the eight-hour day. I declared, before a meeting of eight hundred printers, that the eight-hour day represents an inviolable conquest on the part of the working classes. Today there are those who dream of setting on foot a long discussion because opposing ideas are attributed to this and that member of the Cabinet. I give definite notice that the Government, in one of its forthcoming meetings, will decide once and for all the question of the eight-hour day. This having been said, and I hope that everybody will understand also the sense of all I have not said, I pass on to the subject of foreign policy.

A Circumspect Policy of Activity. In the meantime, I cannot accept the statement of the Hon. Lucci, who makes out that I am original. In the first place, he must give me time. In the second, there is no originality in foreign affairs, and I refuse to be original, if this originality would result in the slightest damage to my country. (Applause.) And I cannot accept, either, his too idealistic point of view. I see the world as it really is, that is to say, a world of unbounded egoism. If the world was Arcadia, it would be pleasant to amuse oneself with nymphs and shepherds; but I do not see anything of all this, and even when the more or less respectable standards of great principles are displayed, I see behind them interests which seek for a footing in the world. If all foreign policy were brought into the region of pure idealism, it would certainly not be Italy who would refuse to join in. But it is not so; hence all that the Hon. Lucci says belongs to the music of the most distant spheres. (Laughter.)

When I first took up my position on this bench, there was a moment of trepidation in certain sections of international politics. It was thought that the advent to power of Fascism would mean, at the very least, war with Yugoslavia. After a few months, international opinion is fully reassured. The foreign policy of Fascism cannot be, especially in these historic times, other than extremely circumspect, though at the same time very active.

The nation, having issued from the splendid and blood-stained travail of the war, is now fully intent on the work of building up its political, economic, financial and moral life. To compel it to make an effort which was not absolutely necessary, would be to follow an anti-national and suicidal policy. At London, as at Lausanne, Italian foreign policy has pursued this direction; at Lausanne, above all, the work of the Italian Delegation has been highly appreciated. If peace was not concluded there, it was not the fault, in any way, of Italy.

On the other hand, it is not good to speak too pessimistically of the development of affairs in the Eastern Mediterranean. It must not be thought that a certain harmless showing of teeth, sometimes the result of reciprocal restlessness, means the beginning of a war. I think that if Greece is prudent and the Entente remains firmly united—as in the case of their ships in the port of Smyrna—that Turkey too, since she has realized a large part of the program laid down at Angora, will become reasonable. There is no reason, therefore, to fear military complications in Europe. Still Italy will keep a careful look-out that the disturbances resulting upon the events in the Ruhr district shall not have serious consequences among the countries of the Danube basin.

The situation on the Ruhr is stationary. I declare once again that Italy could not have followed a different line of policy. The time for fine gestures is past, as they are useless. The attitude which was advocated by certain elements on the Left would have been equally useless. We could not have prevented the French from marching on the Ruhr, and we might have encouraged the German resistance. Also the other plan of our mediation could not have been carried out, because no mediation of any kind is possible if it is not asked for and welcomed. (Applause.) Besides, England has limited herself to non-technical participation in the operations on the Ruhr, but has not pushed her difference of opinion with France to the point of withdrawing her troops from the Rhine. It is opportune to add that France has not asked us, up to now, for formal and concrete assistance. Should this happen, it is evident that Italy should reserve to herself the right of exposing all the complex system of the relations between the two countries. (Loud applause.)

The Last Phase of the Adriatic Drama. As to the Agreements of Santa Margherita, of which the Chamber is asked to approve, they represent the last phase of our sad and lamentable Adriatic drama. I could here reply in detail, I could show the Hon. Chiesa, for example, how only yesterday, February 9th, I received a telegram from Belgrade to this effect:

> The Ministry of Yugoslavia communicates that orders have been sent to the authorities of Spalato that the premises of the school shall be evacuated and put at the disposal of the school itself, and that the house which adjoins the Church of the Holy Spirit shall be emptied and handed over.

I could correct other inaccuracies, but it is not my business, it is not worthwhile to descend to the discussion of detail. I am always of the opinion that this Convention must be carried out in order to test it. At the same time, I do not feel like defending, at too great a length, a treaty of which I did not approve when it was concluded, and which I still hold to be, as regards a great many of its clauses, absurd and harmful to Italian interests. But matters, today, stand thus: either the treaty must be definitely enforced or denounced. Since, in present conditions, it cannot be denounced, for that would mean the reopening of all difficulties, there remains nothing but its loyal and scrupulous application on our part, as loyal and scrupulous as the application on the part of Belgrade will have to be. (Applause.)

To wait indefinitely for events which may occur is the worst of systems at this moment. It is necessary to put an end to a situation which has become unbearable and which gave us all the disadvantages without assuring us of what might be the advantages of clearly defined relations. Moreover it is difficult to understand why the Treaty of Rapallo, of all the treaties which have been made from the beginning of history, should be the only one irreparable and perpetual. No treaty has ever withstood new conditions of affairs developed by the progress of time. The essential thing, to my mind, is to place ourselves in such a position that an eventual revision will enable us to vindicate our eternal rights with dignity and power. (Applause.)

The Government in Favor of Fiume and Zara. By the application of the Agreements of Santa Margherita the Fascist Government gives a solemn proof of its probity, its spirit of decision and of absolute loyalty. Belgrade must do the same. Yugoslavia must take into account the intrinsic value of this act, and follow, where the Italians who remain in Dalmatia are concerned, a policy of freedom and judicious action; as a policy which would tend to suppress the Italian element in Dalmatia would not be tolerated by the Fascist Government. (Applause.) By the ratification of these Agreements the Government offers Yugoslavia the opportunity of furthering the economic relations between the two countries.

The Government, which has already done all it can, within the limits of its possibilities, for Fiume and Zara, will continue to work with the utmost energy and diligence for these two cities. The evacuation of Susak having been carried out—and of Susak only, because the Delta and Porto Baros will still be occupied by our troops until Fiume has become juridically a perfect State—Italy will continue to interest herself in the fate of Fiume, so that she may be restored in a short time to her ancient splendor.

As for Zara, her destiny is serious and difficult, and I, for one, understand the tragedy of that city and the suffering of all the Italians scattered in Dalmatia up as far as Cattaro. But Zara, the sentinel of Dalmatia, is ready to bear, with the spirit of absolute national discipline, the completion of the last act of the Adriatic drama.

The Government will meet its needs immediately, because Zara must live, because Zara beyond the Adriatic represents one of the most vital portions of the Italian people. And the people of Zara and Dalmatia may be sure that the Government will watch over their fate with the most loving care. These are not merely words spoken to help them through this difficult time; deeds will follow them.

As for public, national opinion, it is unanimous in feeling that these Agreements had to be applied in order that Italy might be free in the ever-closer international competition, free to carry out a policy of defense of her interests and free to influence with increasing activity the course of events. I think that the best part of the Italian people agree in this line of home and foreign policy. (Applause.)

Questions of Foreign Policy Before the Senate:
The Ruhr, Fiume, Zara, and Dalmatia

February 16th, 1923, Senate, Rome

◆　◆　◆

Honorable Senators, after having written the prefaces and the intro-
ductions to the Bills, and after the speech made in the other branch
of Parliament, I do not think that there remains much to say.

The very rapidity of the discussion itself bears witness to the fact
that all these treaties and agreements are already, in a certain sense,
superseded. By this I do not wish to deny their importance, but it is a
question of treaties and conventions of some time back, and life today
moves at a very great rate. I do not disguise the fact that in continuing
the eternal theory of conferences, people have reason to show a certain skepticism about the likelihood of results. (Laughter.)

Why Italy Intervenes. Senator Crespi tried to carry the discussion
on to general ground—the burning ground of debts and reparations.
He demands new pacts; but there are none. Perhaps there cannot be
any. With reference to a recent appeal for Italy's intervention in this
matter, if responsible members of Governments, and especially those
engaged or interested in the conflict, turned to Italy, the only nation
in the world which, at this moment, is following a policy of peace—
(Applause)—I should not hesitate one moment in answering the appeal.

There is a new factor, Senator Crespi, which it would be a good
thing to take into consideration, though it is one which tends to stifle
rather than arouse enthusiasm. It is that England and the United
States have come to an agreement. England has undertaken to pay

227

her debts to America. It is no good, therefore, for us to entertain too many illusions about the likelihood of a cancellation of our debts. It would be perfectly just, I think, from the strictly moral point of view; but the criteria and principles of absolute morality do not as yet guide the relations of the peoples. (Approval.)

It was said in a foreign Parliament that Italy had attempted to mediate between France and Germany. No such attempt was ever made. My duty was to make investigations in the European capitals, and I have done so. But having gathered that there was no possibility of proceeding in that direction, I drew back, as to continue would have been a great mistake. I think, however, that the crisis has reached its culminating point. It is a question now of knowing whether the Entente still exists and still will exist. (Comments.)

I do not think that I shall be revealing secrets if I say here what meets the eye of anyone who reads the daily news in the papers. Not a single event has occurred, not a single question arisen, without the problem of the unity of action of the Entente having been brought forward. Of necessity in this political situation there can be no improvised action and still less originality. All foreign policies, not excluding that of Russia, which is simply terrifying in form and method, are of a cautious and circumspect nature at this moment. There is no reason why Italy should follow a different course. When it is a question of the interests of our nation and of 40 million inhabitants who have the right to live, it is necessary to be careful about improvisations, and it is necessary to take into account that, besides our wishes, there are also the wishes of others.

If we had coalfields; if we had in some way solved the problem of raw materials; if we could dispose of large reserves of gold in order to keep up the value of our money, we could follow a given policy, even one of generosity toward Germany. But we cannot afford the luxury of prodigality and generosity when we have to toil to carry on life, when we have to summon all our energies to avoid falling into the abyss.

And so you will agree with me, Honorable Members, that Italy could not keep aloof from that which is taking place on the Ruhr, could not deprive herself of participation in an economical and technical capacity. It is always better, in my opinion, to be present, because sometimes complicated problems find unexpected solutions. It was not possible to run the risk capriciously of not being present, in the event—not at all improbable—of an economic agreement, as regards iron and coal, between Germany and France. (Applause.)

Zara and Dalmatia. Coming to the Agreements of Santa Margherita, I understand perfectly the grief and anguish expressed in the words of Senators Tamassia and Tivaroni. Undoubtedly sentiment is a great spiritual force, both in the lives of individuals and of peoples, but it cannot be the one dominating influence of foreign policy.

It is necessary to have the courage to say that Italy cannot remain forever penned up in one sea, even if it is the Adriatic. Beyond the Adriatic there is the Mediterranean and other seas which can interest us. The Treaty of Rapallo was, in my opinion, a lamentable transaction, which was the result of a difficult internal situation and of a foreign policy which was not marked by its excessive autonomy. And here allow me to repeat that a strong and dignified foreign policy cannot be carried out if the nation does not present a daily example of iron discipline. (Approval.) I do not think that these Agreements of Santa Margherita sign the death warrant of Zara and Dalmatia. With the last concessions we have saved the use of the Italian language for our brothers there. Now I think it was Gioberti who said that where the language is spoken there is the nation. For this reason, if these brothers of ours can speak, write and learn in their mother tongue, I think that already one of the foundations of their Italian nationality is saved.

For a decade the Italians of Zara and Dalmatia have resisted the furious attempts at denationalization made by the Hapsburg Monarchy. In those days Italy could not give active assistance to those brothers; now you see that she has another realization of herself. Those brothers of ours, who might have felt themselves forgotten if the Agreements of Santa Margherita were applied by another nation, cannot feel the same when the definite and necessary application of the Treaty of Rapallo is carried out by the Government over which I have the honor of presiding and of which the members are those who won the victory. (Applause.) We firmly believe that the strict and scrupulous application of the Agreements of Santa Margherita on our part, as well as on the part of Yugoslavia, will save the Italian character of Zara and Dalmatia. There is no need for me to repeat that treaties are transactions, and are like the steps of an equilibrist. No treaty is eternal and perpetual; all that is happening today under our eyes gives us clear warning.

The Question of Fiume. We shall then carry out these Agreements immediately and loyally. It must not be thought that the Third Zone is a kind of vast continent, and that in it we have immense forces. It is a question of the territory round Zara and a group of islands; all told, we have only 120 policemen, eighteen custom-house guards, and twenty soldiers. At Susak we have a battalion of infantry. It will be a case of turning them back to the line of Eneo, because until it is known what is to become of Fiume, Porto Baros and the Delta, they will remain under the control of Italian troops. (Applause.) What is this Arbitration Commission? It represents an attempt to bring about the existence of that more or less vital creature, first conceived at Rapallo, known as the Independent State of Fiume. (Laughter.) One thing is certain, at any rate, and that is that there are three Italians on the Commission. And another thing is certain, and that is that it is not absolutely necessary for Fiume to become a new province of the realm. That there should actually be a prefect at Fiume is to me a secondary matter; the important thing is that Fiume shall keep her spirit sound and intact, that she shall remain Italian, and that such means shall be found that shall make her a city which lives in itself and for itself and not only through the largess of the Italian State. (Loud applause.)

The Government, which sometimes makes deeds precede words, has already taken steps for the provision of Zara, economically, politically and spiritually. The same has been done for Dalmatia. It is necessary to admit frankly that since the coming of the Fascist Government the Yugoslavs have been less intransigent with regard to us. There is no doubt that the definite carrying out of the Treaty of Rapallo is the cause of great grief to the citizens of Fiume and Zara, of Dalmatia and many in the old kingdom.

(Cries of "It is true.")

At other times there might perhaps have been difficulties. But the Government over which I have the honor of presiding does not hesitate; it faces difficulties, I was almost going to say seeks them. I intend to regulate as soon as possible all that more or less successful heritage of foreign policy left me by my predecessors. It is no good being alarmed by what happens. I have what I dare to call a Roman conception of history and life. Things must never be thought to be irreparable. Rome did not believe in the irreparable, even after the Battle of Cannae,[58] when she lost the flower of her generation. On the contrary, you will remember that the Senate went out to meet Terentius Varro, who, having wished to undertake the battle against the advice of Paulus Aemilius, was certainly one of those responsible for the defeat. Rome fell, and rose up again; she marched slowly, but she marched; she had a goal to reach, and she intended to reach it. Italy, our Italy, the Italy which we carry in our hearts, and which is our pride, must be like this; the Italy which accepts her destiny when it is imposed, by hard necessity, but only while she prepares her spirit and her forces to overcome it someday. (Loud and prolonged applause, many Senators advance to congratulate the Prime Minister. Silence being once more established, Mussolini continues.)

I propose that the Senate, having concluded the discussion suspended yesterday evening, should be adjourned. I do not know for how long. The Government must be left free to work and to prepare work for the Chamber and the Senate.

Meanwhile, I feel the necessity of thanking the President, who has directed the proceedings with that tact and high wisdom for which he is known. I am glad that the Senate, in approving of these political and commercial treaties—which are two aspects of the same policy—has thus brought to a conclusion a part of our foreign policy. I beg the President to accept the expression of my profound admiration.

(Tittoni, President of the Senate, replies, reciprocating the words of the Prime Minister and praising his spirit and his patriotic faith. He pays tribute to the way in which the Hon. Mussolini has assumed, with a firm hand, the direction of public interests.)

---

[58] Key engagement of the Second Punic War between the Roman Republic and Carthage, fought on August 2nd, 216 BC, near the ancient village of Cannae in Apulia, southeast Italy. It is regarded as one of the greatest tactical feats in military history and one of the worst defeats in Roman history.

A Review of European Politics in
Their Relation with Italy

March 2nd, 1923, Cabinet, Rome

◆ ◆ ◆

Honorable Colleagues, the situation on the Ruhr has remained stationary during these last weeks. While the two disputants seem to settle themselves more rigidly in their respective positions of passive resistance on the part of Germany and active pressure on the part of Belgium and France, England has not changed her attitude of benign disapproval and Italy has neither increased nor reduced the number of technical experts representing her on the Ruhr. So far there has not arisen the new factor which would lead, in one sense or the other, to the solution of the crisis. This new factor could consist either in a direct proposal made by one disputant to the other, or in a request for mediation, or in the modification, on a political basis, of the aims which France says she has in view—aims of an economic nature, which so far have not gone beyond the limit of the payment of reparations— or else in an increase of the opposition of England which would lead to the withdrawal of her troops from the Rhine.

It seems, however, clear—notwithstanding the solicitations of an element of the advanced democracy—that England maintains her attitude of circumspect waiting, without impatience or precipitation. The war, which at the present moment has for its theatre the basin of the Ruhr, is one of attrition, and it may yet last for some time, in spite of the general expectation all over Europe of a rapid conclusion. As I have already said both in the Senate and the Chamber, Italy will not refuse her assistance in any attempt that may be made to render normal the situation in Central Europe as soon as possible, and of this she has given tangible proof in the help afforded, before any other country, to Austria. The solidarity which Italy was bound to show toward France upon the common ground of reparations, has given rise to projects of greater importance, which might have been interpreted in certain circles as having been directed against other Powers or to the exclusion of some one of them. An official declaration on the part of the Government has established the truth of the matter. The campaign in certain papers has not been approved of and still less authorized. That it is very opportune that friendly and cordial relations should exist between Italy and France is the sincere conviction of my Government. It is very much to be desired that the economic relations between these two neighboring countries shall be intensified and strengthened, and the Government has worked in this direction in concluding the recent commercial agreement. But this has nothing to do with a real treaty of alliance, as has been suggested in certain sections of public opinion. The Fascist Government intends on the whole to follow a line of foreign policy as far as possible autonomous, and it could never adhere to alliances which did not protect the interests of Italy in the highest degree and which did not constitute a solid guarantee of peace and prosperity for Italy in particular and Europe in general.

Fascist Italy cannot and will not adhere to a system of alliances which does not take into account these fundamental premises. For her to pledge herself in any way definitely while the Entente is still in a state of crisis, and there are still many obscure points in the general situation in the world, would be unpardonable.

Turkey and Peace. No reliable news has hitherto reached us as to the intentions of the Government at Angora concerning the acceptance or non-acceptance of the projected treaty presented by the Allies to the Turkish Delegation at Lausanne. Information is contradictory, because, whereas on the one hand it is said that, in spite of the moderating influence of Mustapha Kemal and Ismet Pasha, the Assembly of Angora has shown itself adverse to some of the conditions already accepted by the Turkish Delegation at Lausanne and intends to re-discuss the projects of the treaty, article by article; on the other hand, especially from British quarters, it is continually said that the Turks seem favorably disposed toward the rapid conclusion of peace.

Whatever may be the decision of the Government at Angora, it must be remembered that, once the deliberations of the Assembly are at an end, the Turks will, by means of the Secretary-General of the Conference, who remains for the present at Lausanne, give a definite reply to the Allies concerning eventual requests and proposals.

Between the Governments at Rome, London and Paris there is in consequence an active diplomatic correspondence in progress with the object of establishing the common line of action to be adopted by the Allies in certain important questions, such as that of Capitulations and those concerning the Economic Clauses, as well as the course to be adopted in the eventual resumption of the work of the Conference, if the Turkish proposals are such as to furnish a serious basis for discussion. The British Government is showing itself to be very rigid in this respect and seems not to wish to allow discussion upon other than these three points:

1. The formula of the Turko-Grecian reparations.
2. The formula of the judicial guarantees for foreigners.
3. Economic Clauses.

As regards the first, it is a question of putting in the hands of an Arbitration Commission the reciprocal claims of the two countries, since the Turks do not even admit that the Greeks have any claims to present. For the second, it is a question of finding a formula which will provide more efficient guarantees for foreigners where the searching of private houses and arrests are concerned; and as regards the third, of resuming the discussion and negotiations upon all economic questions and of handing them over to another commission to be dealt with apart from the treaty of peace.

The Italian Government is fully convinced of the necessity of bringing about the conclusion of this peace in order that grave dangers, derived from the actual situation in the East, may be avoided, and in order that normal conditions, favorable to the free exercise of trade and industry, may be re-established. Although we are resolute in demanding from Turkey the acceptance of the really moderate conditions proposed by the Allies, we do not think, however, that every and any request, not connected with the three points mentioned above, made by Turkey, should be excluded *a priori*, but rather that the possibility of examination without preconception should always be considered where some well-defined and limited proposal is concerned.

As to procedure, the British Government would be inclined toward the renewal of the discussion at Constantinople, while the Italian Government, realizing the dangers which would menace the success of the negotiations in the surroundings of the Turkish capital, would prefer that it should take place at Lausanne with a limited gathering of technical delegates.

In any case it will not be possible to make a definite decision about this before knowing the answer of the Turkish Government, which is to be decided by the vote of the Grand Assembly.

Memel and the Polish Frontier. The question of Memel has been solved in theory, and it is not probable that in practice overpowering obstacles will be met with, since in the solution the rights of both the Lithuanians and the Poles have been taken into account.

This incident has afforded an opportunity of examining generally the still uncertain position of Poland with regard to her boundaries. It seemed to the Italian Government that such uncertainty was pregnant with dangers, and that it was of the utmost importance to arrive, as soon as possible, at the recognition of the frontier, the delimitation of which is reserved for the Allied Powers by the Treaty of Versailles. Consequently, at the Conference of Ambassadors at Paris, the Government proposed that such a delimitation should be proceeded with at once, a proposal which, not having appeared at first to meet with the approval of the other representatives, has recently been presented again by the French Government, and to which we, for the sake of consistency, have adhered.

As far as the boundaries between Lithuania and Poland are concerned, we should have preferred the League of Nations to have been called upon to pass an opinion, so that the largest number of States possible should be interested in guaranteeing the decision. Our Allies, however, having drawn attention to the fact that the procedure of the League of Nations is of a length and tediousness which, at the present moment, it is better to avoid, we have also adhered on this point to the French proposal to hand the question over to the Conference of Ambassadors.

We truly hope that Poland and Lithuania will accept the decisions which the Conference of Ambassadors thinks it just to make. And this is one of those typical cases in which Poland and Lithuania must take into account the inevitable necessity of sentiment yielding to reason.

The Problems of the Adriatic: Fiume; Abbazia; Zara. The Italian Delegation and part of that of Yugoslavia have already arrived at Abbazia. At present work has not begun, but will begin as soon as possible. At our request the Government at Belgrade has replaced Admiral Priza by Signor Rybar as her representative. The accusations against Admiral Priza, as a participator in the legal proceedings which led to the condemnation and death of Nazario Sauro, are well known. The Government at Belgrade showed itself to be appreciative of the eminently moral reasons for our objection and consented to the substitution— even at the cost of facing the criticism of the Italophobic opposition— with a good-will which seems an excellent omen for the future.

Our Delegation, too, to the Commission for the Evacuation of the Third Zone is already at Zara, and since the Yugoslav Delegation has also arrived, work can begin at once.

An incident which occurred the night before last, when abuse of Zara and Italy was shouted from a passing Yugoslav steamer within sight of that port, has already evoked spontaneous and immediate apologies from the Yugoslav consul to our prefect. But I have urged Belgrade to prevent such deplorable, although unimportant, incidents from occurring again.

I must say that, hitherto, the Yugoslav Government has shown itself to be animated on the whole by excellent feeling, and loyally cooperates in seeking to smooth the way in this period of important and delicate negotiations which has just begun.

As for the attitude of the national elements at Zara and Fiume, they remain inspired by a high sense of discipline and recognition of the necessity of subordinating private interests to the general welfare of the nation.

The Conference of the Südbahn. The work of the Conference of the Südbahn for the purpose of technical and administrative reorganization has made sufficient progress. Both the States interested and the company have presented their proposals for amendments, in which they try, without interfering with the basis of the projects under discussion, to lessen the financial burden.

The project of the agreement concerning through traffic, which contains regulations guaranteeing the regularity of the organization of the railways, facilities for the customs and sanitary services, and the setting in order of the international stations, as well as regulations regarding the railway rates of the through trains, has already been discussed. The States have shown themselves to be of one opinion with regard to the intentions of the project, which tend to unite in a special convention all the different regulations which have issued from the treaties of peace and the projects of the Convention concluded at Barcelona and Portorose.[59]

The project, moreover, is directed particularly toward reviving the powers of the Convention of Berne in respect of international traffic. The scheme of agreement for the technical and administrative reorganization of the Südbahn admits the possibility of direct control on the part of the State as well as on the part of the company. It aims also at the maintenance of that unity of commercial direction which, without offending the sovereignty of the States with regard to tariffs, will allow of international traffic and the direct dispatching of goods, and will take into account the special exigencies of trade which require particular measures and which, not being prejudicial to the States, will be advantageous as regards the economic relations between them.

The work of the Conference will probably last another week on account of the complicated and difficult character of the various financial, technical and administrative problems to be solved.

---

[59] Portorož, Slovenia

The Italo-Yugoslav Conference
for the Commercial Treaty

March 6th, 1923, Chigi Palace, Rome,
before the members of the conference

◆ ◆ ◆

Gentlemen, I am particularly glad to open this meeting and welcome cordially the delegates of the Kingdom of the Serbs, the Croats and the Slovenes. I attach great importance to this meeting and to its results, which I am confident will be excellent.

You know that at Abbazia the Adriatic question is being settled, so that at the present time the field may be cleared of those special problems which up to today have not permitted an understanding with Yugoslavia.

Along with that of Abbazia, this meeting, convened with the object of linking together more closely commercial relations between the two countries, attains a great importance. Italian public opinion and the Fascist Government consider that, together with political relations, there must be close and profitable economic ties.

I am certain that the Italian delegates will make every effort to arrive at this agreement and I do not doubt that the Yugoslav Delegation will do the same. This will be in the common interest of the two countries. (Applause.)

History Tells Us That Strict Finance Has Brought Nations to Security

March 7th, 1923, Before the Ministry of Finance, where Mussolini officially handed over to the Minister, Hon. de Stefani, the Budgets of Home and Foreign Affairs, to be revised in accordance with a decision of the Council of Ministers.

◆ ◆ ◆

Honorable Ministers, Colleagues, Gentlemen, it might be asked, "Why such fuss, why so many soldiers for a ceremony which could be described as purely administrative, such as the consignment of my two Budgets to the Finance Minister?" We must answer this question thus: For various motives, some more plausible than others. The solemnity which accompanies this ceremony serves to demonstrate the immense importance the Government attaches to a rapid restoration of financial normality. We have formally promised to make a start toward balancing the State Budget, and with this promise we wish to keep faith at whatever cost. We must be convinced that if the whole falls, the part falls too; and that if the economic life of the nation falls in ruin, all that is in the nation—institutions, men, classes—is destined to suffer the same fate.

And why these soldiers? To show that the Government has strength. I declare that, if possible, I want to govern with the consent of the majority of the people, but while waiting for this consent to be formed, to be nourished, to be strengthened, I collect the maximum available force. Because it may happen, by chance, that force may aid in rediscovering consent, and, at any rate, should consent be lacking, force still remains. In all the measures—even the most drastic—the

Government takes, we shall put before the people this dilemma: either accept them from a high spirit of patriotism or submit to them. This is how I conceive the State, and how I understand the art of governing the nation.

I am glad to find myself before you—(continued the President, turning to the officials of the Ministry of Finance present at the ceremony)—because the Minister has spoken very favorably to me of the high officials of the Ministry of Finance. He told me that some of you often work up to sixteen hours a day. Well done! Those are long hours, but it is a splendid example. But if they were not sufficient, it would be necessary to work even twenty hours. Only thus, gentlemen, shall we rise up out of the sea of our present difficulties and reach the shore.

We must inculcate in our spirit a sense of absolute discipline. We must consider that the money of the Treasury is sacred above everything else. It does not rain down from Heaven, nor can it even be made with a turn of the printing press, which, if I could, I would like to smash to pieces. It is made out of the sweat, it might be said of the blood, of the Italian people, who work today, but who will work more tomorrow. Every *lira*, every *soldo*, every *centesimo* of this money must be considered sacred and should not be spent unless reasons of strict and proved necessity demand it. *The history of peoples tells us that strict finance has brought nations to security.* I feel that each one of you believes in this truth, which is fully proved by history.

With this conviction I bid you farewell. (Applause.)

It Is Not the Economic System of Europe Alone That We Have to Restore to Its Full Efficiency

March 18th, 1923, Palazzo delle Esposizioni, Rome, before the
International Congress of the Chambers of Commerce

◆

Gentlemen, the Government over which I have the honor to preside and which I represent is glad to welcome you to Rome and offers you a deferential and cordial greeting, which I extend also to the foreign representatives, who have wished to honor us by their presence. The fact that your important Congress is held in the capital of Italy, only five months after the events which gave the control of public affairs to the youthful forces of war and of victory is the best declaration to the world that the Italian nation is rapidly returning to the full normality of her political and economic life. In a meeting like this I shall not linger on the former, but shall briefly dwell on the latter subject.

The economic policy of the new Italian Government is simple. I consider that the State should renounce its industrial functions, especially of a monopolistic nature, for which it is inadequate. I consider that a Government which means to relieve rapidly peoples from afterwar crises should allow free play to private enterprise, should renounce any meddling or restrictive legislation, which may please the Socialist demagogues, but proves, in the end, as experience shows, absolutely ruinous.

It is, therefore, time to remove from the shoulders of the producing forces of every nation the last remains of that machinery which was called the trappings of war and to examine economic problems, no longer with a state of mind veiled by the influence of particular interests, as they had to be examined during the war. I do not believe that the aggregate of forces, which in industry, in agriculture, in commerce, in banking, in transportation may be called by the world-name of capitalism, is near its downfall, as certain doctrinarians belonging to the Social-Extremists have claimed. One of the great historical experiences of which we have been witnesses proves that all the systems of associated economics which do away with private initiative and individual effort fail more or less pitifully in a short time. But free initiative does not exclude an agreement between groups, which will be realized all the easier when there is a loyal protection of each separate interest. Your Chamber of Commerce follows exactly this program of enquiry, and of stabilization, of coordinating and conciliating the various interests. You are here in Rome to discuss the best means to revive the great currents of trade which, before the war, had increased general wealth and brought all people to a high standard of living. These are weighty and delicate problems which often cause discussions of a political and moral nature. To solve them we must be guided by the conviction that *it is not the economic system of Europe alone that we have to restore to its full efficiency*, but that there are also countries and continents which may offer a field for a larger economic activity in the near future. It is not without significance that the powerful Republic of the United States has sent such a large number of her representatives to Rome. It means that, if official political America still keeps an attitude of reserve, economic America feels that she cannot remain indifferent to what may or may not be done in Europe.

There is no doubt that Governments—beginning with mine—will examine with the utmost care and give due weight to the decisions which are arrived at by this Congress. (Loud cheers.)

Only Those Who Profited by the War Grumbled and Still Grumble, Cursed and Still Curse at the War

March 29th, 1923, Villa Mirabello, Milan, before blind ex-soldiers

◆ ◆ ◆

My dear Comrades! When a little time ago one of your officers told me that you never grumbled at the war, even when Italy seemed overwhelmed, I was not surprised because only those who profited by the war grumbled and still grumble, cursed and still curse at the war. Those who have performed their duty do not grumble, do not curse, but accept their sacrifice with Roman simplicity and austerity.

When I am among the maimed I live again the greatest days of our war. And I declare to you that a Government which did not bear you in mind would be unworthy, and would only be worthy of being overthrown by the fury of the people.

But the Government which I represent is entirely formed of men who have fought from the Stelvio to the sea of Trieste, and such men cannot ignore the sacrifices accomplished.

I express to you here this morning all my brotherly sympathy and admiration as an ex-soldier, as a man, as an Italian, and I embrace you all. And by this act I intend to honor and exalt all those who contributed to the greatness of the mother country by the deeds accomplished and by the shedding of their blood. (Applause.)

Patriotism Is Not Formed by Mere Words

March 30th, 1923, Arosio, near Milan,
before ex-soldiers suffering from shell-shock

◆　◆　◆

Fellow Soldiers, I did well to accept your courteous invitation, in the first place, as it always gives me great pleasure to offer to my comrades of the trenches the proof of my fraternal sympathy as a soldier, as a man, as an Italian, and as the head of the Government.

As I said yesterday to the blind ex-soldiers at Villa Mirabello, so I say to you. The Government intends to protect you, intends to satisfy your requests, to defend your material and moral rights.

Your invitation has given me the opportunity to see this splendid work, which represents the results and the harmonious synthesis of faith in your undertakings and of noble love for our country.

Everything that is done for the maimed and for ex-soldiers is a small thing in face of the sacrifice of so many Italians who gave their life on the battlefields or who shed their blood.

What is done here is not only a manifestation of piety, it is an expression of national solidarity and of conscientious patriotism. Because patriotism is not formed by mere words, it is formed by deeds, by example, by showing oneself worthy before one's own conscience of the quality of being Italian.

The Government intends to exalt all the forces of the country, all the moral forces arising from our victory; it means daily and disinterestedly to defend all those who by their deeds and their blood have contributed to this glorious victory. (Applause.)

Questions of Foreign Policy Before the Cabinet

April 7th, 1923, Cabinet, Rome

◆

The Abbazia Conference. Colleagues, the Commission appointed according to the Agreements of Santa Margherita, which met, as is known, on March 1st, started its work by the arrangement for the evacuation of Susak, which took place on the following day. It is opportune here to note that the Italian Delegation wished to express to the world and to the Italian troops its gratitude for the courteous and chivalrous behavior during the whole occupation of Susak.

The Commission decided, at that time, a provisional settlement for communication and traffic between Fiume and Susak, which was made effective for two months, in view of the eventuality of the prorogation of the sittings of the Commission. The frontier traffic between Castua and the adjacent territories was also organized.

With reference to the military operations, the Serbo-Croatian-Slovak Delegation has at once recorded an objection, on the grounds that with the evacuation of Susak, it did not consider that that stipulated by the Agreements of Santa Margherita had been carried out, seeing that the Delta and Porto Sauro remained occupied by Italian troops. Against this assertion the Italian Delegation replied that Italy had carried out to the letter the provisions of the Agreements of Santa Margherita, which refer purely and simply to the evacuation of Susak.

Apart from this objection, the Commission has continued its work and the Italian Delegation has put forward a project for a Consortium in the port of Fiume between the three interested States. Such a project, in a general way, attributes to Fiume the character of an international port, leaving the possibility of the enjoyment of special privileges and guarantees to each of the contracting States for a freer development of the traffic which affects them. With regard to such a project, the Serbo-Croatian-Slovak Delegation has put forward its objections, presenting on its own account a draft of a project, according to which the Sauro Basin and the Delta would be excluded from the port of Fiume and assigned exclusively to Yugoslavia.

The Italian Delegation has formally declared that it could not accede to any pact whatsoever which, destroying the unity of the port of Fiume, would irremediably damage the future of the new State, and, in answer to the objections raised by the Serbo-Croatian-Slovak Delegation to the Italian project, our Delegation has presented another plan, in which full consideration was given to the said exceptions. But, in the course of the following discussion, the points of view of the two Delegations could not be reconciled. The sittings were suspended on March 24th, to be resumed shortly.

The New Lausanne Conference. Following the counterproposals put forward by the Government of Angora, the British Government has convened in London an Inter-Allied meeting in order to examine what modifications to the drafting and the substance of the Peace Treaty presented to the Turks on last January 30th may be possible. The Allied Representatives at this meeting have decided to invite the Turks to resume as soon as possible at Lausanne the discussion with the Allied experts and have at the same time come to an agreement as to the line of conduct to follow in such a discussion.

In the text of the reply sent to the Government of Angora, which has been published, the Allies have deemed it opportune to insert some remarks and objections on certain points of special importance, as for example that regarding the removal of the Economic Clauses asked by the Turks, to which the Allies cannot accede; that concerning some part of the judiciary declarations and the Turkish demands relative to substantial modifications of the Territorial Clauses already agreed upon, such as that of Castelrosso,[60] whose restoration to Turkey could not be countenanced.

---

[60] Also called Kastellorizo, currently a Greek Island though along the south coast of Turkey.

It is to be hoped that the good-will that both parties have the intention of displaying in the imminent negotiations of Lausanne may bring about speedily the conclusion of peace in the East, which corresponds with the warmest wish and interest of the Italian Government.

Italo-Polish Relations. Mr. Skrzynski came to Milan to express to me the gratitude of Poland for the friendly attitude of Italy in the determination of the Polish frontier, which took place recently. Expressing a personal view, I mentioned to him the advisability of a larger extension of autonomy to the population of Eastern Galicia. I profited by the occasion to examine with the Minister for Foreign Affairs some concrete points, which, with regard to oil and coal, concern more closely our commerce. I recognized with satisfaction the friendly disposition which animates the Polish Government and I was struck with the impression that whenever important Italian enterprises should wish to develop their activity in Poland, they would find there the best of welcomes. The representatives of some Italian firms of standing, moreover, are now already in negotiation at Warsaw, and the results, I hope, will in a short time confirm the favorable attitude of the Polish Foreign Minister.

The Visit of the Austrian Chancellor Seipel. In the conversations I had at Milan with the Austrian Chancellor, both parties expressed the reciprocal desire and interest to improve further relations between the two countries. The Chancellor has warmly thanked the Italian Government for the helpful action on behalf of Austria and has asked our support for the satisfactory solution of all problems which might contribute to the economic reconstruction of the Republic. I gave favorable assurances and, consequently, have accordingly hastened the negotiations already begun for a commercial agreement and I have had examined numerous questions which had been dragging on unsolved for some time.

It is to be hoped that, the last difficulties having been removed, the Commercial Treaty may be signed within a few days. The Clauses of the Portorose Conventions, signed and not ratified by the contracting parties, will be included in it. The Chancellor has asked that the small Austrian properties in Italy and the historical Austrian Institute in Rome should be restored to Austria, as was done for Germany. While I declared myself favorable to his requests, I have, for my part, reminded him of the situation of Italian property in Austria and have obtained from the Chancellor satisfactory assurances concerning this and other subjects. With reference to the Conventions signed at the Conference of Rome, some of which have notable importance for Italy, the Chancellor has promised to proceed to their ratification without further delay.

The Commercial Relations with Austria. The negotiations with Austria are being conducted with a spirit of the greatest good-will on both sides, in order to arrive in a short space of time at an agreement which should establish regular and profitable relations between the two countries and also after the first period, during which the economic relations between the two States are regulated by the Treaty of St. Germain. If some difficulty still remains, this is due in the first place to the fact that it is not the case of negotiating pacts which, with regard to their application and their consequences, could remain restricted to the exchanges between the two neighboring States, but are destined to have a repercussion also on our relations with the other States which, for their imports into Italy, enjoy the "most favored nation" clause.

This fact, independently of the specially favorable conditions by which certain important industries, competing with ours, are working in Austria, compels us to be very cautious in adhering to the many Austrian requests, and all the more that, for financial and other reasons, Austria is herself not in a position to meet our demands to the extent which is essential to us. The two Delegations have, however, already arrived at an agreement on most of the questions which have been the subject of reciprocal demands, and now certain controversies remain to be solved which, although they offer the greatest interests for both sides, it is to be hoped may be solved with satisfaction to all.

Special attention has been paid by the two Delegations to the study of the questions relative to the traffic through the port of Trieste and the regulation of the frontier traffic for the protection of the interests of the populations of the zone near the frontier of the two States. On this subject agreement may be said to be complete.

The Commercial Treaty with Yugoslavia. The negotiations with Yugoslavia, which should lead to the regulation of all the economic and financial questions still pending between the two States, have been conducted so far on the Treaty of Commerce, which, except for the part concerning the Italian proposals on the tariffs, may be said to be already agreed upon by the two Delegations. With reference to the other subjects under examination, of which only a small part has been possible to discuss at the same time as the negotiations for the Commercial Treaty, the Yugoslav Delegation is now awaiting further instructions from Belgrade. Besides the commercial negotiations I have mentioned, there are others proceeding for a Commercial Treaty with Spain. Negotiations will shortly be opened for commercial agreements with Siam, Finland, Estonia, Lithuania, Latvia, and Albania.

(After a short discussion, in which several Ministers participated, the Cabinet approved the declarations of the Prime Minister.)

Mine Is Not a Government That Deceives the People

June 2nd, 1923, Palazzo Municipale, Rovigo, to the contadini

◆ ◆ ◆

Fascists, how shall I find adequate words to thank you for this magnificent welcome? A few moments ago your mayor gave voice to the greeting of the city and the province. Today I have passed through your fertile lands, furrowed by rivers, exploited by your tenacious work. All Italy must be grateful to this industrious people, who, too, having realized the beautiful and supreme interests of the nation, has now all the more the right to be treated with greater friendship and consideration.

I know that I am speaking to an assembly where workers are certainly in enormous majority. Well, I say to them with calm words and with a still calmer conscience that the Government which I have the honor to represent is not, cannot, and will never be against the working classes. (Loud applause.) Six months of Government are still too few for a program to be carried through, but, to my mind, they are sufficient to give an idea of its directives which today are precise and sound. *Mine is not a Government that deceives the people.* (Applause.) We cannot, we shall not, make promises if we are not mathematically sure of being able to fulfil them. The people have been too long deceived and mystified for the men of our generation to continue this low trade.

We have traced a furrow, very clear-cut and deep, between that which was the Italy of yesterday and that which is the Italy of today. In the latter, all classes must have a sphere of action for their fruitful cooperation. The struggle between classes may be an episode in the life of a people, it cannot be the daily system, as it would mean the destruction of wealth, and, therefore, universal poverty. The cooperation, citizens, between him who labors and him who employs labor, between him who works with his hands and him who works with his brains, all these elements of production have their inevitable and necessary grades and constitutions. Through this program you will attain a state of well-being and the nation prosperity and greatness. If I were not sure of my words I would not utter them before you on such a solemn and memorable occasion. (Applause.)

(At this point of the speech an airplane piloted by Ferrarin was executing some daring stunts just above the Palazzo Municipale, from where Mussolini was speaking. The Prime Minister stopped for a few seconds following Ferrarin's stunts, then went on.)

Fascists! The other day I was passing in one of those airplanes over your town. That flight was profoundly significant, as it was meant to show that six months of tenure of office have not yet nailed me down into my Presidential easy chair and that I, as you, as all of you, am still ready to dare, to fight, if necessary, to die, so that the fruits of the great Fascist revolution may not be lost!

Long live Fascism! Long live Italy! (Loud applause.)

In Times Past as in Times Present, Woman Had Always a Preponderant Influence in Shaping the Destinies of Humanity

June 2nd, 1923, Padua, first Women's Fascist Congress

◆ ◆ ◆

Ladies, if I am not mistaken, this, which is inaugurated here today, is the first Women's Fascist Congress of the "three Venices."[61] The title and the field covered by this first Congress of yours are full of profound significance. Fifty years ago one could not speak of the "three Venices"! Venice herself, after the magnificent years of heroism of 1848 and 1849, was still held by the shackles of foreign slavery. In 1866 we liberated Venice, one of the Venices.[62] Fifty years afterwards we liberated the other two—that which has as its boundary the devoted and impregnable Brenner, and the other which has as its boundary the not less devoted nor less impregnable Nevoso.

Fascists do not belong to the multitude of fops and sceptics who mean to belittle the social and political importance of woman. What does the vote matter? You will have it! But even when women did not vote and did not wish to vote, *in times past as in times present, woman had always a preponderant influence in shaping the destinies of humanity*. Thus the women of Fascism, who bravely wear the glorious Blackshirt, and gather round our standards, are destined to write a splendid page of history, to help, with self-sacrifice and deeds, Italian Fascism.

---

[61] Triveneto, comprised of Venezia Euganea (Euganean Venetia), Venezia Giulia (Julian Venetia) and Venezia Tridentina (Tridentine Venetia).
[62] The city of Venice is part of Venezia Euganea.

Do not trust the little stuffed owls, the yelling monkeys or, indeed, any representative of the lower zoological orders, who believe they practice politics, but could be called by a more infamous name. Do not believe those who talk of crises within the ranks of Fascism;— these are details, mere episodes in the great event, and they, after all, concern men, not masses. When Fascists have not to strike the enemy, they can well afford themselves the luxury of internal quarrels. But if the enemy should begin to raise his head again and intensify the character of his more or less stupid opposition, then Fascists will again become solidly united. Then "Woe to the vanquished!" (Applause.) And since the opportunity is propitious, I would like to tell you, women of Fascism, and the Fascists of all Italy, that the attempt to sever Mussolini from Fascism or Fascism from Mussolini is the most useless and grotesque attempt that could be conceived. (Applause.) I am not so proud as to say that I who speak and Fascism are one; but four years of history have now clearly shown that Mussolini and Fascism are two aspects of the same thing, are two bodies and one soul or two souls in a single body. I cannot forsake Fascism, because I have created it, I have reared it, I have strengthened and I have chastened it, and I still hold it in my fist, always! It is, therefore, quite useless for the old screech-owls of Italian policy to pay me their foolish court. I am too shrewd to fall into this ambush of the commercial mediocrities of village fairs. I can assure you, my dear friends, that all these little vipers, all these cheap politicians will be bitterly disillusioned.

To think that I could become brutalized in Parliamentary bureaucracy is to believe an absurdity. Although I come from the working class, I have a spirit too aristocratic not to feel disgust for low Parliamentary maneuvers. We shall continue our march vigorously (added the Hon. Mussolini, raising his voice), because this has been imposed on us by destiny. We shall not turn back, nor shall we even mark time. I have already said that we did not want to push matters to extremes only to see ourselves driven back by the swing of the pendulum. I prefer, as I wrote in an article, which aroused some interest—I prefer to march on continually, day by day, in the Roman way, in the way of Rome who is never reconciled to defeat; of Rome who welcomed Terentius Varro coming from Cannae, although she knew that he had given battle against the opinion of Consul Paulus Aemilius and was, in a certain degree, responsible for the defeat; of Rome who after Cannae forbade matrons to sally forth, so that their grief-stricken bearing should not shake the strength of the citizens; of this Rome who rewrote continually the chapters of her history, who found in every ill-success the incentives to endurance, to steadfastness, to strengthen her spirits, to harden her nerves, to light the flame of passion! This is the Rome of whom we dream; the Rome in whom all hierarchies are respected, those of strength, beauty, intelligence, and human kindness; the Rome who struck hard at her enemies, but then raised them up again and made them share her great destiny; the Rome who left the utmost liberty to the beliefs of her subject-peoples, provided only that they obeyed her!

Giuseppe Mazzini used to say that power is but the unity and perseverance of all efforts put together. Well, Italian power, Fascist power, the power of all the new generations which expand in this superb spring of our life and history, will be the result of the unity of our efforts, of the tenacity of our work. After all, what do Fascists ask for? They are not ambitious or factious. They have the sense of limitation and of their responsibility. And I am sure of interpreting your thought, the deep craving of your soul, if I say that Fascists, from the first to the last, from the leaders to the led, ask only one thing: To serve with humility, with devotion, with steadfastness, our beloved Mother Country, Italy! (The speech was greeted with enthusiastic applause.)

So Long as These Students and These Universities Exist, the Nation Cannot Perish and Become a Slave, Because Universities Smash Fetters Without Allowing the Forging of New Ones

June 3rd, 1923, University of Padua

❖ ◆ ❖

Mr. Chancellor, professors, my young friends, it is not I who honor your university, it is your university which honors me, and I must confess that, although on account of my laborious dealings with men I am a little refractory to emotions, today, being among you, I feel deeply touched.

We have known each other for some time, from 1915, from the days of that May always radiant. I remember that the students of Padua hung up at the doors of this university a big paper puppet representing a politician about whom I do not wish to express any opinion now. But that act meant that the youth of the University of Padua did not want to hear about ignoble diplomatic bargains—(Applause)—did not want to sell its splendid spiritual birthright for a more or less wretched bit of stew.[63] The University of Padua, the students, who were not degenerate descendants of those Tuscan students who went out to die at Curtatone and Montanara,[64] wished then to be the vanguard, to take up their post in the fighting line, carrying with them the reluctant ones, chastening the pusillanimous, overthrowing the

---

[63] Referencing the story in Genesis 25 of Essau selling his birthright to Jacob.
[64] The Battle of Curtatone and Montanara (May 29th, 1848), during which the Tuscan and Neapolitan volunteers bravely defended the Italian formation, part of the First Italian War of Independence.

Government and going out to fight, to sacrifice and death, but also to honor and glory.

From that time I know that among you there are faithful followers and that this university among all the others is truly an active center of faith and of intense patriotism. If I look back for a moment to the rolling by of centuries, I recognize in this university a great fountain at which thousands of men of all countries, of all generations, of all races, have quenched their thirst.

The Government which I have the honor to represent repudiates, at any rate in the person of its chief, the doctrine of materialism and the doctrines which claim to explain the very complex history of humanity only from the material point of view, to explain an episode, not the whole of history, an incident, not a doctrine. Well, this Government prizes individual, spiritual and voluntary qualities, holds in high esteem the universities, because they represent so many glorious strong points in the life of the people. In fact I do not hesitate to state that if Germany has been able to resist the powerful influence of Bolshevism, it is due, above all, to the strong university traditions of that people.

A people with an ardent spirit and with genius like ours is necessarily a well-balanced and harmonious one. The Government understands the enormous historic importance of universities, has a respect for their noble traditions and wishes to raise them to the heights of modern exigencies. All this cannot be done at once, as everything cannot be accomplished in six months. All that we are doing at present is to clear the ground from all the debris which the rotten political caste has left us as a said inheritance. (Applause.) How could a Government composed of former soldiers ever disparage universities? It would not only be absurd but criminal! From the universities have come out by the thousands volunteers and by tens of thousands those magnificent warriors who used to assault the enemy's trenches with a superb contempt of death. They are our comrades whose memory we bear engraved in our hearts. You will write their names on your gates of bronze, but their memory will be more imperishably engraved in our spirit. We cannot forget them, as we cannot forget that out of the universities came by thousands the Blackshirts, those Blackshirts who, at a given moment, put an end to the inglorious vicissitudes of Italian politics, who took by the throat with strong fingers all the old profiteers who appeared, to the exuberant impatience of the new Italian generations, always the more inadequate for their paralyzing decrepitude. (Applause.) Well, so long as there are universities in Italy—and there certainly will be for a long time—and so long as there are young men to attend these universities and to become acquainted with the history of yesterday, thus preparing the history of tomorrow, so long as there are such young men, the doors of the past are definitely shut. I guarantee it formally! But I add further that *so long as these young men and these universities exist, the Nation cannot perish and it cannot become a slave, because universities smash fetters without forging new ones.* (Applause.) If tomorrow it were again necessary, either for causes arising within or without the frontiers, to sound again the trumpet of war, I am sure that the universities would again empty themselves to re-populate the trenches. (Loud applause.)

And now that you have rejuvenated me by twenty years, I would like to sing with you the "Gaudeamus Igitur."[65] After all, Lorenzino dei Medici was right when he sang, "How beautiful is youth!" Well, my young friends, there can never be for us as individuals the certainty of tomorrow, but there is the supreme and magnificent certainty of tomorrow for us as a nation and as a people.

And with the students' hymn, let us utter in Latin a simpler word, *Laboremus.*[66] To work with dignity, with probity and with cheerfulness, to assault life with earnestness and to meet it as a mission, trying to fulfil the categorical injunction left us by our dead. They command us to obey and to serve, they command us discipline, sacrifice and obedience.

We should really be the last of men if we failed to do our clear duty. But we shall not fail. I who hold the pulse of the nation and who carefully count its beats, I who sometimes shudder in the face of the heavy responsibilities which I have assumed, feel in me a hope, nay a vibration, of a supreme certainty which is this: that, by the will of the leaders, by the determination of the people, and by the sacrifice of past, present and future generations, Imperial Italy, the Italy of our dreams, will be for us the reality of tomorrow. (Loud applause.)

---

[65] A popular academic commercium song sung in Latin in many European countries. In English: "So Let Us Rejoice."
[66] "We will work."

Italy's Foreign Policy Regarding German Reparations, Hungary, Bulgaria, Austria, Yugoslavia, Turkey, Russia, Poland, and Other Countries

June 8th, 1923, Senate, Rome

◆　◆　◆

Honorable Senators, the speech that I have the honor of delivering before your illustrious Assembly may appear analytical, because in it I propose to touch on several questions and to speak decisively upon several problems, especially with regard to internal policy.[67] By this I do not delude myself to be able to convince those who are my opponents in *mala fide*, nor to disperse completely the small opposition which nourishes itself on detail, and is the effect of personal temperament.

You will not be surprised if I begin with foreign policy, even if it happens that this is the field in which serious and founded opposition does not exist, and it may be legitimately said that our policy is endorsed unanimously by the nation.

As I have already said on other occasions, the foreign policy of the present Government is inspired by the necessity for a progressive revaluation of our diplomatic and political position in Europe and in the world. It is a fact that, except for territorial acquisitions bounded by the Brenner and the Nevoso, frontiers wrested by long and bloody wars, Italy was excluded in the Peace of Versailles and other successive treaties from all other benefits of an economic and colonial nature. Solemn pacts signed during the war have lapsed and have not

---

[67] Discussed in the following speech in this collection.

been replaced. The position of inferiority assigned to Italy has weighed and still weighs heavily on the economic life of our people. It is useless to dwell upon recriminations of the past. We must rather seek to regain the ground and time lost. There is no doubt that from October to today the situation has notably improved.

The other Powers, whether allied or not, know that Italy intends to follow an energetic and assiduous policy for the protection of her natural and vital interests, intends to be present wherever, directly or indirectly, they are at stake, because this is her right and her definite duty; but at the same time she is in favor of that line of conduct in general policy which tends to bring back as quickly as possible to a normal state the economic situation of our continent. Italy, who too is marching rapidly toward her readjustment, sees this rebirth continually disturbed by general outside factors. There is, therefore, a definite Italian interest in hastening the pacific solution of the European crisis.

The Position of Italy and Reparations. All such crises, since the Treaty of Versailles onwards, have been dominated by the one problem: Reparations. In the face of this problem the fundamental position of Italy is as follows:

1. Germany can and must pay a sum which now seems universally fixed and which is very far from the many hundreds of billions talked of after the Armistice;

2. Italy could not tolerate territorial changes which would lead to a political, economic or military hegemony in Europe;

3. Italy is prepared to bear her quota of sacrifice, if it is necessary to obtain what is called European reconstruction;

4. The Italian Government maintains today more than ever, above all after the last German Note, that the problem of reparations and that of Inter-Allied debts are intimately connected and are in a certain sense interdependent.

There is no doubt that the occupation of the Ruhr has contributed to render the crisis of the Ruhr extremely acute, and therefore to a certain extent hastened a solution.

It will not be inopportune to recall, considering the rapidity of events, that the French and Belgians went to the Ruhr on account of the declarations of a series of failures of the supplies in kind by Germany, admitted also by England, at any rate as regards that of wood, and the failure of the Conference of Paris.

It is certainly worthwhile to fix exactly in their essential lines the main features of the Italian, English, and German projects, in order to have a picture of the situation as regards its agreements and divergencies, and to see what conjectures we can form as to a possible settlement. This will also serve to explain why Italy was not able to accept the Bonar Law scheme at Paris, and why she had to reject the recent Cuno-Rosenberg Memorandum.

The Italian project reduced the German debt to 50 billion gold marks, proposed a moratorium of two years, during which Germany would continue the supply of reparations in kind, accepted the distribution of German payments according to the quotas fixed at Spa, by which the Italian quota was put at 5 billion gold marks, fixed the payment of one part of the "C" bonds by means of the security given by the other ex-enemy States, used the remainder of the "C" bonds to settle the debt to America, agreed to the taking of economic pledges as a guarantee of the German payments, and finally, as regards the payments of the reparations owed by Austria, Bulgaria, and Hungary, asked for a pledge for the acceptance of the proposals that England had deferred putting forward—proposals, that is, of annulling those debts.

The Italian quota of reparations, which the Italian project fixed at 5 billion gold marks, was thus reduced in the English project to less than half; while cancelling the bonds, it partly abolishes to our detriment German solidary responsibility for minor ex-enemy debts and rendered impossible the execution of the agreement of March 1921, which ensures important advantages to Italy upon the basis of the "C" bonds. The larger percentage reserved on the 17 billion, representing the interest of the moratorium capitalized to 1923, could not be used for the payment of American debts, in consideration of the aleatory nature of these 17 billion.

I do not recall all this to reopen discussions, but only to make clear the main outlines of that which was and remains a noteworthy attempt to find a solution for this grave problem; an attempt which contains worthy elements which can be usefully taken up again in case of a definite settlement.

The conclusion of an agreement between England and America on the problem of debts—the work of the then Chancellor of the

Exchequer, Mr. Baldwin, today Prime Minister, followed shortly after the presentation of the English project.

Any idea of this debt being itself cancelled, or even of a simple compensation through the payment of reparations, is excluded from this agreement. The obligation to pay, although facilities may be accorded concerning both the number of years in which it must take place and the interests due, is solemnly affirmed and put into execution. In England the Speech from the Throne strongly emphasized this agreement. Even taking into account the diversity of economic strength and the totality of sacrifices borne, it could not remain without effect upon the importance of the whole question for the other European Powers.

Analysis of the German Project. If we compare the English and Italian projects with the German, the unacceptability of the latter appears evident. As is known, one of the fundamental points of the last German project concerns the consolidation of the actual debt of Germany, especially in kind, at the figure of 20 billion gold marks, with an additional 10 billion, the payment of which depends upon the decision of an International Commission. Deducting the interest, these 20 billion are reduced to 15, and the sums necessary must be found by international loans; and in the very probable eventuality that by 1927 the 20 billion has not been subscribed, an annuity will be paid which represents 5 percent interest plus 1 percent for the redemption of the loan. Finally, in the German project any provision or regulation for the guarantees demanded is lacking. The total German debt, which in the English and the Italian projects is fixed at the figure of 50 billion, in the German project is reduced to less than a third, and it is difficult, if not impossible, to determine in it the Italian quota and the sacrifice demanded from Italy.

In view of the representations, especially of England and Italy, Germany has recognized her proposals as insufficient, and yesterday the German Ambassador, Neurath, presented to me the new German Note, on the contents and nature of which I cannot pronounce an opinion for evident reasons, as in consequence of this Note diplomatic action with all the Allies must be taken up. I will only say that the German Note no longer demands the preliminary evacuation of the Ruhr as a condition for negotiation. This might make us believe in a renunciation on the part of Germany of that passive resistance, the utility of which—even for German aims—appears ever more doubtful, and whose cessation would help toward a more rapid attainment of a solution.

Italy and Hungary. But the problem of reparations is not only Franco-German, it is also Hungarian, Bulgarian and Austrian.

It is useful to define the stage which has been reached with regard to these ex-enemy countries. The total of the Hungarian reparations, which is fixed by the Treaty of Trianon, has not yet been determined by the Reparations Commission, and Hungary up to today has only furnished limited supplies in kind. The Hungarian Government, alleging the disturbed economic and financial conditions of the country caused by the serious depression of the krone, has recently put forward the necessity to contract a foreign loan, which, if it is to succeed, should be guaranteed by the custom duties, by the tobacco monopoly, and, if needs be, by other resources. Hence arises the necessity for such resources to be freed for an adequate period from the claims of reparations. A Memorandum precisely to this effect has been recently presented by the Hungarian Minister in Paris to the Reparations Commission.

The Italian Government, having examined the question from a technical point of view, has deemed it indispensable to concede to Hungary the temporary relinquishment of certain resources, so that she may proceed to her own economic restoration by means of loans to be contracted abroad. Italy has, therefore, shown herself favorable to the above Hungarian request, with the addition of certain conditions necessary to guarantee her own rights, on which point she is in agreement with the British Government.

Agreement with Bulgaria for Payment. With reference to Bulgarian reparations, Italy, Great Britain, and France came to an agreement on March 21st with the Bulgarian Government to facilitate the payment of her debt of 225 billion gold francs fixed by the Treaty of Neuilly, by dividing it in two parts; one of 550 million to be paid by instalments beginning in October of this year, and the other 170 billion not to be claimed before thirty years.

Bulgaria has pledged herself by this agreement to reserve for the regulation of her debt the revenues of her customs and has already passed a law to this effect. The agreement has also been approved by the Reparations Commission, with the reservation of our rights for the reimbursement of the expenses of the army of occupation. In fact, negotiations are proceeding with the Bulgarian Government for the regulation of this credit, which enjoys the privilege of priority over other reparations.

Our Government, animated by favorable dispositions as regards all that concerns the settlement of obligations arising from the war, has had no difficulty in accepting such an agreement.

The Loan to Austria. Fulfilling the pledge taken by its predecessors in the Protocol of Geneva of October 4th, 1922, the Italian Government has co-operated with the Governments which are signatories of the Protocol, in order that the loan in favor of Austria should have a large and ready success. For this purpose the Government has consented to postpone for twenty years, which is the duration of the War Loan, her credits against Austria for the recovery of damages and for bonds of food supply, has given her own guarantee for 25 percent of a maximum loan of 585 million gold kronen, and has authorized Italian banks to contribute directly to the loan up to the maximum of 200 million lire, including the sixty-eight which Italy had previously lent to Austria, and which, by the terms of the Protocol of Geneva, should have been repaid in cash.

Putting off for a further period the exaction of Austrian reparation, and giving a guarantee and a direct and substantial contribution to the loan in favor of Austria, the Italian Government has wished to offer her cooperation toward the political independence and territorial integrity of the Austrian Republic to which the Protocol of Geneva refers, and to which the United States of America also wish to contribute, confidently subscribing for the first time to a European loan.

Relations between Italy and Yugoslavia. Italy's political line of conduct toward the States of the Little Entente and in general toward the States recently created is substantially inspired by the necessity of exacting the respect and the scrupulous fulfilment of the treaties, because, given the present contingencies, only such a policy can produce quick and pleasing results with regard to an economic settlement of the Danubian States which would contribute to the larger one of Central Europe. On several occasions the friendly and moderate policy of Italy has followed such a course with satisfactory results.

With reference to such a policy the relations between Italy and Yugoslavia have a special importance. The clear attitude taken by the

Government with regard to Yugoslavia by proceeding to the definite enforcement of the Treaty of Rapallo has strengthened our legal position, and we are able to rest any further development of our policy on a solid basis. The enforcement of the Agreements of Santa Margherita, which has been necessarily laborious owing to the large extent of the field covered, can be said, however, to proceed on the whole satisfactorily. In spite of the initial difficulties encountered in any exceptional regime, the economic system of the so-called "special zone of Zara" is already in force for the evacuation of the remaining Dalmatian territories, and the various organizations for the regulation of all the intricate questions arising out of the Agreements have been constituted.

Fiume. But naturally the most important question to solve is that of Fiume. As is known, it offers the gravest difficulties, since, in order to ensure the future of the commercial life of the town, there must be solved many complex problems of an economic nature which are often in opposition to those of a political character. Undoubtedly the recent long Parliamentary crisis in Yugoslavia, which for a considerable time forced the Government of Belgrade to confine its attentions almost exclusively to internal problems, has heavily weighed against the rapidity of the solution of such a question.

That Government has repeatedly acquainted us with its wishes to solve the question in a satisfactory way as regards the sentiments and the interests of Italy, and has also frankly made known to us the real difficulties with which the Government is faced in asking the populations interested to accept a solution in agreement with the Italian point of view.

Italo-Yugoslav Commission. With a view to ensure an atmosphere of greater quiet to the Italo-Yugoslav Commission, the Government of Belgrade has, in the meantime, agreed to transfer the seat of the Commission to Rome. The Yugoslav Delegation has arrived, and between it and the Italian Delegation, which is fulfilling its duty with a high sense of patriotism and political probity, preliminary meetings are taking place with the object of fixing certain fundamental points before resuming official discussions, so that the latter may proceed with the necessary speed without lapsing into a deplorable stagnation, which would be otherwise inevitable in such an arduous task.

The Conference of Lausanne and the Definite Cession of Castelrosso to Italy. The Conference of Lausanne, which after the well-known suspension of last February resumed its proceedings on April 23rd, is slowly completing them through the no small difficulties of various kinds caused by the delicacy and complexity of the questions under examination. The course followed by the Italian Delegation under any circumstance has always been inspired by the most calm and impartial attitude, and its efficacy has been recognized and generally appreciated at its just worth.

Italy cannot help considering as her vital interests the speedy restoration of a normal state of trade in the East, as well as the economic development and general progress of all the peoples living on the shore of the Eastern Mediterranean.

Although all the questions under discussion have not yet been solved at Lausanne, on some of them, however, which more directly affect our country, an agreement, satisfactory on the whole, has been reached. The Government of Angora has explicitly withdrawn the objection regarding the cession of the island of Castelrosso to Italy, the possession of which on our part could in no way justify an eventual suspicion of Italian aggressive aims with regard to Turkey. Our flag, which has already been saluted from the moment it appeared in the island as a symbol of peaceful well-being, will in the future continue to protect a population which by plebiscite has entrusted itself to us.

The Juridical Protection of Foreigners in Turkey. The Italian Government has also obtained the cancellation of those clauses, with regard to our colonies in North Africa, which the agreements concluded after the Libyan War had left in existence, and at the same time the interests of Libyan subjects residing in Turkey, whose rights have been equal to those of Italian citizens, were opportunely protected.

From the opening of the Conference the question of the juridical protection of foreigners has been of the greatest importance. The Conference has agreed in fixing the limits of such protection, including it in a formula which establishes for a period of five years the appointment on the part of the Turkish Government of foreign judges, who are authorized to receive complaints of the sentences and of the proceedings of Turkish magistrates.

At Lausanne there still remain under discussion certain important questions of general interest, such as those relative to the management of the Ottoman Public Debt and others of an economic nature, which I hope may be quickly solved.

Relations between Italy and Russia. The present relations with Russia are regulated by the Italo-Russian and Italo-Ukraine Agreements of December 26th, 1921. A few days ago the projects for the conversion into law of the Royal Decree of January 31st, 1922 were presented to Parliament, by whom the said agreements had been approved, though some opposition had been offered to their practical application. This opposition gave the Russians a pretext for violating the agreement. We mean to remove these obstacles in order to render easier the economic relations between the two countries and pave the way for an understanding resting on a wider basis without excessive illusions, but also without dangerous prejudices.

Relations between the two countries, which possess different economic systems, present enormous difficulties. They are, however, not unsurmountable if on both sides there is a good-will to overcome them. Italian policy toward Russia is clear and cannot give rise to misunderstanding.

The presentation before Parliament of these decrees represents another proof of our intentions and gives us the right to expect from the Government of Moscow the scrupulous fulfilment of the pacts, the execution of the pledge taken to abstain from any act hostile to our Government, and from whatsoever direct or indirect propaganda against the institutions of the kingdom.

Relations between Italy and the United States. I do not think it is necessary, considering the brevity of this speech, to enter into further detail. I will only say that the relations between the United States and Italy are particularly cordial, and I am glad to add that both the Government and the American people have fully understood the new political situation in Italy.

Relations with Poland and Other Countries. The initiative of Italy for the definite determination of the Polish frontiers has cemented even more closely the bonds of cordial friendship which have united the two countries for centuries. Their collaboration continues to be strengthened on economic as well as on political grounds. In these last days the Polish Government has placed important orders with Italian manufacturers.

The conversations and the personal relations I have had with the Ministers of Austria, of Romania, of Hungary, the recent journey of His Majesty the King of England, the commercial treaties concluded and to be concluded, are other signs of that progressive revaluation of our diplomatic position which I referred to at the beginning of this speech.

Improvement of the Diplomatic and Consular Services. The Fascist Government, always with the object of this revaluation, as soon as it came into power instructed its representatives abroad to direct their policy outside the confines of the country to the renewed life of Italy, and to face immediately the problem of the means and the men for that end. In fact, the administration of Foreign Affairs, in the face of so many difficulties from outside, already possessed a great difficulty in her own constitution, due to the scanty number of its elements. The tools of our work, which is so delicate abroad, had to be renewed, and rendered suitable, as regards the increase in number of officials and the new conditions of Italy, for the momentous task which they are required to perform.

Instructions have, therefore, been given with effect from the first days of November for the reorganization of the competition for the Diplomatic and Consular Services, and for Interpreters.

In conclusion I wish to repeat that Italian foreign policy, while it intends to safeguard national interests, wants at the same time to constitute a factor of equilibrium and peace in Europe, and by such a policy I think I interpret the tendencies and the needs of the Italian people. (Applause.)

The Internal Policy

June 8th, 1923, Senate, Rome, same speech

◆ ◆ ◆

Honorable Senators, the problems of public order are problems of the authority of the State. There is no real authority in the State if public order is not perfectly normal. Public order and authority of the State are, therefore, two aspects of the same problem. I ask you if conditions have improved or become worse since last October. ("Improved!") Some of you give an affirmative answer. I, too, say they have improved. Although, naturally, I am far from being pessimistic and, therefore, from being discontented, I feel that nothing ever goes well enough. But, Gentlemen, when one speaks of public order, one must make comparisons. Even if they are disagreeable, they are necessary. Unrest, uneasiness and sedition are phenomena to be found not only in Italy. If we glance beyond our frontiers we have reason to repeat that, if Messene weeps, Sparta does not laugh! Look at the vanquished peoples and note what happens in Austria and in Germany. Look at the victorious peoples and you will see that only yesterday there was a strike of public officials in Belgium, which has cost the Treasury hundreds of millions of francs. If, then, you glance at the neutral countries, at Spain, you will find there, too, that life is not excessively bright and easy. All this I say for those who, at every small revolver shot fired in one of the twenty thousand villages of Italy, think they have been wounded by a 17-inch shell!

A Significant Comparison. But, above all, it is worthwhile to look at Italy and consider, on one side, her conditions in the years 1918–20 and in the period following 1920–21. The dominating events of the former two years are the occupation of the factories, the permanent strike of the officials belonging to public organizations, carried out in rotation, and by a displacement of all the powers of State authority (Assent.); and, although the incident is extremely painful, one must recall to mind that in the rank and file of that same glorious army of ours occurred an episode at Ancona which proves how deeply sedition had worked its way into the body of the Italian State.

The dominating event of the following two years is the punitive Fascist expedition. Fascists, from sheer necessity, went out to the assault of the towns in large armed bodies. Today all this is over. Today the officials of public organizations do not and will not strike. (Assent.) When the Fascist employees of the Post and Telegraph Offices came to me to protest because my colleague, the Hon. Colonna di Cesaro, had punished them, I told them that if I had been Minister of Post and Telegraphs I should have punished them twice, and I added that, just because they were Fascists, they would have to recognize the necessity for a strict discipline. (Assent.)

The State Renewed. The conditions of public order reached their zenith of disintegration during the latter part of the year. In August there was the anti-Fascist strike, which completely paralyzed the State. This had no effect; the Fascist forces, in its stead, obtained success. And, from that time, I said that the two must be made one, and that since that State was destitute of all the attributes of virility, while there was a State in power which was rising with great strength and capable of imposing discipline on the nation, it was indispensable for the rising State to substitute itself, by a revolutionary movement, for the other State which was declining. The August anti-Fascist strike was followed by the Fascist occupation of the towns of Bologna and Bolzano. The authority of the State was a complete ruin. There are no more reports of labor conflicts in the papers now.

The Chamber and the Conflicts. I am sufficiently impartial to say that in these last days there has been a slight recrudescence of trouble. What is its cause? I tell you quite frankly: the reopening of the Chamber. (Laughter.) The Chamber is the place of questions. By the spectacle it offers to the nation it sows seeds of conflict and discord among the impulsive and excitable masses.

Further, the attitude of a section of Italian Liberalism is a very welcome piece of good fortune for the subversive elements, because they constitute for them unhoped-for, unexpected allies, who blow enormous bubbles, which I promise myself to prick with the pin of logic and sincerity before closing my speech. (Assent.) Then perhaps there is this, that certain gentlemen, when they found out that they had not to fear the law of Fascism or that of the Government, which is slower because it is bound to move in accordance with legal procedure, resumed their bold attitude.

Elimination of the Subversive Elements. The measures adopted to restore public order are: First of all the elimination of the so-called subversive elements. There was much clamor after the hauling in of the nets, but in reality it was only a very small affair. Of two thousand who were arrested, those who are still in jail do not reach the figure of one hundred and fifty. They are in the hands of the judges. They were elements of disorder and subversion. Following each conflict I gave the categorical order to confiscate the largest possible number of weapons of every sort and kind. This confiscation, which continues with the utmost energy, has given satisfactory results. (Assent.) I had to repress every illegal act.

The High Grades of the National Militia. There was another problem with regard to the National Militia: namely the necessity of filling the superior posts, to which had to be appointed men coming from the army with a large personal military experience; this necessity had to be harmonized with the gratitude due to the small heads of Fascist squadrismo,[68] the body which, by leaving thousands of glorious dead, had crushed the subversive demagogic elements.

We have solved this problem. All the ranks of superior officers above those of Seniore have been assigned to the officers coming from the regular army; all the inferior grades and those of sub-officers have been given to military men, to squadristi who had previously seen military life.[69]

Moreover, statistics are always worth more than speeches. Ninety-seven percent of the officers of the Militia having a rank superior to that of Seniore come from the officers of the regular army. Out of about two hundred and thirty officers superior to the rank of Seniore, six are decorated with the Military Order of Savoy, two with Gold

---

[68] The movement of squadre d'azione (action squads), the fascist militias which ultimately became the Blackshirts.
[69] Squadristi is the name given to individuals in the squadrismo movement.

Medals, one hundred and thirty with Silver Medals, eighty with Bronze Medals.

As this is a day of explanations, even at the risk of abusing your patience, I must read the list of rewards bestowed on the Chiefs of the National Militia: *General Cesare De Bono*, Field Marshal of the regular army: three Silver Medals, special promotion for war services, "Croce di Guerra"; *General Gandolfo*, Field Marshal of the regular army: two Silver Medals, special promotion for war services; *Hon. Cesare Maria De Vecchi*: four Silver Medals, two Bronze Medals, two "Croci di Guerra"; *Italo Balbo*: one Silver Medal, one "Croce di Guerra"; *Gustavo Fara*, the general well-known through all Italy: one Gold Medal, two Silver Medals, special promotions for war services; *Stringa*, Major-General of the regular army: three Silver Medals, one Bronze Medal, disabled in the war; *Ozol Clemente*, Major-General in the regular army: two Silver Medals, "Croce di Guerra"; *Ceccherini*, Major-General in the regular army: three Silver Medals, two Bronze Medals; *Zambon*, Major-General of the regular army: Silver Medal and Bronze Medal; *Guglielmotti*, Major-General of the regular army: two Silver Medals.

After these follow:

Giuriati, with two Silver Medals; *Acerbo*, with three Silver Medals (voices: "Bravo!"); *Caradonna*, with three Silver Medals; *Finzi*, with a Silver Medal and two "Croci di Guerra."

Not to embarrass the modesty of my friends, I shall not continue to read the list of these officers of the National Militia—(Laughter)—but this is enough to prove to you that this is a serious institution. And I add that every day it becomes more so, because I mean that it shall be so, because all its chiefs mean it.

It might be asked of us: "Why does the Militia remain?" I shall tell it to you at once: for a very simple reason, to defend Fascism at home and also abroad. The word "abroad" might alarm you. Well, I tell you that abroad there is a difficult atmosphere for Italian Fascism. Difficult for the parties of the Right, which, being formed of national elements, cannot feel enthusiasm for a movement that exalts our national qualities; difficult for the parties of the Left, because those elements are our adversaries from the social point of view, knowing that the Fascist movement is clearly anti-Socialist. It is well, therefore, that it should be known that there is in Italy a mighty army of volunteers to defend that special form of political organization called Fascism.

The Militia, moreover, has the object of enabling the army to do its own work. The army must fight, must get ready for war. It must not do police work, especially of a political nature, except under absolutely exceptional circumstances, of which now I do not wish to think, even hypothetically. As an example, I can tell you that last night, upon my personal instructions, a whole section of Leghorn was blockaded. Well, one hundred carabineers and three hundred Blackshirts sufficed, while the army, the official troops, were sleeping peacefully in their barracks, as was their duty and their right. Moreover, believe me, so long as in Italy they know that, besides some tens of thousands of faithful carabineers, there is this enormous force, attempts at revolt or at sedition will never be dared.

Modifications to the Statute Law. Finally, and this is a maneuver of the last few days, have burst forth in Italy the bold defenders of the Statute, of Liberty and of Parliament. (Laughter.) It seems, listening to these gentlemen, who had for a long time forgotten the existence of the Statute, even as a simple historical document,—(Laughter)—that the Statute runs a serious risk and that one cannot even discuss nor examine it.

Well, I think that none of you can consider Camillo Cavour as a Bolshevist and a Fascist of 1848. Everybody knows that the Constitutional movement of Piedmont was the work of Cavour. Everybody knows how the political Constitution was granted. At Genoa a tumult arose against the Jesuits, believed supporters of Absolutism. A Commission of Genoese went to Turin and asked for the expulsion of the Jesuits and the calling out of the Civic Guard. But Cavour answered, "This is too little; the times are ripe for something more!" Cavour wrote in his paper, Il Risorgimento, "The Constitution must be demanded." And this was promulgated on March 4th. In its preamble it says, "The Statute is the fundamental, perpetual law of the Monarchy." Four days afterwards the first Constitutional Ministry of Coalition was formed with the Moderate Balbo and the Democratic Pareto.

The phrase "The Statute is the fundamental, perpetual and irrevocable law of the Monarchy" had wounded the ears of the Democrats. Cavour hastened to interpret it in a relative sense. It is worthwhile to listen attentively to this paragraph of Cavour:

How is it possible, how can it be expected that the legislator would have wished to pledge himself and the nation not to make the slightest direct change, to bring the smallest improvement to a political law? But this would mean the removal from the community of the power of revising the Constitution; it would mean the deprival of the indispensable power of modifying its political form according to new social exigencies; this would be such an absurd idea that no one of those who co-operated in the making of this fundamental law could conceive it. A nation cannot renounce the power of changing by legal means its common law.

After a short time history had to register a first violation of the Statute, which assumed or presumed that, in order to become a member of Parliament, it was necessary to be an Italian citizen. On October 16th, there was a division between the Right, among which there were the Moderates and the Municipals, and the Left, to which belonged the Democrats, called the "burnt heads," and the Republicans. On the following day these two parties were agreed in unanimously proclaiming above the Statute that all Italians could belong to the Subalpine Parliament. The first to benefit by this violation of the Statute was Alessandro Manzoni; but he declined the mandate by a letter which represents a fine example of correctness and political probity. (Approval.)

Nobody, Gentlemen, wishes to overthrow or destroy the Statute, which rests solidly on firm foundations; but the inhabitants of this building from 1848 up to today have changed. There are other exigencies, other needs. There is no longer the Piedmontese Italy of 1848! And it is very strange to notice among the defenders of the Statute those who have violated it in its fundamental laws, those who have curtailed the prerogatives of the Crown, those who wanted the Crown to be entirely outside the politics of the nation, and to become a dead institution. (Loud applause.)

The Abolition of Parliament? They say that this Government does not like the Chamber of Deputies. (Comments.) They say that we want to abolish Parliament and deprive it of all its essential attributes. It is timely to say that the collapse of Parliament is not desired by me, nor by those who follow my ideas. Parliamentarism has been severely affected by two phenomena typical of our days: on one side syndicalism, on the other journalism. Syndicalism gathers by its various organizations all those who have special interests to protect, who wish to withdraw them from the manifest incompetence of the political Assembly. Journalism represents the daily Parliament, the daily platform where men coming from the universities, from science, industry, from the experience of life itself, dissect problems with a competence that is very seldom found on the Parliamentary benches.

These two phenomena typical of the last period of capitalist civilization are those which have reduced the enormous importance which was attributed to Parliament. To sum up, Parliament can no longer contain all the life of the nations, because modern life is exceptionally complicated and difficult.

But this does not mean that we wish to abolish Parliament. We wish rather to improve it, to make it more perfect, make it a serious, if possible a solemn institution. In fact, if I had wished to abolish Parliament, I would not have introduced an Electoral Reform Bill. This Bill logically presupposes the elections, and through these elections there will be deputies—(Laughter)—who will form Parliament. In 1924, therefore, there will be a Parliament.

But must the Government be towed along by Parliament? Must it be at the mercy of Parliament? Must it be without a will, or a head before Parliament? I cannot admit that.

The Grand Council of Fascism. They say that Fascism has created duplicate institutions. These duplicates do not exist. The Grand Council of Fascism is not a duplicate of the Council of Ministers or above it. It met four times and never dealt with problems which concerned the Council of Ministers. With what, then, did the Grand Council of Fascism deal? In the February meeting it devoted itself to the National Militia and Freemasonry; it paid a tribute to the Dalmatians and to the people of Fiume, and dealt with Fascism abroad. In the March meeting it arranged the ceremony for the anniversary of the foundation of Rome and dealt with syndicalism. In its fourth meeting it devoted itself to the Congress of Turin and again to syndicalism.

All the great problems dealing with State administration, with the reorganization of armed forces, with the reform of our judiciary circuits, with the reform of the schools, all the measures of a financial nature have been adopted directly by the responsible body, the Council of Ministers.

And then what is the Grand Council of Fascism? It is the organ of co-ordination between the responsible forces of the Government and those of Fascism. Among all the organizations created after the October revolution, the Grand Council of Fascism is the most characteristic, the most useful, the most efficient. I have abolished the High Commissioners, because they duplicated the Prefects and also embarrassed the authority of the latter, who alone have the right to wield authority. But I could never think of abolishing the Grand Council of Fascism, not even if tomorrow by chance the Council of Ministers were composed entirely of Fascists.

Our Magnanimity Must Not Be Taken Advantage Of! This Government, which is depicted as hostile to liberty, has been perhaps too generous. The October revolution has not been bloodless for us; we have left dozens and dozens of dead. And who would have prevented us from doing in those days that which all revolutions have done, from freeing ourselves once for all from those who, taking advantage of our magnanimity, now render our task difficult? Only the Socialists of the newspaper *La Giustizia*, of Milan, have had the courage to recognize that if they still exist they owe it to us, who did not wish that, in the first moments of the March on Rome, the Blackshirts should be stained with Italian blood. But our generosity must not be taken advantage of!

Nobody Must Hope for a Crisis in Fascism. The Membership of Fascism. But nobody must hope for a crisis in Fascism, which is and will remain simply a formidable party. If you happen to notice that in one of its innumerable sections in Italy there is dissension, do not thus draw the conclusion that Fascism is in a state of crisis. When a party holds the Government in its hands it holds it, if it wishes to hold it, because it possesses formidable forces to use to consolidate its power with increasing strength. Fascism is a Syndicalist movement which includes one and a half million workmen and *contadini*, who, I must say in their praise, are those who give me no trouble. There is, moreover, a political body which has 550,000 members, and I have asked to be relieved of at least 150,000 of these gentlemen. (Laughter.) There is, still, a military section of 300,000 Blackshirts, who are only waiting to be called. These bodies are all united by a kind of moral cement, which might be called mystic and holy, and through which, by touching certain keys, we would hear tomorrow the sounds of certain trumpets!

The Associations Included in Fascism. They ask us, "Will you then camp out in Italy as an army of enemies which oppress the remainder of the population?" Here we have the philosophy of force by consent. In the meanwhile I have the pleasure to announce that imposing masses of men who deserve all the respect of the nation have joined Fascism, such as the Association of the Maimed and the Disabled, the National Association of Ex-soldiers. In the wake of Fascism, moreover, are also included the families of the fallen in war. There are a great many members coming from the people in these three Associations, while there is a great solidarity among these disabled ex-soldiers and families of the fallen in war. They represent millions of people, and, in the face of this collaboration, must I go and simply seek all the fragments, all the relics of the old traditional parties? Must I sell my spiritual birthright for a bit of stew which might be offered to me by those who have followed no one in the country? (Loud assent.) No! I shall never do this.

The Collaboration I Welcome. If there is anybody who wishes to collaborate with me, I welcome him to my house. But if this collaborator has the air of a controlling inquisitor, or of the expectant heir, or of the man who lies in ambush, with the object of being able at a given moment to record my mistakes, then I declare that I do not want to have anything to do with this collaboration. (Bravo!)

Besides, there is a moral force in all this. What was the cause after all which affected Italian life in past years? Italy was passing through a transformation. There were never definite limits. Nobody had the courage to be what he should have been.

There was the bourgeois who had Socialistic airs, there was the Socialist who had become a bourgeois up to his fingertips. The whole atmosphere was made up of half tones of uncertainty. Well, Fascism seizes individuals by their necks and tells them: "You must be what you are. If you are a bourgeois you must remain such. You must be proud of your class, because it has given a type to the activity of the world in the nineteenth century. (Approval.) If you are a Socialist you must remain such, although facing the inevitable risk you run in that profession." (Laughter.)

Taxation and the Discipline of the Italian Population. The sight which today the nation offers is satisfactory, because the Government exercises a stern and, if you like to say so, a cruel policy. It is compelled to dismiss by thousands its officials, judges, officers, railway men, dock-workers; and each dismissal represents a cause of trouble, of distress, of unrest to thousands of families. The Government has been compelled to levy taxes which unavoidably hit large sections of the population. The Italian people are disciplined, silent and calm, they work and know that there is a Government which governs, and know, above all, that if this Government hits cruelly certain sections of the Italian people, it does not do so out of caprice, but from the supreme necessity of national order.

The Government is One. Above this mass of people there are the restless groups of practicing politicians. We must speak plainly. In Italy there were several Governments which, before the present one, always trembled before the journalist, the banker, the grand master of Freemasonry, before the head of the Popular Party, who remains more or less in the background—(Applause)—and it was enough for one of these ministers *in partibus* to knock at the door of the Government, for the Government to be struck by sudden paralysis. Well, all this is over! Many men gave themselves airs with the old Governments; those I have not received, but have reduced them to tears. (Assent.) For the Government is one. It knows no other Government outside its own and watches attentively, because one must not sleep when one governs, one must not neglect facts, one must keep before one's eyes all the panorama, notice all the composition and decomposition, the changes of parties and of men. Sometimes it is necessary, as a tactical measure, to be circumspect; but political strategy, at least mine, is intransigent and absolute.

My Only Ambition Is to Make the Italian People Strong, Prosperous, Great, and Free. I should have finished; in fact I have finished, but I must still add something that concerns me a little personally. I do not deny to citizens what one might call the "Jus murmurandi"—the right of grumbling. (Laughter.) But one must not exaggerate, nor have one's ears always open to dangers which do not exist. And, believe me, I do not get drunk with greatness. I would like, if it were possible, to get drunk with humility. (Approval.) I am content simply to be a Minister, nor have I ambitions which surpass the clearly defined sphere of my duties and of my responsibilities. And yet I, too, have an ambition. The more I know the Italian people, the more I bow before it.

(Assent.) The more I come into deeper touch with the masses of the Italian people, the more I feel that they are really worthy of the respect of all the representatives of the nation. (Assent.) My ambition, Honorable Senators, is only one. For this it does not matter if I work fourteen or sixteen hours a day. And it would not matter if I lost my life, and I should not consider it a greater sacrifice than is due. My ambition is this: I wish to make the Italian people strong, prosperous, great and free! (The end of the speech is hailed by a frantic and delirious ovation. All the Senators rise, and the Tribune applauds loudly, while the great majority of the Senators go to congratulate the Hon. Mussolini.)

(The sitting is adjourned.)

As Sardinia Has Been Great in War, So Likewise Will She Be Great in Peace

June 10th, 1923, Palazzo della Prefettura, Sassari, Sardinia

◆

Citizens of Sassari! Proud people of Sardinia! The journey which I have made today is not, and should not be interpreted as, a Ministerial tour. I intended to make a pilgrimage of devotion and love to your magnificent land.

I have been told that, since 1870 to today, this is the first time that the head of the Government addresses the people of Sassari assembled in this vast square. I deplore the fact that up to this day no Prime Minister, no Minister, has felt the elementary duty of coming here to get to know you, your needs, to come and express to you how much Italy owes you! (Applause.)

For months, for years, during the long years of our bloody sacrifice and of our sacred glory, the name of Sassari, consecrated to history by the bulletins of war, has echoed in the soul of all Italy. Those who followed the magnificent effort of our race, those who steeped themselves in the filth of the trenches, young men of my generation—proud and disdainful of death—all those who bear in their heart the faith of their country, all those, O men of the Sassari Brigade, O citizens of Sassari, pay you tribute of a sign, of a testimony of infinite love. (Applause.)

What does it matter if some lazy bureaucrat has not yet taken into account your needs? Sassari has already passed gloriously into history. I was grieved today when I was told that this town has no water. It is very sad that a city of heroes has to endure thirst. Well! I promise you that you will have water; you have the right to have it. (Applause.) If the National Government grants to you, as it will grant, the 3 or 4 million necessary for this purpose, it will only have accomplished its duty, because while elsewhere young men with broad shoulders worked at the lathe, the people of Sardinia fought and died in the trenches.

We intend to raise up again the towns and all the land, because he who has contributed to the war is more entitled to receive in peace.

A few days ago, on the anniversary of the war, I went by airplane to the cemeteries of the Carso. There are many of your brothers who sleep in those cemeteries the sleep which knows no awakening. I have known them, I have lived with them, I have suffered with them. They were magnificent, long-suffering, they did not complain, they endured, and when the tragic hour came for them to advance from the trenches they were the first and never asked why. (Loud applause.)

The National Government which I have the honor to direct is a Government which counts upon you, and you can count upon it. It is a Government sprung forth from a double victory of the people. It cannot, therefore, be against the working classes. It comes to you so that you may tell it frankly and loyally what are your needs. You have been forgotten and neglected for too long! In Rome they hardly knew of the existence of Sardinia! But since the war has revealed you to Italy, all Italians must remember Sardinia, not only in words, but in deeds. (Loud applause.)

I am delighted, I am deeply moved by the reception which you have given me. I have looked you well in the face, I have recognized that you are superb shoots of this Italian race which was great when other people were not born, of this Italian race which three times gave our civilization to the barbarian world, of this Italian race which we wish to mold by all the struggles necessary for discipline, for work, for faith. (Applause.)

I am sure that, as Sardinia has been great in war, so likewise will she be great in peace. I salute you, O magnificent sons of this rugged, ferruginous, and so far forgotten island. I embrace all of you in spirit. It is not the head of the Government who speaks to you, it is the brother, the fellow soldier of the trenches. Shout then with me: Long live the King! Long live Italy! Long live Sardinia!

(An enthusiastic ovation greeted the last words of Mussolini.)

Men Pass Away, Maybe Governments Too, but Italy Lives and Will Never Die

June 12th, 1923, Palazzo della Prefettura, Cagliari, Sardinia

◆ ◆ ◆

Citizens! Blackshirts! Chivalrous people of Cagliari! Of late I have visited several towns, including those which belong to the place where I was born. Well! I wish to tell you, and this is the truth, that no town accorded me the welcome you gave me today. I knew that the town of Cagliari was peopled by men of strong passions, I knew that an ardent spirit of regeneration throbbed in your hearts. The cheers with which you welcomed me, the crowd crammed into the Roman amphitheater, all this tells me that here Fascism has deep roots. I thank you, therefore, Citizens, from the depth of my heart.

I have come to Sardinia not only to know your land, as forty-eight hours would not be enough for that purpose, and still less would they be enough to examine closely your needs. I know them; statesmen have known them for the last fifty years. Those needs are already before the nation, and if up to today they have not yet been solved, this is due to the fact that Rome was lacking that iron will for regeneration which is the pivot, the essence of the Fascist Government's faith in the future of our country. (Applause.)

Passing through your land, I have found here a living, throbbing limb of the mother country. Truly this island of yours is the western bulwark of the nation; is like a heart of Rome set in the midst of our sea. Among all the impressions I have received in coming here, one has struck my heart. I was told that Sardinia, for special local reasons, was refractory to Fascism. Here, too, there was another misunderstanding. But from today the cohorts and the legions, the thousands of strong Blackshirts, the syndicates, the fasci, the whole youth of this island is there to show that Fascism, representing an irresistible movement for the regeneration of the race, was bound to carry with it this island where the Italian race is manifested so superbly. (Applause.)

I salute you, Blackshirts! We saw each other in Rome and the groups coming from Sardinia were cheered in the capital. You bear in your hearts the faith that at a given moment drove thousands and thousands of Fascists from all the cities, from all the villages of Italy, to Rome. (Applause.)

Nobody can ever dream of wrenching from us the fruit of victory that we have paid for by so much blood generously shed by youths who offered their lives in order to crush Italian Bolshevism. Thousands and thousands of those who suffered martyrdom in the trenches, who have resumed the struggle after the war was over, who have won—all those have ploughed a furrow between the Italy of yesterday, of today and of tomorrow.

Citizens of Cagliari! You must certainly play a part in this great drama. You, undoubtedly, wish to live the life of our great national community, of this our beloved Italy, of this adorable mother who is our dream, our hope, our faith, our conviction, because men pass away, maybe Governments, too, but Italy lives and will never die! (Loud applause.)

Today I have visited the marvelous works of the artificial Lake Tirso. They are not only a glory to Sardinia; they represent a masterpiece of which the whole nation may be proud.

I feel, almost by intuition, that Sardinia also, too long forgotten, perhaps too patient, Sardinia today marches hand in hand with the rest of Italy. Let us then salute each other, O Citizens!

After this speech of mine, which was meant to be an act of devotion, a bond of union between us, let us salute each other by shouting: Long live the King! (Cheers.) Long live Italy! (Cheers.) Long live Fascism! (Loud cheers.)

Fascism Will Bring a Complete Regeneration to Your Land

June 13th, 1923, Palazzo Municipale, Iglesias, Sardinia

◆

Citizens of Iglesias! Blackshirts! Fascists! Your welcome, so cordial and so enthusiastic, surpasses any expectation. Iglesias has really been the cradle of Sardinian Fascism. From here sprang the first groups of Blackshirts; it was, therefore, my definite duty to come and get into touch with you.

You deserve that the Government should remember you, as in this island there is a large reserve of faith and ardent patriotism: I go back to Rome with my heart overcome with emotion.

Since Italy has been united this is the first time that the head of the Government is in direct touch with the people of Sardinia.

One thing only I regret, and that is that the shortness of my visit has not given me an opportunity of seeing more of your beautiful land. But I formally pledge myself to come again and visit your towns and your villages. As the head of the Government I am glad to have found myself among industrious, quiet and truly patient people, who have been too long forgotten, indeed almost considered as a far-away colony.

It is well it should be known that Sardinia is one of the first regions of Italy, and it should be known, too, that she gave the largest contribution of lives to our glorious victory.

As the head of the Government I am glad to find myself among the heroic Blackshirts and to have seen the splendid flourishing conditions of Fascism, which will bring a complete regeneration to your land.

Here (said the Hon. Mussolini, putting his hand on the standard of Iglesias, which was hoisted near him)—here is the standard, the symbol of pure faith. I kiss it with fervor, and with the same fervor I embrace you, O magnificent people of Sardinia. (Loud applause.)

As We Have Regained the Mastery of the Air, We Do Not Want the Sea to Imprison Us

June 19th, 1923, balcony of the Palazzo Vecchio, Florence

◆

Blackshirts of Florence and Tuscany! Fascists! People! Where shall I find the necessary words to express the fullness of my feelings at this moment? My words cannot but be inadequate for the purpose. Your solemn, enthusiastic welcome stirs me to the depths of my heart. But it is certain that it is not only to me that you pay this extraordinary honor, but also, I think, to the idea of which I have been the inflexible protagonist.

Florence reminds me of the days when we were few. (Deafening applause.) Here we held the first glorious meeting of the Italian "Fasci di Combattimento." You remember, we had often to interrupt our meeting to go out and drive away the base rabble. ("Bravo!" Frantic applause.) We were few then! Well, in spite of this huge crowd here assembled, I say that we are still few, not with regard to the enemies who have been put to flight forever, but with regard to the enormous tasks that lie before our Italy. (Applause.) I said that our enemies have been put to flight, as we shall no more do the honor of considering as enemies certain corpses of the Italian political world—("Bravo!")—who delude themselves that they still exist simply because they abuse our generosity. Tell me, then, Blackshirts of Tuscany and of Florence, were it necessary to begin again, should we begin again? (Deafening applause and cries of "Yes! Yes!") This loud cry of yours, more than a promise, is an oath which seals forever the Italy of the past, the Italy of the swindlers, of the deceivers, of the pusillanimous, and opens the way to "our" Italy, the Italy whom we bear proudly in our hearts, who belongs to us who represent the new generation who adore strength, who is inspired by beauty, who is ready for anything when it is necessary to sacrifice herself to struggle and to die for the ideal.

I tell you that Italy is going ahead. Two years ago, when the bestiality of the red demagogy raged, only twenty airplanes entered for the Baracca Cup. Last year they were thirty-five; this year, up to now, ninety. And as we have regained the mastery of the air, so we do not want the sea to imprison us. It must be, instead, the way for our necessary expansion in the world. (Great applause.)

These, O Fascists, Citizens, are the stupendous tasks which lie before us. And we shall not fail in our aim if each of you will engrave in his own heart the words by which is summed up the commandment of this ineffable hour of our history as a people: "Work," which little by little must redeem us from foreign dependence; "Harmony," which must make of the Italians one family; "Discipline," by which at a given moment all Italians become one and march hand in hand toward the same goal.

Blackshirts! You feel that all the maneuvers of our adversaries tending to sever me from you are ridiculous and grotesque. And I hope it will not seem to you too proud a statement if I say that Fascism, which I have guided on the consular roads of Rome, is solidly in our hand—("Bravo!")—and that if anybody should delude himself in this respect I should only need to make a sign, to give an order: "A noi!"[70] (Deafening applause.)

Raise up your standards! They have been consecrated by the sacred blood of our dead. When faith has thus been consecrated it cannot fail, cannot die, *will not* die! (Prolonged applause.)

---

[70] "To us!"

I Promise You—and God Is My Witness—That I Shall Continue Now and Always to Be a Humble Servant of Our Adored Italy

June 19th, 1923, historical Salone dei Cinquecento, Florence, where the Municipal Council solemnly bestowed on Mussolini the freedom of the city of Florence.

◆ ◆ ◆

Mr. Mayor, Councilors, People of Florence, the capital for many centuries of Italian art, you will notice that—on account of the honor which you pay me—I feel moved. To be made a citizen of Florence, of this city which has left such indelible traces on the history of humanity, represents a memorable and dominating event in my life. I do not know if I am really worthy of so much honor. (Cries of "Yes"; "May God preserve you for the future of our Italy." Applause.)

What I have done up to now is not much; but oh! Citizens of Florence, my determination is unshakable. ("Bravo!") Human nature, which is always weak, may fail, but not my spirit, which is dominated by a moral and material faith—the faith of the country.

From the moment in which Italian Fascism raised its standards, lit its torches, cauterized the sores which infected the body of our divine country, we Italians, who felt proud to be Italians—("Bravo! Bravo!" Applause)—are in spiritual communion through this new faith.

Citizens of Florence! I make you a promise, and be sure I shall keep it! I promise you—and God is my witness in this moment of the purity of my faith—I promise you that I shall continue now and always to be a humble servant of our adored Italy! (Prolonged applause.)

The Victory of the Piave Was the Deciding Factor of the War

June 25th, 1923, Palazzo Venezia, Rome, commemoration of the anniversary of the Battle of the Piave[71]

◆　◆　◆

Fellow Soldiers! After your ranks, so well disciplined and of such fine bearing, have marched past His Majesty the King, the intangible symbol of the country, after the austere ceremony in its silent solemnity before the tomb of the Unknown Warrior, after this formidable display of sacred strength, words from me are absolutely superfluous, and I do not intend to make a speech. The march of today is a manifestation full of significance and warning. A whole people in arms has met today in spirit in the Eternal City. It is a whole people who, above unavoidable party differences, finds itself strongly united when the safety of the common Motherland is at stake.

On the occasion of the Etna eruption, national solidarity was wonderfully manifested; from every town, every village, one might say from every hamlet, a fraternal heart-throb went out to the land stricken by calamity.

Today tens of thousands of soldiers, thousands of standards, with men coming to Rome from all parts of Italy and from the far-away Colonies, from abroad, bear witness that the unity of the Italian nation is an accomplished and irrevocable fact.

After seven months of Government, to talk to you, my comrades of

---

[71] The Second Battle of the Piave River (or Battle of the Solstice), June 15th–23rd, 1918, was a decisive victory for the Italian Army against the Austro-Hungarian Empire during the First World War.

the trenches, is the highest honor which could fall to my lot. And I do not say this in order to flatter you, nor to pay you a tribute which might seem formal on an occasion like this. I have the right to interpret the thoughts of this meeting, which gathers to listen to my words as an expression of solidarity with the national Government. (Cries of assent.) Let us not utter useless and fantastical words. Nobody attacks the sacred liberty of the Italian people. But I ask you: Should there be liberty to maim victory? (Cries of "No! no!") Should there be liberty to strike at the nation? Should there be liberty for those who have as their program the overthrow of our national institutions? (Cries of "No! no!") I repeat what I explicitly said before. I do not feel myself infallible, I feel myself a man like you.

I do not repulse, I cannot, I shall not repulse any loyal and sincere collaboration.

Fellow soldiers! The task which weighs on my shoulders, but also on yours, is simply immense, and to it we shall be pledged for many years. It is, therefore, necessary not to waste, but to treasure and utilize all the energies which could be turned to the good of our country. Five years have passed since the battle of the Piave, from that victory on which it is impossible to sophisticate either within or beyond the frontier. It is necessary to proclaim, for you who listen to me, and also for those who read what I say, that the *victory of the Piave was the deciding factor of the war.* . . . On the Piave the Austro-Hungarian Empire went to pieces; from the Piave started its flight on white wings the victory of the people in arms. The Government means to exalt the spiritual strength which rises out of the victory of a people in arms. It does not mean to disperse them, because it represents the sacred seed of the future. The more distant we get from those days, from that memorable victory, the more they seem to us wonderful, the more the victory appears enveloped in a halo of legend. In such a victory everybody would wish to have taken part!

We Must Win the Peace! Too late somebody perceived that when the country is in danger the duty of all citizens, from the highest to the lowest, is only one: to fight, to suffer and, if needs be, to die!

We have won the war, we have demolished an Empire which threatened our frontiers, stifled us and held us forever under the extortion of armed menace. History has no end. Comrades! The history of peoples is not measured by years, but by tens of years, by centuries.

This manifestation of yours is an infallible sign of the vitality of the Italian people.

The phrase "we must win the peace" is not an empty one. It contains a profound truth. Peace is won by harmony, by work and by discipline. This is the new gospel which has been opened before the eyes of the new generations who have come out of the trenches; a gospel simple and straightforward, which takes into account all the elements, which utilizes all the energies, which does not lend itself to tyrannies of grotesque exclusivism, because it has one sole aim, a common aim: the greatness and the salvation of the nation!

Fellow soldiers! You have come to Rome, and it is natural, I dare to say, fated! Because Rome is always, as it will be tomorrow and in the centuries to come, the living heart of our race! It is the imperishable symbol of our vitality as a people. Who holds Rome, holds the nation!

The Blackshirts Buried the Past. I assure you, my fellow soldiers, that my Government, in spite of the manifest or hidden difficulties, will keep its pledges. It is the Government of Vittorio Veneto. You feel it and you know it. And if you did not believe it, you would not be here assembled in this square. Carry back to your towns, to your lands, to your houses, distant but near to my heart, the vigorous impression of this meeting.

Keep the flame burning, because that which has not been, may be, because if victory was maimed once, it does not follow that it can be maimed a second time! (Loud cheers, repeated cries of "We swear it!")

I keep in mind your oath. I count upon you as I count upon all good Italians, but I count, above all, upon you, because you are of my generation, because you have come out from the bloody filth of the trenches, because you have lived and struggled and suffered in the face of death, because you have fulfilled your duty and have the right to vindicate that to which you are entitled, not only from the material but from the moral point of view. I tell you, I swear to you, that the time is passed forever when fighters returning from the trenches had to be ashamed of themselves, the time when, owing to the threatening attitudes of Communists, the officers received the cowardly advice to dress in plain clothes. (Applause.) All that is buried. You must not forget, and nobody forgets, that seven months ago fifty-two thousand armed Blackshirts came to Rome to bury the past! (Loud cheers.)

Soldiers! Fellow soldiers! Let us raise before our great unknown comrade the cry, which sums up our faith: Long live the King! Long live Italy, victorious, impregnable, immortal! (Loud cheers, while all the flags are raised and waved amidst the enthusiasm of the immense crowd in the square.)

The Relations Between Italy and the United States

Speech by the American Ambassador to Rome

On June 28th, 1923 the Italo-American Association held in Rome a banquet in honor of Mr. Richard Washburn Child, American Ambassador to Italy, and of the Hon. Mussolini, President of the Italian Council. The two distinguished guests delivered the following speeches,[72] which have a special importance, both with regard to Fascism and to Italo-American relations.

The object of this meeting was clearly explained by the Hon. Baron Sardi, Italian Under-Secretary of State for Public Works, in an appropriate address to the illustrious guests (published in full by the *Bulletin of the Library for American Studies* in Italy, No. 5), in which, after having thanked them in the name of Senator Ruffini, President of the Association, still detained on account of important duties in Geneva, and also in the name of the other members, for the honor they conferred on the Society by their presence, went on to lay stress on the purpose for which the Association exists, namely, to promote a better reciprocal understanding between the American and Italian peoples through the manifold activities of their respective countries.

The Hon. Sardi announced that during the summer months of this year courses of preparation will be inaugurated again for American students who wish to come and visit our country and study our language, literature and history, while for next October, under the patronage of the American Ambassador and the Italian Premier, with the cooperation of American and Italian professors, special industrial and commercial courses are in preparation. The American students will be able to benefit by the use of the valuable library of the Association, which is daily enriched by the competent work of Commendatore Harry Nelson Gay and his collaborators.

The Hon. Sardi, after referring to the fraternity of arms, which during the Great War brought together the soldiers of Italy and America, said that, having returned now to the peaceful spheres of industry and culture, these forms of

---

[72] The two speeches have been courteously given at his request to Baron Quaranta di San Severino for publication by the American Ambassador, Richard Washburn Child.

effort contribute strongly to cement between the two countries that spiritual fraternity which arises out of a better mutual acquaintance with the respective virtues and qualities and a clearer realization of our aspirations.

The orator concluded by expressing the wish that the Italo-American Association, by the indissoluble union of cultured minds, might be able to intensify the bonds already uniting the United States of America and Italy.

❖   ◆   ❖

Mr. President and Gentlemen, it is my privilege to propose a toast to the King and to the spirit of an Italy now stronger and more united than ever before.

I wish to express the earnest hope that my country and yours will continue to stand together in upholding ideals which make men strong instead of tolerating those which make men weak.

During the last eight months Italy has made an extraordinary contribution to the whole world by raising ideals of human courage, discipline, and responsibility. I would be unfaithful to my beliefs and to those of hosts of Americans if I failed to acknowledge the part played by your President of Council, Mussolini, with the people of Italy, in giving to all mankind an example of courageous national organization founded upon the disciplined responsibility of the individual to the State, upon the abandonment of false hopes in feeble doctrines, and upon appeal to the full vigorous strength of the human spirit.

We have heard a great deal in the last few years about the menace which war brings before the face of the world. I am confident that my people and your people are willing to act together to contribute anything possible to reduce the dangers of war, but I hold the belief, and I think your Premier holds the belief, that worse menaces than war now oppose the progress of mankind. Folly and weakness and decay are worse.

These menaces of weakness are often fostered by men of good intentions, who talk about the need to rescue mankind and about the necessity to establish the rights of mankind.

I want to see leaders of men who, instead of teaching humanity to look outside themselves for help, will teach humanity that it has power within itself to relieve its own distress. I want to see leaders who, instead of telling men of their rights, will lead them to take a full share of their responsibilities.

I do not doubt that the spirit of benevolence is a precious possession of mankind, but a more precious possession is the spirit which raises the strength of humanity so that benevolence itself becomes less of a necessity. He who makes himself strong and calls upon others to be strong is even more kind and loving of the world than he who encourages men to seek dependence on forces outside themselves or upon impracticable plans for new social structures. I do not doubt the good faith of many of those who put forth theories of new arrangements of social, economic and international structure, but they may all be sure that more important than any of these theories is individual responsibility and the growth and spread of self-reliance in the home and in the nation.

I do not doubt that we, Italians and Americans, have a full appreciation of the pity which we ought to confer upon weak or wailing groups or nations or races which clamor for help or favor; but I trust that, even in the competition of peace or war, I shall be the last ever to believe that weak groups or nations or races are superior or are more worthy of my affection than those who mind their own business with industry, strength and courage, and stand upon their own strong legs.

I do not question the motives of many of those who, feeling affectionate regard for the welfare of their fellow men, hope for a structure of society in which international bodies shall hand down benefactions to communities, and communities shall hand down benefactions to individuals. I merely point out that some nations, such as yours and mine, are beginning to believe that these ideas come out of thoughts which, though easily adopted, are the offspring of a marriage of benevolence with ignorance. In any structure of society which can command our respect and our faith the current of responsibility runs the other way. The doctrine that the world's strength arises from the responsibility of the individual is a sterner doctrine. The leaders of men who insist upon it are those who will be owed an eternal debt by mankind.

The strength of society must come from the bottom upward. The world needs now more than anything else the doctrine that the first place to develop strength is at home, the first duty is the nearest duty. A strong cooperation of nations can only be made of nations which are strong nations, a strong nation can only be made of good and strong individuals.

When one makes the *fasces*, the first requirement is to find the individual rods, straight, strong, and wiry, such as you have found, Mr. President, and so skillfully bound together in the strength of unity. But if they had been rotten sticks you could not have made the fasces. Unity in action would have been impossible. The rotten sticks would have fallen to pieces in your fingers.

Mr. President, what the world needs is not better theories and dreams, but better men to carry them out. The world needs a spirit which thinks first of responsibilities before it thinks of rights. It was this spirit which you have done so much to awaken into new life in Italy.

Not long ago I heard a speech made by a foreigner in Italy who is used to dealing with economic statistics. He was trying to account for the new life in Italy on the basis of comparative statistics. I told him he could not do it until he could produce statistics of the human spirit. I told him he could not account for everything in Italy until he could reduce to statistics that wonderful record of the human spirit which in scarcely more than half a century has created the new Italy. I told him he would have to account for the number of Italians who in 1848 and 1859, in the Great War and 1923, had a cause for which they were willing to die. I told him that I was always a nationalist before I was an internationalist, and I would go on being a nationalist, believing in the spirit of strong and upright and generous nationalism, and believing not in theorizing nations or whining peoples, but in nations and peoples who develop a national spirit so finely tempered that they offer to the world an example of organization, discipline and fair play, because they themselves are upright and strong men and can contribute valuably to international cooperation. I said to him that when he could produce statistics on human virtues and human spirit he would be nearer to understanding what made progress in the world. I asked him if he had figures to show the difference between nations which breed men who are ready to die for their beliefs and nations which produce no such men. I asked him to put his figures back in his pocket and go out and talk to the youth of Italy.

Mr. President, the youth of Italy, as in any other country, are the trustees of the spirit of tomorrow. It is a fact which goes almost unnoticed, that the training of masses of youth in the spirit of discipline and fair competition and of loyalty to a cause is largely to be found in athletic games. It is a fact which almost always is forgotten, that nations of history or those of today which have engaged in athletic games are the strong nations, and those which have had no athletics are the weak nations. It is a fact almost neglected that nations which can express their spirit of competition in athletics are the nations which have the least destructive restlessness within and are the most fair and, indeed, are the most restrained in their dealings with other nations.

Athletic games teach the lesson that every man who competes must win by reason of his own virtue. No help can come from without. There is no special privilege for anyone. He who wins does so by merit alone. Athletic games, whenever they are carried on by teams, teach the lesson that the individual must put aside his own interests for the good of his group. There must be a voluntary submission to discipline and absolute loyalty to a captain in order to avoid the humiliation of disorganization and defeat.

Athletic games are not for the weak and complaining, but for the strong and for the lovers of fair play.

Finally, they furnish oft-repeated lessons of the truth that when flesh and muscles and material agencies seem about to fail, human will and human spirit can work miracles of victory.

Because I believe in these ideals for my own country and for yours, I offer through you, for the purposes which the Olympic Committee of Italy will set forth, a small but friendly token of my deep interest in the youth of Italy. (Loud applause.)

The Italian Prime Minister's Reply

Mr. Ambassador, the discourse which your Excellency has pronounced at this reunion strengthens the bonds of sympathy and fraternity between Italy and America, and has profoundly interested me in my capacity as an Italian and as a Fascist. As an Italian, because you have spoken frank words of cordial approval of the Government which I have the honor to direct. I have no need to add that this cordiality is reciprocated by me and by all Italians. There is no doubt that the elements for a practical collaboration between the two countries exist. It is only a question of organizing this collaboration. Some things have been done, but more remain to be done.

I will not surprise your Excellency if I point out, without going into particulars, a problem which concerns us directly. I speak of the problem of immigration. I limit myself only to saying that Italy would greet with satisfaction an opening in the somewhat rigid meshes of the Immigration Bill, so that there could be an increase in Italian immigration to North America, and would greet with similar satisfaction the employment of American capital in Italian enterprises. As a Fascist, the words of your Excellency have interested me because they reveal an exact understanding of the phenomenon and of our movement, and constitute a sympathetic and powerful vindication of it. This fact is the more remarkable because the Fascism movement is so complex that the mind of a stranger is not always the best adapted to understand it. You, Mr. Ambassador, constitute the most brilliant exception to this rule. Your discourse, I say, contains all the philosophy of Fascism and of the Fascism endeavor, interwoven with an exaltation of strength, of beauty, of discipline, of authority, and of the sense of responsibility. You have been able to show, Mr. Ambassador, that in spite of the numerous difficulties of the general situation, Fascism has kept faith to its promises given before the March on Rome. The time intervening since those promises were made has been short, so that only a stupid person would pretend that the work is already completed. I limit myself to saying that I find corroboration by your Excellency that it is well begun.

I am certain, Mr. Ambassador, that all Italians will read with emotion the words which you have pronounced on this memorable occasion. I ask you especially to believe this. I have heard, just now, not a discourse in the manner and strain of an ordinary conventional speech, but a clear and inspiring exposition of the conception of life and history which animates Italian Fascism. I do not believe that I exaggerate when I say that this conception finds strong and numerous partisans even on the other side of the ocean, among the citizens of a people who have not the thousands of years of history behind them

which we have, but who march today in the vanguard of human progress. In this affinity of conceptions I find the solid basis for the fraternal understanding between Italy and America. The announcement
that you, Mr. Ambassador, are giving a wreath of gold to the Italian
youth who will be victor in the next Olympic competition games will
win the hearts of all Italian athletes, and of these there are, as you
know, innumerable legions.

I thank your Excellency in the name of Italian youth, almost all of
whom have put on the Blackshirt, especially the young athletes, and,
at the same time that I encourage the Italo-American Society to per-
severe in the execution of its splendid program, I declare that my
Government will do whatever is necessary to develop and strengthen
the economic and political relations between the United States and
Italy.

I raise my glass to the health of President Harding and the fortunes
of the great American people. (Loud applause.)

The Greatness of the Country Will Be
Achieved by the New Generations

July 2nd, 1923, Palazzo Venezia, Rome

This speech was given before the schoolboys of Trieste, Nicastro, Castel Gandolfo, Vetralla, and Perugia and their masters, who were accompanied by representatives of the Roman Balillas, and had come to Rome to pay homage at the tomb of the Unknown Warrior, before which they laid a wreath of beaten iron and kneeling repeated the oath of love and loyalty to the King and the Country. The Hon. Mussolini with the Minister of War, General Diaz; the Under-Secretary of State for the Presidency, Hon. Acerbo; General De Bono, the Director General of Police; Signor Lombardo Radice, the Director General of Primary Schools; and other officials, greeted them. The Hon. Mussolini thus addressed the meeting.

❖　◆　❖

On this radiant morning you have offered the capital a magnificent spectacle. Romans, having lived through many millenniums of history, are rather slow in being impressed by events and are not easily to be carried away by excessive enthusiasm. They have certainly however been filled today with admiration at this scene of promising youth which has been offered them by the schoolboys here gathered from all parts of Italy and especially from the Venezia Giulia, particularly dear to the heart of all Italians. It was well said that in the dark pre-war days the schools of the National League and in general the schools entrusted to Italian masters represented the center around which were nursed the hopes and the faith of the Italian race. I am glad to express to you the feelings of my brotherly sympathy. I am pleased to add that the National Government, the Fascist Government, holds in high esteem the scholarly characteristics and has deep respect for the teachers of all grades, of all schools.

The Fascist Government feels and knows that the *greatness of the country, to which all of us must consecrate the best of our energies, will be achieved by the new generations.*

You (continued the Hon. Mussolini, turning especially to the masters), you must be the artificers—as you show you are—of this great Italian restoration.

The task falls on you of blending together in increasing intimacy the intellectual life of the Italians who were slaves to Austria with that of the Italians who rose and sacrificed themselves by hundreds of thousands to break their fetters.

You passed before the Unknown Warrior, and you certainly gathered his spirit; take it to Trieste near the other great spirit of him who was the forerunner of your liberation and of ours: Guglielmo Oberdan![73] (Loud applause.)

---

[73] Considered a martyr of the Italian unification movement, Guglielmo Oberdan was an irredentist who was executed after a failed attempt to assassinate Austrian Emperor Franz Joseph in 1882.

The Situation on the Ruhr and Other
Questions of Foreign Policy

July 3rd, 1923, Council of Ministers, Rome

◆ ◆ ◆

Honorable Ministers and Colleagues, from my last detailed declarations of Foreign Policy made at the Senate up to today the salient events of international politics are the following:

The Bulgarian Coup d'état. The first is the Bulgarian *coup d'état*, following which the opponents of the Fascist Government fell into certain paradoxical misunderstandings. The end of Stamboliyski and the advent of Tsankov aroused a certain ferment in some of the countries of the Little Entente. Italy at once took a moderating action in the right quarters and the complications feared were averted.

The Treaty of Lausanne. The signing of the Peace Treaty of Lausanne seems imminent.[74]

The Situation in the Ruhr. In the last few days the situation in the Ruhr has become aggravated. On one side the passive resistance continues; on the other, the occupation is extended and intensified by measures of a nature increasingly political and military. A general repercussion of this crisis, which seems to have reached its acute stage, is felt by the European exchanges, which are all falling, not excluding the English sovereign, as compared with the dollar.

The attempt made by the Pope, so noble in its humanitarian and European aims, has not modified the situation. On the day after the letter to Cardinal Gasparri there was, on the part of the French,

---

[74] Indeed, it was signed three weeks after this speech, on July 24th, 1923.

Poincaré's speech, which had the unanimous approval of the Senate, and, on the same day, the fearful act of "sabotage" which cost the lives of many Belgian soldiers. All this does not represent a detente but an aggravation of the situation.

In the meanwhile, following the solution of the Belgian crisis, it has been possible to resume diplomatic action. Italy participates directly in it, and as soon as she sees the problem on its way to complete solution, will signify her consent to those propositions of the Memorandum of London, from which none of the projects presented afterwards has departed, that is to say: connection of the problem of Reparations with that of Inter-Allied debts; sufficient moratorium to Germany; the fixing of a definite amount; rational scheme for payment; solid guarantees of an economic nature and, hence, renunciation on the part of France of the territorial occupation of the Ruhr.

As for passive resistance, the Italian Government thinks that it is not in Germany's interest to prolong it, because she cannot hope to weaken France nor can she delude herself that she may obtain outside help.

It is certainly necessary urgently to hasten the possibility of an agreement, as the occupation of the Ruhr has weighed heavily on the economic life of Europe, delaying its recovery.

Fiume. As to the question of Fiume, representations have been made to Belgrade so that negotiations might be conducted more equably, in view of the situation of the town and of the necessity of putting on a normal footing the relations between the two countries. (The Council approves the declarations of the Hon. Mussolini.)

The Electoral Reform Bill

July 16th, 1923, Chamber of Deputies, Rome

♦

Honorable Gentlemen, I should have preferred to speak to this Assembly on that question of Foreign Policy which at this moment interests Italy and fills the world with excitement: I mean the Ruhr. I should have proved that the action of Italy is autonomous, and is inspired by the protection of our interests and also by the need generally felt to get out of a crisis which impoverishes and humiliates our continent. (Assent.) I promise myself to do so shortly, if the Chamber does not have the whim today of dying before its time. (Laughter and prolonged comments.) My speech will be calm and measured, although fundamentally forceful. It will be composed of two parts: one that I should like to call "negative," and another which I shall call "positive."

After all, I am not sorry that the discussion has gone, little or far, beyond the limits in which it could have been confined. The discussion on the Electoral Bill has offered opportunity to the Opposition to reveal itself, to move, from all its sections, from all its benches, to an attack against the policy and the political system of my Government. It will not surprise you, therefore, if, although not entering into details of all the speeches, I pick out from what has been said by the principal speakers those arguments and those propositions which I must definitely refute.

Warning to the Popular Party. As the speech by the Hon. Petrillo was favorable to the Government, it is not worthwhile to busy ourselves with it. (Laughter.)

I shall give my attention to the speech delivered by the Hon. Gronchi, a speech fine as regards its form, and perhaps still finer as regards its contents. The Hon. Gronchi has once again offered the Government a collaboration of convenience, as in those marriages of convenance which do not last or which end in ceaseless yawns. (Comment.)

Your collaboration, Gentlemen of the Popular Party, largely consists of details omitted. Your party, too, shows the same weakness. You should set to work and clear them up.

I do not know for how long these elements who wish to collaborate legally with the National Government can still remain united with your party, together with those who would wish to do so but cannot, because their inmost feelings do not allow them this step and this collaboration. You certainly know me well enough to understand that, as far as political discussion goes, I am intransigent. The small fry of the two-fifths and of the three-quarters or some other fraction of this electoral arithmetic does not interest nor concern me. Politics cannot be compared to a retail business. (Assent and comment.) To be or not to be! I am such a poor electoralist that I could even let you have the thirty or forty deputies who satisfy you; but I do not give them to you, as this would be immoral, because it would represent a transaction which must be repugnant to your conscience, as it is to mine. (Assent and comment.) In fact, I cannot accept a kind of Malthusian collaboration! (Laughter and approval.)

The Russian and the Italian Revolutions Both Tend to Overcome All Ideologies. The speech delivered by the Hon. Labriola was certainly powerful. He said that Ministerial crises are a substitute for revolution. He should have said "Ersatz," because substitutes, since the war, are of German origin. That is too like the opinion of an herbalist to be accepted. It may be that the want of Ministerial crises leads to revolution, but here you have an example that shows how excessive Ministerial crises lead also to revolution. But, above all, it astounded me to hear the Hon. Labriola still employ the old vocabulary of second-class Socialist literature, speaking of bourgeoisie and proletariat—two entities clearly defined and perpetually in a state of antagonism. It is certainly true that there is not one bourgeoisie, but there are, perhaps, twenty-four or forty-eight bourgeoisies and under-bourgeoisies. The same can be said of the proletariat. What relation can there be between a workman of the "Fiat" factory—specialized, refined, with tendencies and tastes already bourgeois, who earns thirty to fifty lire a day—what relation can there be between this so-called proletarian and the poor peasant of Southern Italy, who despairingly scrapes his land burnt by the sun? (Assent and comments.)

The Hon. Labriola has said that only the proletariat can give itself the luxury of a dictatorship. This is a mistake which is proved and can be proved. The only example of dictatorship is offered us by Russia. But the Hon. Labriola has written dozens of articles to prove that dictatorship does not exist in Russia and that dictatorship is not *of* but *upon* the proletariat. All those who govern the Russian States are professors, lawyers, economists, literary men, men of talent; that is to say, men coming from the professional classes, from the bourgeoisie.

The fault which the Hon. Labriola lays on us, finding an analogy between the methods and the evolution of the Russian and of the Italian revolution, does not exist. And here I make a simple statement of historical order. It is a fact that both revolutions tend to destroy all the ideologies and in a certain sense the Liberal and Democratic institutions which were the outcome of the French Revolution.

Italy pulled herself together after Caporetto, because the necessary Discipline of War was imposed on her. During the last few days use and abuse of a polemic method have been made, that of unearthing the writings and opinions of the past to employ them as a weapon in the present dispute. This is a very wretched system which I am going to use against those who have adopted it.

In his speech the Hon. Alessio has stated that the defeat of the Central Empires was due to the deficiency of their representative organs. This is a totally one-sided explanation. There has been a war; millions of men have fought against the Central Empires and defeated them. Another mistake is to say that after Caporetto Italy pulled herself together because she had regained her liberty. Nothing of the kind! The reason is that the necessary war discipline was imposed upon her. (Loud applause on the Right.) I am not one of those who think that Caporetto was due entirely to the disintegration of the country in rear of the fighting front. It was a military reverse in its causes and development; but there is no doubt that the atmosphere of the country, an atmosphere of leniency and of excessive tolerance, has produced disturbing moral phenomena which must have contributed to our reverse.

***The Dawn of Italian Risorgimento Came from the Bourgeoisie of
Naples***. The other statement made by the Hon. Alessio, that the Italian
Risorgimento represented the efforts of the Italian lower classes, is
superficial. Alas! it is not so. The Italian lower classes were absent and
often hostile to it. The first dawn of the Italian Risorgimento came
from Naples, from that bourgeoisie of intelligent and gallant professional men which in Southern Italy represents a class historically, politically and morally well-defined. (Applause and assent.) Those who
at Nola in 1821 hoisted the standard of revolution against the Bourbons were two cavalry officers. All the noble martyrology of the Italian
Risorgimento is formed out of elements of the bourgeoisie. Nothing is
sadder than the useless sacrifice of the Bandiera brothers. And when
you think of the tragedy of Carlo Pisacane you are thrilled! (Applause.)
I should like to deny that Giuseppe Mazzini himself can be included
in Democracy. His methods were certainly not democratic. He was
very consistent in his aims, but how many times was he not incoher-
ent and changeable in his means?

***The Expedition to the Crimea Really Prepared the Way for the
Unity of Italy***. And what about Cavour? I think that the event which
really prepared the way for the unity of the country was the expedition to the Crimea—(Comment)—which represents one of the most
noteworthy in history. I recall it because it shows how in solemn
hours the decision is left to one man, who must consult only his own
conscience. (Applause and comment.) When General Dabormida refused to sign the Treaty of Alliance with France and with England, Cavour, on the same evening of January 1st, 1855, signed it without con-
sulting Parliament or the Council of Ministers, and signed it above all
at his discretion without imposing any condition whatsoever. It was a
stroke of rashness that you might call sublime. Cavour himself recognized it, and when writing to Count Oldofredi, he said, "I have taken a
tremendous responsibility on my shoulders. It does not matter. Let
happen what may. My conscience tells me that I have fulfilled a sacred
duty!"

When the soldiers of the small and valiant Piedmont were on the
point of leaving, the discussion in the Subalpine Parliament took
place, and Angelo Brofferio, a kind of Cavallotti of the time—(Comment)—accused Cavour of not having a definite political line of conduct. It is really worthwhile to read part of this speech, because it

closely recalls the speeches which during the present week have been made in this hall:

> Our Ministers, represent all ideas and all convictions. At one time they become Conservatives and withhold the Jury from the Press; another time they ape the Democrats and raise cries against usurpations of Rome; still another time they throw off the mask and become retrogrades in order to unite with Austria!

Angelo Brofferio ends with these really singular words: "Where is in this system respect for convention and for constitutional morality?" and, referring to the Treaty, he added, "May God preserve us from that sinister eventuality! But if you agree to this Treaty, the prostitution of Piedmont and the ruin of Italy will be accomplished facts!"

It is curious, also, that another powerful ideologist, certainly sacred to the memory of all Italians, Giuseppe Mazzini, was very much against this Treaty, even to the extent of calling "deported" the Piedmontese soldiers who were leaving for the Crimea and of inciting them to desert! But Garibaldi, a far more practical leader, had an intuition of the fundamental importance of the Treaty of Alliance between Piedmont and Western Powers. "Italy," said Garibaldi, "should lose no opportunity of unfurling her flag on the battlefield which might recall to European nations her political existence."

Today you certainly all agree in recognizing that history has shown that Angelo Brofferio was in the wrong and Camillo Benso, Count of Cavour, was entirely in the right. (Assent.)

The Moral Unity of the Italian People. The speech delivered by the Hon. Amendola is, after that of the Hon. Labriola, more worthy of being analyzed. He said, "The Italian people are affected by a moral and spiritual crisis, which is certainly connected with our intervention, with the war, and with the after-war period," and he concluded by suggesting that it is necessary to give to this Italian people its moral unity. Well, we must be clear, what means "moral unity of the Italian people"? A minimum common denominator, a common field for action, in which all the National Parties meet and understand each other, a general levelling of all opinions, of all convictions, of all parties? For me it is sufficient that moral unity should exist in certain decisive hours of the life of the people. We cannot expect to have it on all days and on all questions. On the other hand I firmly believe that this moral, fundamental unity of the Italian people is already at work. We ourselves see it realized, perhaps not so much by our political work as by the war, which has made Italians know one another, and has thrown them together, making of this small peninsula of ours a kind of family.

Many local boundaries which separated provinces and regions have disappeared. Now we must complete the work. The Hon. Bentini, speaking of the freedom of the Press, to which subject we will return later, quoted the episode of Garibaldi and Dumas. I fully approve the answer given by Garibaldi. But I ask you—if the newspaper *Indipendente* had, by chance, published news concerning the movements of the Garibaldian troops or discrediting the military action, do you think that Garibaldi would not have suppressed that paper? (Assent and comment.)

We have the Power—We Shall Hold It and Defend It Against All! But in the speech by the Hon. Bentini, what is particularly singular is the confusion between tactics and political strategy. Today it is possible to win many battles and the war can be lost or won. What happened? You had brilliant tactical results, but afterwards you had not the courage of undertaking what was necessary to reach the final goal. You conquered a great many outlying communes, provinces and institutions, and you did not understand that all this was perfectly useless if, at a given moment, you had not become masters of the brains, of the heart of the nation—(Interruptions on the Extreme Left)—if, that is to say, you had not the courage of making use of a political strategy. Today your chance is over, and do not delude yourselves!

History offers certain chances only once. (Assent on the Extreme Right.) But to understand this law it is necessary, Honorable Gentlemen, to keep before you two very simple considerations, and they are these: there has been a war which has shifted interests, which has modified ideas, which has exasperated feelings, and there has also been a revolution. To make a revolution it is not necessary to play the great drama of the arena. We have left many dead on the roads to Rome and naturally anybody who deludes himself is a fool. *We have the power and we shall hold it. We shall defend it against anybody!*

The revolution lies in this firm determination to hold power! (Assent and comment.)

The Italian People Under the Domination of a Liberticidal Government, Groaning Under the Fetters of Slavery? And now I come to the practical side of the discussion.

They speak of liberty. But what is this liberty? Does liberty exist? After all, it represents a philosophical and moral concept. There are various manifestations of liberty. Liberty never existed. The Socialists have always denied it. The liberty of work has never been admitted by you. You have beaten the blackleg when he presented himself at the factories when the other workmen were on strike. (Applause: interruptions by the Extreme Left.)

But then is it really true and proved that the Italian people are under the domination of a liberticidal Government, and groans in the fetters of slavery? Is mine a liberticidal Government?

In the social field, No! I had the courage to transform the eight-hour work day into a law of the State. (Comments on the Extreme Left.) Do not despise this victory; do not undervalue it. (Assent.) I have approved all the social and pacifist Conventions of Washington. What has this Government done in the political field? It is said that democracy lies where suffrage is widened. Well, this Government has maintained universal suffrage. And, although Italian women, who are intelligent enough to exact it, had not done so, I have given it, be it only as regards the municipal elections for 6 to 8 million women! No exceptional laws were passed—(Comments on the Extreme Left)—and the regulation of the Press is not an exceptional law.

You forget a very simple thing, that the revolution has the right of defending itself. (Approval from the Right: comments.) Is there in Russia liberty of association for those who are not Bolshevists? No! Is there liberty of Press for them? No! Is there liberty of meeting, of vote? No! (Applause: comments on the Extreme Left.) You who are the defenders of the Russian regime have not the right to protest against a regime like mine, which cannot, even distantly, be compared with that of the Bolshevists. (Approval on the Right: comments on the Left.)

I am not, Gentlemen, a despot who remains locked up in a castle protected by strong walls. I circulate freely among the people without any concern whatsoever, and I listen to them. (Loud assent.) Well, the Italian people, up to now, have not asked for liberty. (Assent on the Right: comments on the Extreme Left.) At Messina the population which surrounded my carriage said, "Take us out of these wooden huts." (Assent.) In Sardinia—(you will notice that I am speaking of a region where Fascism has not tens of thousands of followers as in Lombardy)—in Sardinia, at Arbatax, men came to me with drawn faces; they surrounded me and, pointing out to me a track with a putrid river among the marshy reeds, said to me, "Malaria is killing us!" They did not speak to me of liberty, of the Statute, of the Constitution. It is the emigrants of the Fascist revolution who create this idol which the Italian people, and now, too, foreign public opinion, has largely dismantled. (Loud applause on the Right.)

Every day I receive dozens of Committees, and hundreds of applications are flung on my desk, in which one might say that the urgent needs of each of the eight thousand communes of Italy are represented.

Well, why should all those not come to me and say, "We suffer because you oppress us"? But there is a reason, a fact to which I wish to draw your attention. You say that the ex-soldiers fought for liberty. How does it happen, then, that these ex-soldiers are in favor of a liberticidal Government? (Applause.)

Are force and consent antagonistic elements? Not at all! In force there is already consent, and consent is force in itself and for itself.

But tell me, have you found on the face of the earth a government, of whatsoever kind, which claimed to make happy all the people it governed? But this would mean the squaring of the circle! Whatever government, be it even directed by men participating in the divine wisdom, whatever measure it takes, will make some people discontented. And how can you check this discontent? By force! What is the State? It is the police. All your codes of law, the laws themselves, all your doctrines are nothing if, at a given moment, the police by their physical strength do not make felt the indestructible weight of the law. (Comments and assent.)

We Do Not Want to Abolish Parliament. They say that we want to abolish Parliament. No! It is not true. First of all, we do not know what we could substitute for it. (Comment.) Parliaments, the so-called Technical Councils, are still in the embryonic stage.

Maybe they represent some principles of life. With such subjects one can never be dogmatic or explicit; but, in the face of today's state of affairs, they represent only attempts. Maybe that in a second stage it may be possible to allot to these Technical Councils a portion of the legislative work.

But, Gentlemen, I beg you to consider that Fascism is in favor of elections. That is to say, it calls for the elections, in order to conquer the communes and the provinces. It has called for them in order to send Deputies to Parliament; it does not, therefore, seek to abolish Parliament. On the contrary, as I said before and I repeat it, the Government wants to make of Parliament a more serious, if not more solemn institution: it wants, if possible, to bridge over that hiatus which undeniably exists between Fascism and the country.

Fascism Is Not a Transitory Phenomenon. Do Not Hope that Its Life Will Be Short! Gentlemen, we must follow Fascism, I will not say with love, but with intelligence. There must be no illusions. How many times from those benches it was said that Fascism was a transitory phenomenon! You saw it. It is an imposing phenomenon which gathers in its followers, one might say, by millions. It is the largest mass party which has ever existed in Italy. It has in itself some vital, powerful force, and since it is different from all others, as regards its extent, its organization, its discipline, do not hope that its life be short!

Today Fascism is going through the travail of a profound transformation. You will ask, "When will Fascism grow up?" Oh! I do not wish it to grow up too soon! (Laughter.) I prefer that it should continue still for some time as it is today till all are resigned to the *fait accompli,* and have its fine armor and its virile warlike soul.

There is a fact which is rapidly transforming the essence of Fascism. The Fascist Party, on one side, becomes a Militia, and, on the other, becomes an administration and a Government. It is incredible what a change the head of a squadra undergoes when he becomes an alderman or a mayor. He understands that it is not possible to attack abruptly the Communal Budgets without preparation, but that it is necessary to study them and devote himself to the administrative part, which is a hard, dry, and difficult task. (Applause.) And as the communes conquered by Fascists number now several thousands, you will conclude that the transformation of Fascism into an organ of administration is taking place and will be soon an accomplished fact.

Liberty Must Not Be Converted into License, and License I Shall Never Grant! You ask, "When will this moral pressure of Fascism end?" I understand that you are anxious about it. It is natural, but it depends on you. You know that I should be happy tomorrow to have in my

Government the direct representatives of the organized working classes. I would like to have them with me; I would like also to entrust them with a Ministry which requires delicate handling, so as to convince them that the administration of the State is a thing of the utmost complexity and difficulty, that there is little to improvise, that *tabula rasa* must not be made, as in some revolutions, because afterwards it is necessary to rebuild. You cannot take a corporal of the division of Petrograd and make of him a general, because afterwards you have to call in a Brusilov![75] (Comment.) To sum up, so long as opponents exist who, instead of resigning themselves to the *fait accompli*, contemplate a reactionary movement, we cannot disarm. But I say further that the last experience after your attempt at the strike of last year must also have convinced you by now that that road will lead you to ruin; while, on the other hand, you ought to take into account, once and for all, if you have in your veins a little Marxist doctrine, that there is a new situation, to which (if you are intelligent and watch over the interests of the classes you say you represent) you should conform. And, moreover, Colombino, who is a friend of Ludovico d'Aragona, can say if I am an enemy of the working classes. I dare him to deny my statement that six thousand workmen belonging to the Italian Metallurgic Consortium work today because I helped them and because I did my duty as citizen and head of the Italian Government. (Comment and assent.)

But liberty, Gentlemen, must not be converted into license. What they ask for is license, and this I shall never grant! (Loud applause and comment.) You can, if you wish, organize and march along in processions and I shall have you escorted. But if you intend to throw stones at the carabineers or to pass through a street where it is forbidden to do so, you will find the State which opposes you, if necessary by force. (Loud applause on the Right: comment on the Left.)

Close Analysis of the Electoral Reform Bill. But this Electoral Law which harasses us so much: is it really a monster? I declare it to you that, were it a monster, I should like to hand it over at once to a museum of monstrosities. (Laughter.) This law, of which I have traced the fundamental lines, but which afterwards has been successively

---

[75] Aleksei Brusilov, "The Iron General" of the Russians in the First World War, whose victories resulted in heavy casualties that seriously weakened the Russian army, which was unable to replace its losses.

elaborated by my friend the Hon. Acerbo, and re-elaborated by the Commission, I do not know whether for better or for worse—(Much laughter)—is a creation, and, like all creations of this world, has its qualities and defects. One must not condemn it as a whole; it would be a great mistake.

You must consider—I say this to you with absolute frankness—that it is a law for us—(Comments)—but it involves principles which are ultra-democratic—that of the State election schedule; that of the national constituency, which was the vindication of Socialism, as just now Constantino Lazzari recalled. You say that the struggle is impersonal, that the elections will cause unrest. But who tells you that the elections are near? (Laughter: prolonged comments.) The working of this law is such that a fourth part of the seats is guaranteed to the minorities, while I think that, calling the elections by the present law, the minorities would, perhaps, be further sacrificed. (Assent and comment.) At any rate the impersonality of the struggle withholds from the same struggle that character of harshness which might preoccupy from the point of view of public order. As things stand today, elections held on the uninominal constituency or even on the proportional basis would certainly lead to excesses. (Assent.)

The Government Cannot Accept Conditions. Either You Give It Your Confidence or Deny It. I declare that I shall not call elections until I am sure that they will be held in independence and order. (Comment and applause.) I add that while on principle I am, and I must be, intransigent, I entrust myself, in a certain sense, as regards technical discussion, to the competent elements. In this hall there are very many competent elements. They will say how this law can be even more abused or improved. (Comment.) But this is the business of the Chamber, and the Government declares to you that it does not refuse to accept those improvements which would render easier the exercise of the right to vote.

This concerns in a certain sense the Popular Party, which must decide for itself. I have spoken plainly, but I must say not as plainly as has been spoken from those benches. The Government cannot accept conditions. Either you give it your confidence or you deny it. (Assent and comment.)

On Your Vote Will Depend in a Certain Sense Your Fate! I agree with all the speakers who have declared that the country wishes only to be left alone; to work in peace with discipline. And my Government makes enormous efforts to achieve this result and will go on, even if it has to strike its own followers, because, having wished for a strong State, it is only just that we should be the first to experience the consequences of strength. (Loud applause.) I have also the duty of telling you—and I tell you from a debt of loyalty—that on your vote depends in a certain sense your fate! Do not delude yourselves, even in this field, because nobody gets out of the Constitution—neither I nor the others—as nobody can suppose that he is not amply guaranteed according to the spirit and the letter of the Constitution. (Comment.) And then, if things are thus, I tell you, take into account this necessity. Do not let the country have once again the impression that Parliament is far from the soul of the nation and that this Parliament, after having maneuvered for an entire week in a campaign of opposition, has achieved sterile results at the end. Because this is the moment in which Parliament and country can be reconciled. But if this chance is lost, tomorrow will be too late, and you feel it in the air, you feel it in yourselves. And then, Gentlemen, do not hang on political labels, do not stiffen yourselves in the formal coherence of the parties, do not clutch at bits of straw, as do the shipwrecked in the ocean, hoping vainly to save themselves. But listen to the secret and solemn warning of your conscience; listen also to the incoercible voice of the nation!

◆   ◆   ◆

The last words of the speech of the Hon. Mussolini, which had been listened to all through with the greatest attention by the Assembly and the Tribunes, are greeted by frantic, repeated applause by the benches of the Right, by the Centre, and by many Deputies of the Democratic Left. The ovation lasts for a long time and is intensified by that paid by all the Tribunes.

When the applause is over, all the members of the Government shake hands with the President of the Council, while from the benches of the Right all the Deputies come down to congratulate the Hon. Mussolini, among them the Hon. Fera, ex-Minister of Justice, and the ex-Prime Ministers, the Hon. Giolitti, the Hon. Salandra, the Hon. Orlando, and the President of the Chamber, the Hon. De Nicola, who exclaims, "It is the finest speech in the annals of Parliamentary history."

The sitting is suspended for half an hour. When it is resumed at 8:10 a.m., the Hon. Mussolini agrees to accept the order of the day proposed by Larussa: "The Chamber, reaffirming its confidence in the Government, approves the principles contained in the Electoral Reform Bill, and passes to the discussion of the Articles of the project."

At 11:10 a.m., the operation of voting having been completed, the result is proclaimed: "The Chamber of Deputies votes in favor of the Government by a large majority."

The sitting is adjourned.

The Massacre of the Italian Delegation for the Delimitation of the Greco-Albanian Frontier

August 29th, 1923, Chigi Palace, Rome

On August 27th, General Enrico Tellini, President of the International Commission for the Delimitation of the Greco-Albanian Frontier, the medical officer, Major Luigi Corti, and Lieutenant Mario Bonacini, members of the Mission, were atrociously murdered in Greece, while motoring from Janina to Santi Quaranta.

In consideration of preceding assassinations, of all the concordant information from different sources gathered on the scene of the massacre, and of the persistent campaign of libel and instigation on the part of the Greek Press against Italy and the Italian Military Mission, the Royal Government (the Stefani Agency informs us) has come to the conclusion that the moral as well as implicitly the material responsibility of the massacre falls on the Greek Government. On these grounds the head of the Government, certain of interpreting the sense of indignation of the whole Italian nation, has instructed Commendatore Montagna, Minister at Athens, to present to Greece the following Note containing Italy's demands.

◆ ◆ ◆

Hon. Mussolini's Note to Greece demands on behalf of Italy:

1. Apologies in the most ample and official form, to be presented to the Italian Government at the Royal Italian Legation at Athens through the highest Greek authority;

2. Solemn funeral ceremony for the victims of the massacre, to be celebrated in the Catholic Cathedral at Athens, with the presence of all the members of the Greek Government;

3. Honors to the Italian flag to be paid by the Hellenic Fleet in the bay of the Piraeus to one of our naval divisions, which will proceed there purposely, and this by means of a salute of twenty-one shots fired by the Hellenic ships, while the Greek Fleet flies the Italian flag from the masthead;

4. A strict inquiry will be held by the Greek authorities on the scene of the massacre, with the assistance of the Royal Military Italian Attaché, Colonel Perrone, for whose personal safety the Hellenic Government holds itself absolutely responsible. Such an inquiry will have to be conducted within five days of the acceptance of these demands;

5. Capital punishment of the guilty;

6. Indemnity of 50 million Italian lire—to be paid within five days of the presentation of this Note;

7. Military honors to the remains of the victims upon their embarkation at Preveza on Italian warships.

ENJOYED THIS BOOK?

TO READ MORE, VISIT US AT

ANTELOPEHILLPUBLISHING.COM